The
Complete Guide to
WALLPAPERING

David M. Groff

CREATIVE HOMEOWNER PRESS®

Illustrator: Cynthia Stancil Groff
Cover Design: Warren Ramezzana
Cover Photograph: Greg Plachta

Printed at: Banta Company

Current Printing (last digit)
10 9 8 7 6 5 4 3 2 1

The Complete Guide to Wallpapering
LC: 93-72177
ISBN: 1-880029-24-3 (paper)

CREATIVE HOMEOWNER PRESS®
A Division of Federal Marketing Corp.
24 Park Way
Upper Saddle River, NJ 07458

Disclaimer

The Complete Guide to Wallpapering contains many facts about wallpaper and wallpapering. The subjects and information described in this book are a direct result of personal experience in the field and interviews with people in various segments of the industry including other professional installers, manufacturers, chemists, product sales representatives, and retailers.

To the best of the author's knowledge, all the information and detailed product knowledge is factual and up to date; nonetheless, in view of the many sources of information that have been accumulated, the author cannot and does not warrant that the information contained in the book is flawless in every respect or entirely free from error.

Within the ever-changing world of wallpaper and the technologies associated with it, the products, techniques, and production methods are also continuously changing.

Whenever an exceptional situation arises, such as an adhesive requirement or cleaning instruction, the manufacturer of the specific wallcovering in question should be consulted. They frequently have pre-tested solutions to many of the problems that may arise. **The Complete Guide to Wallpapering** is intended to provide a communication bridge for all who are involved in the wallpapering industry, including manufacturers, distributors, retailers, professional installers, and the do-it-yourselfers.

The terminology section in the back of the book applies entirely to the field of wallpapering. Even though some of the terms are not defined the same as in a dictionary, they are field terms that are used in the wallpapering industry and by the author. The purpose of the terminology section is to furnish a reference by which all individuals within the industry may clarify for each other the jargon used in their individual areas of the trade.

The techniques described and illustrated in **The Complete Guide to Wallpapering** are methods used by the author, and are intended to help the reader better understand the techniques of wallpapering.

Acknowledgments

I would like to extend special thanks to several individuals who helped make **The Complete Guide to Wallpapering possible.**

Jean Utley, the executive editor, has spent many hours helping to put this book together. Her time, dedication, and personality are greatly admired and appreciated. Merel Utley, her husband, sacrificed many hours of time with Jean and helped provide personal support in our efforts. Special thanks to both of you.

I want to thank my wife Cynthia for encouraging me to write **The Complete Guide to Wallpapering** and supporting me during the entire time it has taken to write and publish it. Daniel and D.J., our two sons, have also been very patient and supportive during this effort.

Special thanks go to my dad, Bob Groff, who took the time to train me beginning as early as age seven. Without his patience and strict training, **The Complete Guide to Wallpapering** may have never existed.

Thank you all!

Introduction

Wallpaper has been around for many years--dating back as far as 1481--and is related to a basic historical need. The cold climates and rough construction of the north European houses made some sort of wall covering a necessity if dwellings were to be livable. For the very rich, this necessity was provided by luxurious silks, tapestries, marble, wood paneling, and so forth. But these materials were far beyond the reach of the mass population in the 15th and 16th centuries--just as they are today. The technological innovation that really met the major need for wall-coverings was the invention of the printing press and printed paper.

Wallpaper, as we know it today, has progressed a tremendous amount from those early days, and is available in thousands of different patterns and many different backings and decorative surfaces.

Wallpapering has become a creative business because of the simplicity of the installation process. It is important, however, to realize that individuals who are seeking very highly skilled craftsman in the business, should not be mistaken by the do-it-yourselfer entrepreneurs.

Wallpapers that are manufactured today have a wide variety of substrates (back-ings) and require different types of adhesives to install them. Some of them require specific adhesive viscosities (thickness) as well as prescribed applications.

It is usually advisable for the do-it-yourselfer to start with the lightweight wallpapers that are pre-pasted. Most wallpapers that are not pre-pasted will generally require a pre-mixed adhesive and will require a certain amount of experience. This may prevent a first-time do-it-yourselfer from yielding a successful job.

Manufacturers all across the world have spent millions of dollars on research and development to create wallcoverings that can be installed with a minimum amount of experience and knowledge; however, the chore of installing wallcoverings has become increasingly difficult because of the many types of wallcoverings available. This is not to mention the many different types of adhesives, primer/sealers, and wall conditions that must be taken into consideration in order to produce a satisfactory job.

There are many topics that should be discussed and taught before the decorative prints of the designer's studios can be transformed to the consumer's walls. One of the major topics is wall preparation.

This is the main reason for most wall-papering failures. Proper preparation of the wall surface is absolutely critical to acquire a satisfactory job.

There are various important steps involved with the wallpapering procedure that a professional or do-it-yourselfer may not ever understand--without a tremendous amount of trial and error. This book will indoctrinate you with the actual procedures to follow, which in turn will assure you a successful and fruitful job, even as a first-time wallpaper installer.

A wallpapering glossary of terms has been selected for **The Complete Guide to Wallpapering** to help each reader better understand and interpret the language that is used throughout the wallpaper industry. It is essential that every individual be able to communicate with each other, to determine the correct procedures to use during the installation or when determining the actual amount of wallpaper needed.

The Complete Guide to Wallpapering is not intended to replace the professional schools for wallpapering; and there is no better teacher than hands-on-training. However, this book will serve as a bridge to better improve knowledge and communication for everyone.

Table of Contents

Basic Understanding of Wallcoverings

The word "wallpaper" has been changed to "wallcovering" by many individuals during the past few years simply because there are so many different wall decorating products that are used on today's market that do not contain any paper in their makeup. Wallcoverings may vary from the very lightweight papers that are made from very basic pulp, to the commercial heavyweight wallcoverings that contain either a scrim, osnaburg, or drill backing laminated to a heavy plastic-type finish. Many individuals are applying fabrics, textiles, cork veneers, suedes, wood laminates, etc., which are all considered wallcoverings rather than wallpapers.

Packaging and Selling
Single, Double, & Triple Rolls

Wallcoverings are made and packaged in many different widths and lengths. The standard American single roll will contain between 34 and 36 square feet, ranging from 12 to 24 feet in length and between 18 and 36 inches in width.

The metric size single roll will include between 27 and 30 square feet per single roll, and will range from 13½ and 16½ feet in length and between 20½ and 28 inches in width. The most common size roll is 20½ inches wide by 16½ feet long.

The metric size roll consists of approximately 25% less wallcovering than does the American size roll, and will require 25% more to cover an equivalent wall surface.

There are many types of wallcoverings that are created along with infinite styles of patterns and designs from which to choose. One of the facts that must be understood about wallcoverings is the different variables that are affiliated with each of them including packaging, selling, and the installation processes.

Most residential or lightweight commercial-type wallcoverings are sold by the single roll, nonetheless they are packaged in double or triple roll bolts. The heavier commercial-type wallcoverings are commonly sold by the linear yard and are packaged with 30 yards in a continuous bolt. These will generally be either 48″ or 54″ in width.

This process of packaging and selling wallcoverings has created a bit of confusion among individuals that sell, buy, or install the many different wallcovering products that are available on today's market. The manufacturers established these methods of packaging to yield more usable full length strips per bolt (double or triple roll package), which, in turn, reduces the amount of waste that is involved during the installation process.

To understand this, think of wallpaper as you would fabric. Fabric is priced and sold by the single yard, just as wallcovering is sold by the single roll or linear yard. When five yards of fabric are purchased, the salesclerk will remit the entire five yards to the customer in one continuous piece; however, the receipt indicates the purchase of five individual yards at a given price per yard. This enables the seamstress to obtain as much usable yield as possible without splicing the separate yards together.

The same standard applies in wallcoverings. For instance, wallpaper that is 27 inches wide is 5 yards long per single roll. **Fig.1** indicates the usable yield from this single roll on a standard eight-foot high wall. **Fig. 2** reveals the usable yield that is available from a double roll bolt that is 27 inches wide and 10 yards long.

By being packaged in double roll bolts, the wallcovering does not have to be spliced in order to acquire the third full length strip. Some wallcovering distributors will cut a single roll for a small fee, but it is often advantageous to buy the packaged quantities in order to guarantee the completion of the job.

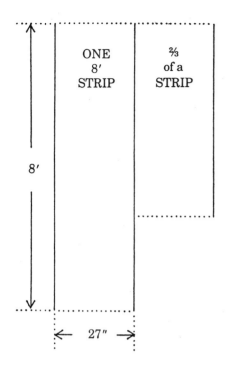

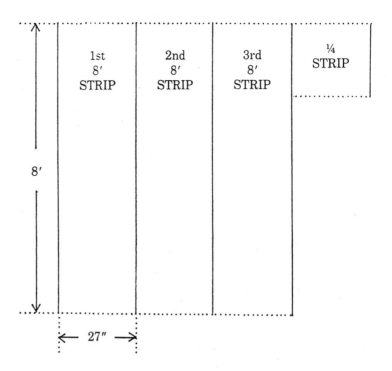

Fig. 1

One single roll 27" wide and 5 yards long

Fig. 2

One double roll 27" wide and 10 yards long

Pattern and Dye-Lot (Run) Numbers

When wallcoverings are manufactured at the factory there is a pattern number and dye-lot number printed on each roll.

A pattern number is designated by the manufacturer to identify a particular design and color way (color schemes) of a pattern. The pattern number may be indicated by letters as well as numbers. For example: A pattern number selection from a book entitled "Crazy Kids Only" may be CK1001. The CK is used to identify the book in which the pattern is located with this particular manufacturer. The number 1001 is used to indicate the color way used when printing the pattern.

There are times when the same identical pattern is being printed; however, the color scheme will change only very slightly. For example: Pattern # CK1001 may include colors of red, green, and yellow. Pattern # CK1002 may be made up of red, green, and blue colors. Since the pattern design is the same and only the colors are different, it is imperative to check each individual roll of an order to insure uniformity in color as well as pattern.

The dye-lot number represents a particular batch (group of rolls) which are printed at the same time. The dye-lot number will change each time there is an alteration in the printing process. This will alert the consumer to variables such as: a possible change of a color (referring to the tonal values of the colors); a change in the vinyl coating and/or consistency; or a change in the embossing process (whether hot or cold) that is being used during the production of the wallcovering.

Estimating

When measuring for wallpaper, the one thing to remember is: there is no easy way to figure the exact amount of wallpaper you will need. Pattern repeats, size of doors and windows, odd-shaped rooms, special areas such as archways, bay windows, soffits, cathedral ceilings, etc., are just a few of the variables that can cause any estimate not to be 100% accurate.

The following guidelines will help you figure, as close as possible, the amount of wallpaper that will be needed. It is advisable to have all the available information concerning the variables of the new wallpaper which should include: the wallpaper pattern repeat, the pattern match (straight-across, half-drop, multiple-drop, or random), the length and width of the wallpaper, the square footage per single roll (American size or metric), the available packaged bolts (double-rolls or triple rolls), etc. All of these factors are important when estimating the quantity of wallpaper required to complete a room or wall. Just remember, "It's always better to get too much than to run out!" Even professional installers can make mistakes!

Square Foot Method

Since wallpaper is packaged by square footage, the amount of wall space to be covered will need to be figured in square feet. A yardstick or steel tape measure is recommended to figure the square footage.

Start by measuring each wall individually. Measure from one corner to another, (include all doors and windows as you go) to determine the length of the wall. Multiply the length of the wall by the height to determine the square footage for that wall.

In **Fig. 1** each individual wall is 12' long by 8' high. To measure the first wall, multiply 12' by 8' to have a total of 96 square feet, including the door. **(Fig.1)**

Figure the same for WALLS 2, 3, and 4. Each wall in this room contains 96 square footage. Therefore, 96' x 4 (walls) is equal to 384 total square feet for the room.

So far, the windows and doors have not been subtracted. The total square footage (384) will need to be divided by the number 30. This is the average amount of usable square footage that a standard American single roll will yield. Even though there are approximately 35 to 36 square feet on a single roll, about six square feet will be wasted when matching patterns from one strip to another and when trimming allowances around obstacles such as windows, doors, moldings, or baseboards.

Dividing 384 by 30 will equal 12.8 single rolls of wallpaper needed to complete all four walls in **Fig. 1**. The next step is to subtract ½ single roll (about 15 square feet) for each normal sized door and window. Important: Do not subtract the entire amount of the opening because there will be waste involved due to the necessity of keeping a pattern sequence in harmony on the wall surface.

In **Fig.2** a door that is 36" wide, will have about 15-16" of wasted wallpaper in hanging around it.

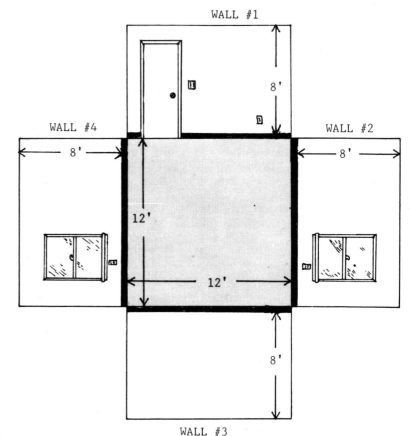

Fig. 1

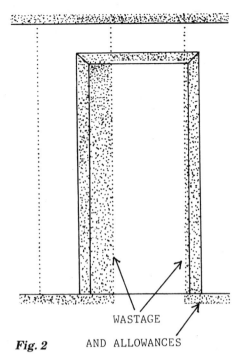

Fig. 2

WASTAGE
AND ALLOWANCES

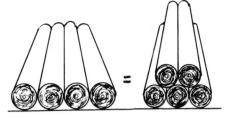

Fig. 3

16 single rolls (8 double rolls) American
= 20 single rolls (10 double rolls) metric

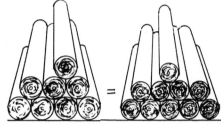

Fig. 4

Remember: American size rolls equal approximately 35 to 36 square feet per single roll, regardless of width and length. Metric (Euro) size single rolls, equal approximately 28-30 square feet per single roll which is about 25% less square footage than American size rolls.

Since there are two windows and one door, three (½ single rolls) or, 1½ can be subtracted from the subtotal.

Equation: 12.8 = total rolls including doors and windows
 - 1.5 = ½ roll x three openings

 11.3 or 12 = American single rolls needed

Note: Always round a fraction amount to the next highest number!

Metric Conversion Method

Once the American size roll quantity is figured, it can be converted to metric by following this basic rule:

Add one single roll for every four single rolls figured for the American size single roll.

Examples:
8 single rolls (4 double rolls) American = 10 single rolls (5 double rolls) metric **(Fig.3)**

Large Pattern Repeats (Square Foot Method)

Whenever a wallpaper selection is made with an 18″ vertical repeat or larger, there are 5 basic steps to determine if additional wallpaper will be needed, and if so, five more steps to recalculate exactly how much more would be required. To help better understand these steps, an example of questions and answers is listed (in sequence) to recalculate the estimate.

Step 1: There will be some basic information concerning an original estimate and the wallpaper itself to determine if more

rolls will be needed.
 Q: How many single rolls of wallpaper were originally estimated for the room?
 A: 16 single rolls.
 Q: Does this represent American or metric size rolls?
 A: American.

Note: If the answer had been **metric** size, then convert it to the **American** size for the purpose of recalculating the estimate.
 Q: What is the wall height in inches?
 A: Standard 8′ (96″). (Be sure the allowance cuts, 3″ for the top, and 3″ are included in the 96″. If not, it must be added).
 Q: What is the actual pattern repeat of the wallpaper that has been chosen?
 A: 30″.
 Q: Is the pattern match straight across, or is it a half-drop match?
 A: Straight-across match.

Note: The pattern match information is found on the back of each page of wallpaper samples found in every wallpaper samples catalog. If this information is not **known,** assume that a straight-across match will be used in order to be on the safe side.

Step 2: Divide the wall height in inches (96) by the pattern repeat in inches (30) to determine how many times the pattern will repeat itself within each strip.

Example: 96 ÷ 30 = 3.2 repeats per strip. Round this figure, 3.2 , off to the next highest figure, which is 4 . This is how many repeats that will be used per strip during the installation.

Step 3: Multiply the number of repeats (4) by the inches of the repeat (30) to determine how long each strip must be to allow for the usable yield and waste.

Example:
 4 Number of repeats per strip
 x 30″ Distance of one vertical repeat

 120″ Number of inches required per strip for usable yield and waste

Step 4: Subtract the number of inches of the wall height (96) from the required inches per strip (120,... answer from Step 3)

Example:

120″ Number of required inches per strip

- 96″ Height of wall in inches

24″ Waste used for matching each strip **(Fig.5)**

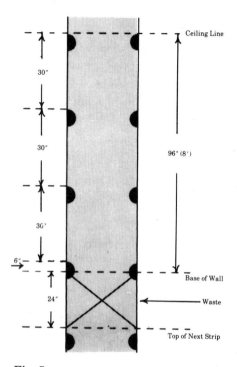

Fig. 5

Notice: 24″ will be wasted between each strip in order to match the pattern designs together from one strip to another. If a half-drop match is being used, the amount of waste could be cut in half by alternating rolls, and the total waste would be less than the 18″ maximum.

Since the waste is 24″, you must continue the following steps. **Caution:** During the original estimate, a maximum of 18″ (waste) should have been allowed for matching patterns per strip. Any amount over 18″ must be recalculated.

Step 5: Refer to Step 3 and convert the length of each strip from inches back to length in linear feet.

Example: 120″ ÷ 12″ = 10 feet

This is the new wall height needed to recalculate the room.

Step 6: Convert the amount of American rolls (16) to the usable square footage (30) required to do the room.

Example:

16 American single rolls originally estimated

x 30 Usable square feet per American single roll

------

480 Total square feet originally required to cover the room

Step 7: Divide the original wall height (8′) into the square footage (480) to determine the distance around the room.

Example:
480 ÷ 8 = 60 feet around the room

Step 8: Multiply the distance around the room (60) by the new wall height as figured in Step 5 (10′).

Example:

60 Distance around the room

x 10 New wall height

------

600 New square footage required to recalculate the estimate

Step 9: Divide the new square footage total in Step 8 (600) by the usuable yield of an American single roll (30).

Example:
600 ÷ 30 = 20 American single rolls

Twenty American single rolls is the new amount required to do this room. This will allow for approximately 24″ to be wasted per strip, in order to correctly match the pattern designs. Be sure to convert this figure to the metric quantity, if the wallpaper quantity originally figured was the metric size.

Important! If you are a professional, inform clients about large pattern repeats, and have this variable stated on the estimate/contract form. This will eliminate an adverse situation and also prevent you (the installer) from loosing a day's work. Be professional when estimating the wallpaper requirements. Don't get embarrassed by coming up short, especially if you have made a special trip to estimate the job.

Special Reminder: When installing a half-drop match pattern, the amount of waste can be minimized by alternating between two different rolls during the strip cutting process.

Large Pattern Repeats (Percentage Method)

The same first four questions required in Step 1 of the square foot method will be required for the percentage method.

Step 1: The customer or retailer will need to provide some basic information in order to determine whether more rolls will be needed.

Q: How many single rolls of wallpaper were originally estimated for the room?

A: 24 single rolls.

Q: Does this represent American or metric size rolls?

A: American.

Q: What is the wall height in inches?

A: Standard 8′ (96″). (Be sure the allowance cuts, 3″ for the top, and 3″ for the bottom of the strips, have been added).

Q: What is the actual pattern repeat of the wallpaper that has been chosen?

A: 47″ vertical repeat.

Q: Is the pattern match straight across, or is it a half-drop match?

A: Straight-across match.

Note: The pattern match information is found on the back of each page of wallpaper samples in every wallpaper samples catalog. If this information is **not** known, assume that a straight-across match will be used to prevent coming up short!

Step 2: Divide the wall height in inches (96) by the pattern repeat in inches (47) to determine how many times the pattern will repeat itself within each strip.

Example: 96 ÷ 47 = 2.04 repeats per strip. Round this figure off to the next highest figure, which is 3. This will determine how many repeats will be used per strip during the installation.

Step 3: Multiply the number of repeats (3) by the actual repeat itself in inches (47) to determine how long each strip must be to allow for the usable yield and waste.

Example:

```
    3   Number of repeats per strip
x 47"   Distance of one vertical repeat
------
  141"  Number of inches required per
        strip for usable yield and waste
```

Step 4: Subtract the wall height in inches (96) from the required inches per strip (141). (Answer is from Step 3.)

Example:

```
  141"  Inches required per strip
-  96"  Height of room
------
   45"  Waste involved while matching
        each strip
```

Notice: 45" will be wasted between each strip in order to match the pattern designs together from one strip to another.

Since the waste is 45", you must continue the following steps. Remember, during the original estimate, a maximum of 18" (waste) was allowed for matching patterns per strip. Any amount over 18" should be recalculated.

Step 5: After determining the amount of waste involved per strip (Steps 2 through 4), divide that amount in inches, into the wall height in inches to figure what percent of wallpaper is wasted.

Example:
(Step 2) 96" ÷ 47" = 2.04, or 3 repeats
(Step 3) 47" x 3 = 141" per strip
(Step 4) 141" - 96" = 45" waste per strip
(New Step 5) 45" ÷ 96% = 46.8 or 47%

The answer reveals that 47% more wallpaper will be wasted than was originally figured for the estimate, therefore, 47% more wallpaper will be required to complete the job.

Step 6:
```
   24   Original estimated rolls
+ 47%   percentage of extra
        wallpaper required
------
 35.2 or 36 single rolls
```

Note: When using the percentage method, it is not necessary to convert metric to American to recalculate the estimate as would be required in Step 1 (B) in Method 1. The answer from Step 1 (A) would be increased by 47% in this example, regardless of whether it is American or metric. If you are a professional, make sure the customer knows which quantity to order from your estimate form.

Count Strip Method

The count strip method is the most accurate method of calculating the quantity of rolls needed to complete a job. However, it is important that every specific detail about the new wallpaper is known in order to determine the exact number of usable strips that a packaged bolt (double-roll or triple-roll) will yield based on the size of the pattern repeat. The following method can be used to establish the quantity of rolls needed for the standard American-size roll with a vertical repeat of 18" or less.

Count Strip Method (Eight Foot Strips)

Note: This method applies **only to** American-size rolls. See Metric Conversion Method. Using the following method, measure the distance around the entire room in inches. Divide by 21" to determine the amount of strips required to install the room.

Every 4 strips 21" wide by 8' long = one American double roll.

Every 3 strips 21" wide by 5' long = one American single roll.

Note: Using the count strip method may work out the same, even if other size width rolls are ordered. **(Figs. 6 & 7)**

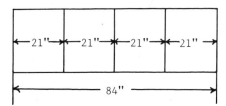

Fig. 6

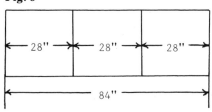

Fig. 7

However, it is important to realize that some types of wallcoverings will not yield as many 8' length strips per bolt (packaged roll) as others, therefore, it will become necessary to determine the quantity based on the useable yield factors of an odd sized roll or package.

Deduct one single roll for every **two** standard doors or windows on 8' high walls.

Deduct one single roll for every three standard doors or windows when installing wallpaper only over the chair-rails.

Important: Deduct for door and window openings **only** if you have included them when counting individual strips.

18" Pattern Repeat Rule

It is important to understand the reason why 18 inches or less is used as a standard pattern repeat when using the count strip method for estimating standard eight foot high walls. Since a 20½ inch wide American double roll contains 42 linear feet it will yield five full length strips. **(Fig.8)**

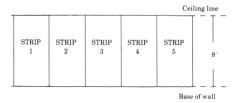

Fig. 8

If the pattern chosen has a vertical repeat of 18″ or less, and there is any waste involved in matching, then the usable yield will be only four strips per double roll instead of five. Therefore, every 2 strips 8′ long will equal one single roll. In **Fig.9** the illustration reveals the waste and remaining usable yield factors involved.

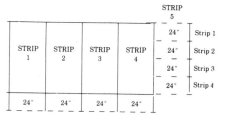

Fig. 9

Assume the match of STRIP 2 is established to align with STRIP 1, and the pattern waste involved is the maximum allowance of 18″.

Remember: Add the allowance cut of 3″ for the top and 3″ for the bottom of each strip. This makes the total waste per strip 24″ or 2′. This waste will have to be utilized from the fifth strip every time a new strip is cut from the roll. After four consecutive strips are cut to match, there will be a total of 96″ wasted, therefore, the entire square footage of STRIP 5 will be used up.

Anytime more than 24″ is wasted per strip (including matching and the allowance cuts of 6″), the quantity should be recalculated to compensate the waste involved during the installation of the wallpaper.

Count Strip Method (Strips Over Eight Feet)

Use the following steps to determine the amount of usable strips a double or triple roll will yield according to its width and length.

Step 1: Determine the total amount of wall height in inches, and add 6″. This allows

for the top and bottom allowance cuts of three inches each.

Step 2: Divide this figure by 12″ to get the average length per strip in feet.

Step 3: Divide this length into the double-roll or triple-roll length (in feet) to determine how many strips each bolt will yield.

Step 4: Divide the number of strips required for the room by the yield factor (Step 3) and this will equal the number of bolts required for the room.

EXAMPLE

The example below does not specify a vertical repeat, therefore it is assumed to be a random match or texture.

Specifications:
a. 20 ½″ wide wallpaper =
  42 linear feet per double roll
b. ceilings: 9′ high

9 x 12″	=	108″ wall height
		+ 6″ allowance cuts
		------
wall conversion	=	114″ total requirement for strip height to inches (feet)

| 114″ total strip inches | ÷ | 12 conversion to feet | = | 9.5′ average length per strip in feet |

| 42′ length of double roll in feet | ÷ | 9.5 length of strip | = | 4.4 usable strips per double roll |

Remember: This example does not allow for vertical repeats or waste involved in matching patterns.

Stairway/ Cathedral Walls

When estimating a stairway wall or cathedral wall remember that there will be an extra amount of waste involved to allow for the slope of either the stairway steps or the ceiling line pitch. In order to properly measure the stairway wall, divide the wall in either squares or rectangles to determine the square footage. In the following illustration, the upstairs ceiling height is standard 8′ and the downstairs ceiling height is also standard 8′. **(Fig.10)**

In **Fig.10** the top half of the wall is 8′ by 15′, and equals 120 square feet. The bottom section of the stairway rectangle is covered by the steps, however **do not** measure just 50% (half) of the square footage for the bottom section, because extra wallpaper is required to allow for the waste that will be involved in order to reach the lower section of each strip. This extra waste will require about 15% more wallpaper, so you must multiply 120 (8′ x 15′) by 65% (50% + 15%) to determine the total square footage needed to allow for the slope of the stairs.

In **Fig.11** is a stairway with a sloping ceiling, and the figures for estimating.

The top imaginary rectangle will require 78 square feet and so will the bottom, therefore a total of 156 square feet would be figured for this stairway wall.

Ceilings

The best method to use when estimating ceilings is the count strip method. Of course, the width and the length of the wallpaper roll must be known.

Step 1: Determine the direction that the wallpaper will be installed and the length of each strip.

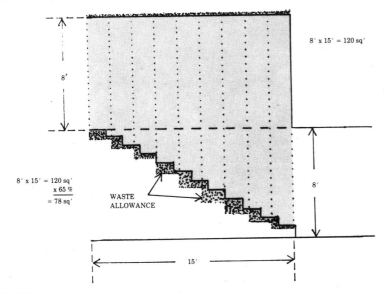

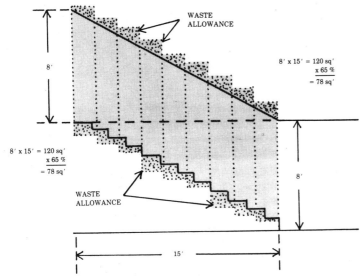

Fig. 10

Step 1: Determine the length of each strip in inches:

15'   Length of room in feet

x 12" Inches per feet

180" Exact length in inches

Step 2: Allow 6" for allowance cuts:

180" Exact strip length (Step 1)

+ 6" Allowance cuts

186" Total length in inches required per strip

Step 3: Divide the repeat into the total length required (Step 2) to determine the amount of repeats required per strip.

186" ÷ 19" = 9.47 or 10 repeats (rounded off)

Step 4: Multiply (10) (Step 3) times the repeat to determine the exact length required per strip to allow for matching patterns:

10   Amount of repeats

x 19 Repeat

190" Total per strip required for matching patterns

Step 5: Convert this figure to feet:

190" ÷ 12" = 15.83' or 16' (rounded off)

Step 6: Divide this figure into the length of the double roll to determine how many usable strips it will yield:

42' ÷ 16' = 2.62 or 2 usable full length strips

This means that the double roll will yield only 2 full length strips, therefore, every strip will equal a single roll. The fraction (.62) will be wasted.

A 15' (180") wide wall would require 8.78 or nine 20½" wide strips. Therefore, since each strip is equal to a single roll, this ceiling would require 9 single rolls.

If the standard square foot method had been used, the measurements would be as follows:

15' x 15' = 225 (total square feet)

If the standard rule of 30 usable square feet per roll had been used for estimating the quantity of rolls; this room would have only required 7.5, or 8 single rolls. (225 sq. ft. ÷ 30 sq. ft. = 7.5)

The only way to complete the job would require splicing a couple of long strips that

The top immaginary rectangle will require 78 square feet and so will the bottom, therefore a total of 156 square feet would be figured for this stairway wall.

Fig. 11

Step 2: Add for the allowance cuts and vertical repeat waste, (if applicable), to determine the exact length that each strip will be, including the waste.

Step 3: Determine how many usable full length strips are available per double roll or triple roll bolt that will be ordered.

Step 4: Divide this amount into the number of strips that are required for the ceiling and this will equal the number of double or triple rolls required.

Note: If a texture is being used, the di-

rection of the strip placement may yield more usable strips in one direction as opposed to the other. It is usually undesirable to splice ceiling strips together. This could result in a two-thirds long strip wasted per bolt, therefore a tremendous amount of waste could occur. The count strip method based on the useable yield of the wallpaper bolt is always the best policy.

Example Specifications

Length of ceiling (15')

Width of ceiling (15')

Vertical repeat (19")

Width of paper (20 ½")

Length of double roll (42')

may not be satisfactory, therefore this method should not be used.

Note: Whenever textures or "no match" patterns are being used, there are no repeats or waste involved for matching.

Commercial Wallcoverings

Commercial wallcoverings are usually sold by the linear yard opposed to square feet and single rolls. The linear yards are usually packaged in 30-yard bolts. This provides a high usable yield factor whenever the wallcovering is installed in large areas, such as hospitals, motels, or office buildings.

The following steps and examples will illustrate and determine the amount of linear yards required to do a room.

Step 1: Determine the total distance around the room (in inches); be sure to include all standard doors and windows.

Step 2: Divide this distance by the width of the wallcovering (54" or 48"). **Note:** If the material being used is untrimmed be sure to deduct a minimum of 4" (2" for each edge) from the width of the wallcovering to allow for double-cutting. This will be the usable yield of width (in inches). This division will equal the number of strips required to do the room.

Step 3: Determine the height of the wall in feet (rounded off to nearest foot).

Step 4: Multiply the number of strips required (Step 2) times the height of the wall in feet (Step 3). This will equal the total amount of linear feet required to do the room.

Step 5: Divide the number of linear feet required for the room by three to determine the number of linear yards it will require.

Example Specifications: Room size 15' x 10'
Wall height 9'
Wallcovering 54" untrimmed

Step 1:
15' + 10' + 15' + 10' = 50' feet (distance around the room in feet)
50' x 12" = 600" (distance around the room in inches)

Step 2:
54" - 4" = 50" usable yield width (the 4" is the allowance needed for double-cutting)
600" ÷ 50" = 12 strips (total strips to cover room)

Step 3:
9' wall height

Step 4:

12	number of strips
x 9'	height of walls

108	linear feet (required for room)

Step 5:
108' ÷ 3 = 36 (linear yards required for room)

Note: Do not subtract for normal sized doors or windows. The **only** openings that are deducted must be larger than the width of the wallcovering.

Conversion Method

Total square footage of room ÷ 12.75 = linear yards of 54" random
Total square footage of room ÷ 11.25 = linear yards of 48" random

Conversion using previous example:

15' + 10' + 15' + 10" =	50' distance around room
	x 9' height of wall
	------
	450 total square footage for room

450 total square footage for room	÷	12.75 54" conversion factor	= 35.29 or 36 yards total yards required (same as other method)

Important: Never underestimate a job, because it is practically impossible to obtain the exact shade and/or dye-lot number.

Borders

Borders generally are packaged in either a continuous strip, a 5-yard spool, or 7-yard spool. Other length spools are sometimes available. This information should be known before establishing the quantity required to do a room. Borders have variables in estimating just as regular wallpaper does. Each individual spool must be re-matched during the installation, therefore a minimum of one-half yard should be added for each spool required to allow for matching.

Example: If a room required 15 yards of border that came packaged in 5-yard spools, it would require 3 spools (5-yard segments) plus 1½ yards for rematching them during the installation. This is a total of 16½ yards required which means that four spools (five yards in length) will have to be purchased.

If the border comes packaged in a continuous strip, a minimum of two yards should be added to compensate for crooked corners and for any possible damage that may occur to the ends of the roll.

Whenever border is being installed around door or window frames, an extra foot (minimum) should be allowed for every mitered cut that will be made. See chapter on **Borders.**

Murals

When estimating the quantity for a mural, some basic information will be needed about the mural itself, and how it will be installed on the wall. First of all, does the mural have extra background or filler paper available to complete a large wall? Second, is the mural interlocking, meaning, it can be joined together in a series or extra panels can be added?

These questions should provide the answers to how many murals or how much filler paper will be required to install a wall or room. Sometimes the selection of the mural itself will be very important.

Example: If a single non-interlocking mural is chosen for a large wall, it may appear too small, and therefore would not be attractive once installed. If the mural is extra large with many panels, it may overpower the wall or may not even fit at all.

Some murals that are interlocking can be mixed together to form the illusion of a single picture. **Fig.12** illustrates a single four-paneled interlocking mural.

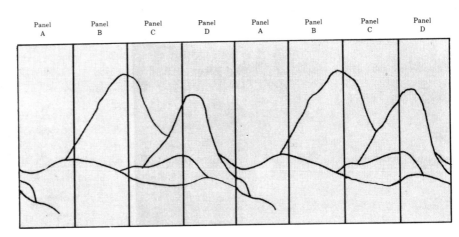

Panel A   Panel B   Panel C   Panel D   Panel A   Panel B   Panel C   Panel D

Fig. 13

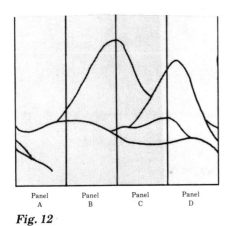

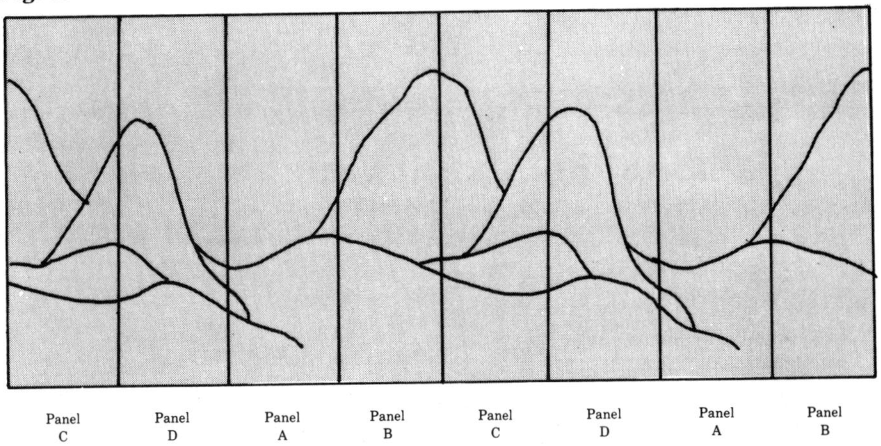

Panel A   Panel B   Panel C   Panel D

Fig. 12

Fig.13 illustrates the same mural installed directly beside the other. The scenic picture appears twice.

Fig.14 illustrates two identical murals being installed together; however, PANELS A and B are installed to the right of the center mural, PANELS C and D are installed to the left of the center mural. This creates an illusion of one large mural.

When estimating for photo murals be sure to check the same basic information as required for standard murals. Photo murals are usually full wall height as opposed to a single picture and are also divided into quarter panels as opposed to single full-length panels. See **Fig.15** to understand the quarter panel layout of photo murals. Note: Some photo murals will interlock with each other just as a standard mural.

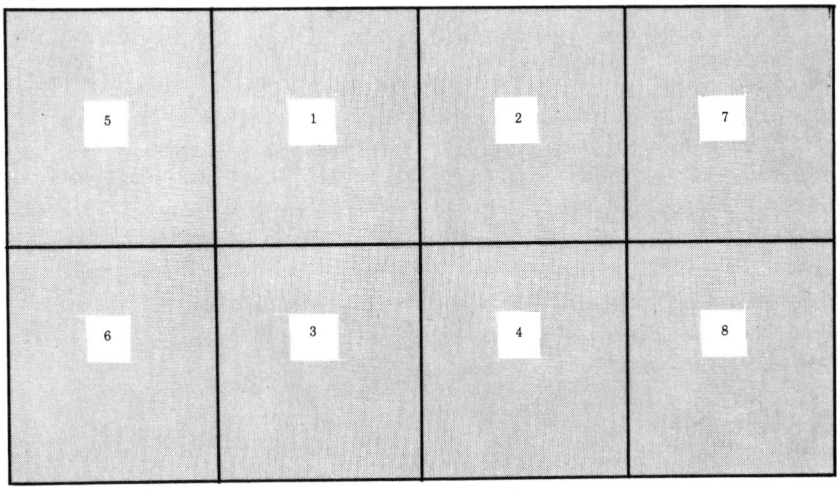

Panel C   Panel D   Panel A   Panel B   Panel C   Panel D   Panel A   Panel B

Fig. 14

5	1	2	7
6	3	4	8

Fig. 15

Blueprints

There are many times that it becomes necessary to calculate the quantity of wallpaper requirements from a blueprint. A blueprint is a scaled version of the structure and is generally scaled as ¼ inch equals one linear foot.

It is relatively simple to figure from blueprints using a standard one-foot ruler. It is important, however, that all the variables are known about the structure which may or may not be indicated on the blueprint at a glance. These variables may include cabinets, soffits (deep or shallow), counter-top laminate requirements (such as the back-splash wall between kitchen cabinets), chair-railing, cathedral (vaulted) ceiling lines, etc. It is generally advisable to have someone (superintendent/customer) available to provide any missing information from the blueprint.

Once all the variables are known, then the square foot method or the count strip method may be used to calculate the number of rolls of wallpaper that will be required to do a room or wall.

Note: When the count strip method is being used; the width of the wallpaper and the length of the packaged bolts must also be known to establish an accurate estimate.

Wall Preparation

Introduction

This chapter will provide the information to establish a secure foundation for wallpapering. If all wall surface preparations are done correctly, the proper installation of wallpaper will provide many years of satisfaction.

It is also just as important to prepare the walls for future redecorating, which would include removing the wallpaper from the wall surface without causing extensive damage.

Almost every dilemma that arises in wallpapering can be traced to the original wall surface preparation: the walls may have lacked the correct primer/sealer; the walls may not have been sanded smooth; the old wallpaper may not have been removed; loose edges of existing wallpaper may not have been secured; grease or penetrating stains may not have been treated; mildew problems may not have been eliminated; etc.

The list could go on and on. The fact of the matter is, if wall preparation is not performed properly, problems will arise...maybe not right away, but eventually. The biggest problem is that most individuals are in such a hurry to see the finished product or meet a closing date, that they either completely ignore the wall preparation procedures or don't carry them out properly. There are definite steps that must be followed in order for the new wallpaper to remain beautiful, last a long time, and be easily removed when desired.

Do-It-Yourselfers

If you are a do-it-yourselfer, this chapter is intended to insure your job will last a long time. All too often, many failures result because a do-it-yourselfer did not ask the necessary questions to obtain the correct advise. Just because you're doing the job yourself, don't ignore wall preparation. It is really sad when a good job turns into a disaster because important procedures were eliminated!

Customers Employing Professional Installers

If you are a customer wishing to employ a professional installer, this chapter will assist you in selecting an individual to install the wallpaper. All too often, customers fall victim of a bad wallpapering job simply because they did not know the correct procedures to expect from a wallpaper installer. By reading this chapter, you will know exactly what to expect from a true professional wallpaper installer.

Wallpapering Entrepreneurs

If you are an entrepreneur thinking of wallpapering for a living you should immediately constantly strive to establish a professional status. This chapter will serve as a foundation for you to grow on. The first and major rule is: don't ignore wall preparation! As it was stated at the outset, most every single problem that is associated with wallpaper coming loose, can be traced to the original wall surface preparation.

Professional Installers

If you are already a professional wallpaper installer this chapter will help you establish high standards for wall preparation procedures that will set you apart from **amateurs.** Always insist that the preparation of the wall surface be done according to high standards in order to secure your reputation as a professional.

If someone else is preparing the walls for you, such as a home owner or painting contractor, the job should be done according to your precise specifications, simply because, if something goes wrong, it will be blamed on you, the installer. Don't ever compromise!

Most all customers are (or at least should be) willing to pay the difference for a first-class professional job if they are informed of the difference between an amateur and a professional installer--especially in the area of wall preparation. Properly estimating jobs will insure that all procedures are covered in wall preparation, and you should be justly compensated.

Note: It is impossible for the manufacturers of wallcoverings to explain on each roll of wallpaper or instruction sheet, all the different wall preparation procedures that exist. Therefore, this chapter is intended to provide a valuable source for this very important information.

It is important that all wall surfaces be cleaned of any type of grease or wax build-up before applying sizings or primer/sealers.

> **WARNING**
>
> Never use a detergent or cleansing agent that contains phosphorous to wash the wall surface. This will prevent the sizing or primer/sealer from properly bonding to the wall surface, and may cause the product to dry to a spongy or rubbery feel. It is better to use an equal mixture of ammonia and water to clean wall surfaces prior to applying sizings or primer/sealers.

Primer/Sealers and Sizings

Wall preparation including primer/sealers and sizings is critical to a successful wallpapering job; however, there is probably less information available about this subject than any other area of wallpapering. There so many types of primer/sealers and sizings available on the market that it is important to realize their differences. Some primer/sealers are made specifically for paint applications and other primer/sealers are made especially for wall surface preparation for wallpapering. The different types are discussed within this chapter.

The Purpose of Sizing and Primer/Sealers

One of the first things that must be understood is why a primer/sealer or sizing needs to be applied to the wall surface in the first place. Primer/sealers and sizings have two major purposes:

(a) To aid in the adhesion of the wallpaper to the wall surface

(b) To aid in the future removal of the wallpaper when redecorating is desired.

Whenever wallpaper is applied to a wall surface the adhesive must go through a drying-out period which is referred to as the dissipation process. This will usually require 24 to 48 hours, though some conditions such as high humidity, heavy viscosities (thicknesses), or non-breathing wall surfaces and/or wallpapers will take longer.

A tremendous amount of torque (pressure) occurs during this drying-out period. If the paint on the wall surface has not formed a sufficient bond or is of poor quality, then the wallpaper will adhere to it (the paint) and pull it entirely off the wall surface during this drying-out process. This may take only a few days or may take as long as six or eight months. If the wallpaper is still secure to the wall surface after a full year has passed--chances are there will be no problems due to the original installation.

For this reason it is important to have or give a full year's written warranty. There are however, several conditions, which the installer cannot control, that may cause the wallpaper to come loose. Some of these are as follows:

(a) Settling of the structure

(b) Paint separation from another paint or wall surface, particularly when several layers of paint or wall surfaces are present

(c) Mildew problems that occur because of poor ventilation and/or the lack of a proper vapor barrier

(d) Sand-painted finishes

There are several adhesions that must take place once the wallpaper has been installed on the wall surface in order to produce a successful job. Picture a chain with different links called **adhesions.**

The first link of the chain is the wall surface. This may be the kraft paper (facing) bonding to the gypsum composition of drywall, or the first layer of paint on a plaster or cinder-block wall.

The second link is the primer/sealer or sizing. This must be compatible with and secured to the first link.

The third link is the adhesive.

The fourth link of the adhesion chain is the substrate (backing) of the wallpaper (which is bonded to either the intermediate layer or the decorative surface).

If any single one of these links of adhesions fail, then the wallpaper will not stay on the wall. Whenever it is time to remove the existing wallpaper, the weakest link of the chain will determine the strippability of the wallcovering. It may be the substrate from the decorative surface, the adhesive from the substrate, the primer/sealer from the adhesive, or the facing paper from the gypsum composition of the drywall.

If the facing paper of the drywall is the weakest link, it could be severely damaged when the wallpaper is removed, and very costly to repair.

Sizings

The term sizing is used rather loosely within the field of wallpapering. Some individuals think of sizing as an action verb, meaning, the act of preparing the wall surface. If this is the case it is important to understand all the fundamentals associated with wall preparation. The term sizing should never be used as a synonym of wall

Adhesion Chain

preparation, especially when a professional is dealing with a customer. This is because it may be very misleading.

When the term sizing is referred to as a product, it has basically two purposes: to provide uniform porosity to the wall surface and provide extra tooth (holding power) for the wallpaper. Both of these reasons are good, however they do not eliminate the major problems of the industry, which are:

(1) the wallpaper fails to adhere properly to the wall surface frequently due to a poor quality latex paint that will not withstand the drying pressures associated with the adhesive's dissipation.

(2) the wall surface is not protected from damage that results from future removal of the wallpaper.

There are basically three types of sizings on the market today. They are as follows:

Starch and Cornflower

Starch and Cornflower: This type of sizing is generally sold by the pound and packaged in small bags or milk cartons. The starch holds together the cornflower once it is mixed with water and applied to the wall surface. It should only be used on a good quality latex or oil-based paint. It should never be used underneath a non-breathing type of wallcovering because it usually does not contain any or enough preservatives against mildew. Starch sizings will not protect new drywall during the removal of wallpaper and will not guard against the poor qualities of latex paint.

Cellulose and Pine Flower

Cellulose and Pine Flower (Sawdust Form): This type of sizing is generally sold by the ounce and is packaged in small boxes. The cellulose holds the pine flower together after it is mixed with water and applied to the wall surface. It sometimes comes packaged in a pre-mixed container

and resembles the viscosity (thickness) of thin milk.

Cellulose sizings will not cause a mildew problem such as starches will, however no sizing or primer/sealer will guard against an already existing mildew problem. Cellulose sizing will not protect walls covered with a poor grade of latex paint and will not aid in the future removal of wallpaper.

Homemade

Homemade Sizing: This type of sizing is frequently made from the same adhesive that is being used to install the wallpaper, however, it has been thinned down to the viscosity of buttermilk or paint. The purpose of this sizing is to provide extra tack (holding power) during the wallpaper installation process simply because the moisture from the adhesive will re-activate the diluted adhesive sizing.

Some installers use a thinned down clay-based adhesive as a sizing because of the solids in it. The clay will act as a blotter that absorbs the excess moisture from the adhesive during the installation, which in turn, will speed up the drying process. This will create a faster tack (drying time) of the new wallpaper during the installation and is especially useful when installing around small corner returns, such as soffits or recessed windows or doors.

The clay (thinned down as sizing) does not add much adhesion to the wallpaper, therefore an acrylic resin or vinyl-over-vinyl adhesive is sometimes added to the mixture which will increase the bond of the wallpaper to the wall surface. The homemade sizings will not protect against the problems of poor latex paints or protect drywall during the removal of the wallpaper.

Primer/Sealers

Since sizing, when referred to as a product, does not aid in the protection of drywall or a poor grade of latex paint--the need for primer/sealers has emerged on the scene. There are many different types of primer/sealers, and each has a different application. Some of the most common types are listed below with a brief description of their makeup and purpose.

Pigmented Acrylic

Pigmented Acrylic Primer/Sealers: This type of primer/sealer is sometimes referred to as a universal primer/sealer. This is because it can be used on all possible surfaces including existing wallpapers and vinyls, poor latex paints, glossy surfaces, and hard laminates including glass and Formica, etc. It cleans up with water and is economical to use. Since it is pigmented, it will prevent the show through of existing wall conditions with a semi-transparent wallcovering. The pigmented acrylic wallpaper primer/sealers will protect drywall from excessive damage during the future removal of wallpaper. The main drawback involved in using this primer/sealer is the cost factor. It is more expensive than a clear acrylic primer/sealer. **Note:** This type of primer/sealer will not secure stains such as grease, crayon, magic markers, ink, food stains, nicotine, or smoke.

Fast-Drying Alkyd (Oil)

Fast-Drying Alkyd (Oil): This type of primer/sealer can be used under all types of wallcoverings and on all surfaces except existing wallpapers and vinyls. The old dyes (inks) of existing wallcoverings may bleed through this type of primer. **See stain-killer primer/sealers.** The clear types of fast-drying oil-primers will not hide existing colors from wall conditions, therefore the pigmented (white) types would be required if this were the case.

Fast-dry alkyds will generally dry within 2 to 4 hours and will provide excellent protection against damage of drywall during any wallpaper removal. If the primer/sealer is thinned down with paint thinner (one to two pints of thinner per gallon), it will soak into and help re-bond poor latex paints to the wall surface. It is not advisable to use a clear pre-mixed adhesive over oil primer/sealers because of the time lapse that is required for the adhesive to dry. This time lapse could cause the wallpaper to shrink, or cause the adhesive to sour or even mildew.

A clay-based type of adhesive is the better type to use over an oil-based primer/sealer, especially when a non-breathing wallcovering is being applied.

Slow-Drying Alkyd (Oil)

Slow-Drying Alkyd (Oil): This type of primer/sealer will require from 10 to 24 hours of drying time after it has been applied to the wall. It may be used under all wallcoverings, and on top of most all surfaces except glossy walls and vinyl wallcoverings.

It has all the same drawbacks and the same advantages as the fast-drying alkyds.

Acrylic

Acrylic Primer/sealers: This type of primer/sealer drys clear, and therefore would not hide wall colors when a semi-transparent wallpaper is being installed. It is useful under most all wallcoverings and on most wall surfaces including existing wallpapers and vinyls. It does not guard against poor latex paints, and will not protect new drywall whenever the wallpaper has to be removed

Heavy-Duty Acrylic

Heavy-Duty Acrylic Primer/sealers: This type of primer/sealer will dry clear and have a tacky (sticky) feel. It positively promotes the adhesion of wallpaper--especially with the commercial types--simply because of the acrylic resins in it. It will not guard against poor latex paint and is even worse for protecting new drywall for strippability. This is because the acrylic primer/sealers soak into the drywall and actually become part of the wall. The heavy commercial wallpaper will bond great to the acrylic primer/sealers, therefore the weakest link of adhesions is the kraft paper (facing) of the sheetrock.

Stain-Killers

Stain-Killer Primer/Sealers: This type of primer/sealer is used exclusively for sealing (protecting against) special stains including inks, lipstick, water circle damage, grease, crayon marks, markers, smoke, graffiti, nicotine, food stains, etc. Whenever these types of stains are present, they must be controlled against bleeding through an acrylic primer/sealer and/or the new wallpaper.

Since stain killer primer/sealers are NOT wallpaper primer/sealers, they must have an acrylic wallpaper primer/sealer applied over it, otherwise the new wallpaper may not properly bond. Caution: Whenever a stain-killer primer/sealer is applied to the wall surface, it will generally seal the wall surface, making it water-proof. This may require the use of a clay-based adhesive or a liner paper whenever non-breathable wallpaper is being applied.

The inks on some types of wallpapers, especially metallic vinyl wallcoverings, will bleed through standard wallpaper primer/sealers. Therefore, a special stain-killer primer/sealer must be applied to prevent the ink from penetrating the new wallpaper. Bleeding inks may be tested by rubbing with ammonia and water. If the inks are colorfast they will not change color. If they are bleeding inks they will turn a greenish-blue.

IMPORTANT!!!

Since a stain-killer primer/sealer is not a wallpaper primer/sealer, it is important to apply a wallpaper acrylic primer/sealer over the stain-killer in order to insure a secure bond of the new wallpaper.

Preparing Wall Surfaces

Properly preparing the wall surface is the most important procedure towards insuring a successful wallpapering job. The following procedures should be reviewed and employed whenever they apply. It is important to realize that every wall surface cannot be made perfectly smooth. Therefore, the selection of the new wallpaper will be very important. A matt or dull finished wallpaper should be selected for uneven or problem wall surfaces that are exposed to a direct light reflection such as on stairways, long hallways, etc.

Textures and embossed wallpapers are likewise considerable choices for unsmoothed wall conditions. The following procedures should be followed wherever they apply.

Removing Wall Fixtures

The wall preparation procedures as well as the job of installing the wallpaper can be made much easier if every obstacle is removed from the wall surface prior to beginning the job. Most all bathroom accessories can be easily removed by using a very small screwdriver to loosen a set (small) screw on towel racks, soap holders, toothbrush holders, toilet paper holders, etc. Some accessories will require a small Allen wrench to unloose the screw.

Most mirrors should be removed that are not too large to jeopardize breaking. If one is too large to move, it should remain mounted on the wall and the wallpaper should be installed around it. Frequently, a set of clips are supporting the mirror. The clips on top of the mirror are usually spring-loaded, and will lift up with a small screwdriver.

Professional wallpaper installers should replace the light fixtures with a temporary light (75-watt recommended) as well as replace large mirrors with a small temporary cosmetic mirrors for the convenience of their customers.

Important: Before removing or replacing any type of electrical obstacle, it is imperative to disconnect the source of electricity.

Most light fixtures are simple to remove. There is generally a screw or bolt (nut) that is supporting the light fixture to a bracket. Once it is removed, there will commonly be a black wire, white wire, and ground (naked) wire to be disconnected. These should be connected with a wire cap or electrical tape. Disconnect them, and place the loose wires into the outlet box after the wire caps (or tape) have been re-applied.

Note: Do not remove electrical outlets or switches. Only remove the plates that are on them. It is advisable to replace the screws into the holes of each electrical obstacle in order to keep from losing them. It is also a good idea to keep all accessories in a household self-fastening clear plastic bag while they are dismounted from the wall.

Once the wall preparation and wallpaper installation are complete, the obstacles can be replaced in the reverse manner that they were removed. The time that is involved (loss) when removing any obstacle will usually be made up (regained) during the wallpaper installation itself.

By taking the time to remove the obstacles, you save time and definitely perform a better, more attractive wallpapering job.

Note: Draw a wiring diagram either on scrap paper or on the back side of an electrical obstacle prior to disconnecting or removing it. This will insure it is wired properly once the new wallpaper has been installed.

Dirty or Greasy Walls

All dirty or greasy walls especially in between kitchen cabinets and behind stoves, should be washed with a solution of equal parts of warm water and ammonia. After the cleaning is complete and the walls have been allowed to dry, (a minimum of several hours), a high quality wallpaper primer/sealer should be applied according to the type of paint and/or wall condition that exists. **Warning: DO NOT EVER USE a detergent that contains phosphorus such as floor cleansers or washing powders. These detergents will prevent the primer/sealers from drying and bonding properly.**

Spot Patching and Sanding

All walls, regardless of the type of paint or surface, must be sanded smooth. It is

advisable to use a coarse sandpaper (80-grit recommended) to eliminate all little bumps or grit that may be on the wall surface. After the walls have been sanded, they should be spot patched with a light-weight water-based non-shrinking spackling, and re-sanded after it has dried. **Never use any type of oil-based spackling prior to wallpapering, because it may bleed through the primer/sealer and stain and/or leave oily spots on the new wallpaper.**

Spot patching is a technique used to correct any wall problems such as nails backing out of drywall (popped nails), old picture hook holes, large paint runs or roller marks, dents from new construction or furniture being moved, door knob holes in the wall, old bathroom fixture holes, oversized holes for electrical switches or receptacles, bad sheetrock seams, or cracks in plaster.

It is advisable to use a 150-watt light bulb to highlight any problem areas during the wall preparation. Use a hammer to slightly indent any protruding places just below the wall surface (such as popped nails, molly bolts, or places where nails or picture hooks were removed). Fill the indented places with spackling, and allow sufficient time to dry. Then sand the spackling smooth and even with the wall surface.

When a problem exist such as flaking paint or dried flaking adhesive, the loose substances should be removed (scraped off) using a broad knife or putty knife. Apply a very light skim coat (application) of thinned-down water-based spackling over the scraped areas using a broad knife or other smoothing tool. This will fill in all slight indentations. After the spackling has been sanded, it will provide a smooth surface for applying the wallpaper primer/sealer and the new wallpaper.

Hard Laminated and Glass

All hard compressed laminates such as Formica or glass should be etched with a coarse sandpaper (50 - 80 grit recommended). This will engrave the surface and give it something for the primer/sealer and the wallpaper to bond to.

When installing over hard surfaces, a heavy-duty acrylic wallpaper primer/sealer should be applied and allowed to completely dry (film cure) a minimum of 24 hours prior to the new wallpaper installation.

Semi-Transparent Wallpapers

If any shadows from the existing wall conditions such as: new drywall (sheetrock) patches and/or seams, old existing wallpaper, dark walls with light painted trim (vice/versa), or dark painted walls with light patching would become visible through the new wallcovering, then a special white-pigmented wallpaper acrylic primer/sealer should be applied.

If you are in doubt about the semi-transparency of the new wallpaper, move behind it a piece of plain white paper with a dark pencil mark on it. If it (the dark pencil mark) is visible through the new wallpaper, it indicates that the wallpaper is semi-transparent and any existing wall conditions with a contrast of color will also show through as a shadow.

If the pencil mark is not visible and shadows are not present, then a high quality clear wallpaper acrylic primer/sealer may be applied.

Stained Areas (Spots)

Stained areas may include **water circle stains, lipstick, grease spots, ink or pencil marks, smoked areas, graffiti, crayon marks, nicotine, food stains, markers, etc.** Every stained place on an existing wall should be spot primed with a good quality pigmented stain killer.

Either a clear or white pigmented wallpaper primer/sealer must be applied over the stain before the new wallpaper is installed. Special stain killer primer/sealers are also necessary for sealing bleeding inks from existing wallpapers such as vinyl metallic wallcoverings. See previous section on primer/sealers.

Important: Do not get a wallpaper primer/sealer confused with a stain killer primer/sealer! A stain killer will prevent stains from returning, and a wallpaper primer/sealer will not.

Moisture Problems

Moisture can be a disastrous enemy to a wallpaper job because it can make the new wallpaper come loose and/or mildew, therefore it must be controlled prior to the application of new wallpaper. If it is not known whether excess moisture is inside or outside of a structure, a simple test will reveal the answer.

Moisture Problem Test:

Tape a piece of aluminum foil (about 12″ x 12″) to the problem wall using duct tape around the edges of it. Leave the foil in place for at least a week and then remove it. If the moisture is between the foil and the wall, it is coming from the exterior of the structure or inside of the wall. If this is the case, a vapor barrier or waterproof silicone may be applied to the exterior of the structure. If the problem wall is within the interior walls of the structure, there may be a leaking water pipe, which would need to be repaired.

There may be excess moisture beneath the structure, which may be corrected either by applying ground draining or air vents in the foundation of the structure.

If the moisture is on the outside of the aluminum foil, then the problem is caused by moisture inside the room and not from behind the wall surface. An exhaust fan or dehumidifier will frequently solve a problem of this type.

Installing Over Pre-Finished Paneling

There are several steps that are required to insure a satisfactory job whenever wallpaper is installed over pre-finished paneling. They are as follows:

(a) Re-check all loose edges of the paneling and re-nail wherever necessary.

(b) Wash all paneling with a solution of equal parts of ammonia and water, to remove any wax or dirt build-up that may be present. Allow to dry.

(c) Lightly sand the paneling with a 80-grit sandpaper to etch it, so the primer/sealer will properly bond.

(d) Apply a wallpaper acrylic primer/sealer to the entire paneling area, including the edges beside windows and doors, and allow to dry a minimum of 24 hours.

(e) Install a medium-weight liner paper horizontally on the paneling to bridge over all the vertical grooves. Allow the liner paper to dry a minimum of 24 hours.

(f) Re-check (using a 150-watt light and drop cord) for any places where the liner paper may have sunken into the grooves of the paneling. Spackle if necessary with a lightweight water-based spackling. Do not use an oil-based product because it will penetrate the final layer of wallpaper and cause it to stain.

> **Warning: It is sometimes recommended to spackle the grooves of pre-finished paneling prior to the application of the wallpaper or liner paper. In this case, the adhesive along with its moisture will bond to the spackling and may cause it to shrink, therefore this procedure may be in vain because the grooves may need to be re-spackled after the liner has been applied. If a liner wallpaper is not used over the pre-spackled grooves, the new wallpaper may end up with permanent groove indentions.**

(h) Apply the final layer of wallpaper onto the liner paper. If a pre-pasted wallpaper is being used for the final layer, it is advisable to apply another application of wallpaper acrylic primer/sealer over the liner. This will help prevent the liner from soaking up the moisture from the adhesive. It may even be necessary to apply an additional paste to the pre-pasted wallpaper to insure a good final bond. It is generally not necessary to apply a second application of primer/sealer if the final wallpaper is not the pre-pasted type.

Cement Block or Brick Walls

One fact that must be understood about cement blocks or brick walls is they are commonly uneven when they are installed. Because of the nature of these wall surfaces, they cannot be sanded smooth, therefore, whenever wallpaper is installed over them, the uneven appearance will continue to be visible.

It is not unusual for individuals to desire to cover the cement block or brick walls simply because they are not very attractive just painted. Most people think of them as being used in institutional or commercial buildings. The application of wallpaper has been used for many years, however, the walls must be properly prepared in order for the wallpaper to bond properly.

Since the walls are uneven, the final selection of decorative wallpaper should be considered. A pattern that has a floral print will hide the unevenness much better than a plain texture or stripe. Also a heavily embossed texture with a dull (matt) finish, will obscure the imperfections better than a smooth shiny surface.

As far as the wall preparation, the first factor to consider is the vaporescence factor (the production or formation of vapor or moisture) that is present either inside or outside the structure. If any excessive amount of moisture is present, it could cause an adverse reaction to the wallpaper's adhesive.

A mildew problem may result or the wallpaper simply may not adhere properly to the walls. It has been established that cement block structures with artificial gas heat can cause a moisture problem in the cold months; whereas in the summer months, it is not a problem. All moisture problems must be resolved before any wallpaper is ever installed.

The second factor to consider is the available lighting conditions, meaning the amount of light that will glare on the wall once the final decorative wallpaper has been installed. The more glare (reflected light) there is, the more the imperfections of the wall will be apparent. It is advisable to have an indirect light reflection to these wall conditions as opposed to a direct lighting arrangement.

A heavyweight liner paper is recommended to help bridge over the mortar joints as well as camouflage the bulge of the walls. An acrylic wallpaper primer/sealer must be applied to the cement block or brick walls and allowed to dry a minimum of 12 hours before the application of the liner paper.

Note: If the cement block or brick walls are new, they should be sealed with a block sealer prior to the application of the acrylic wallpaper primer/sealer.

After the liner paper has been applied, any major places that still look bad may be spackled prior to the application of the final decorative wallpaper. If the brick or masonry walls are too uneven to provide a satisfactory appearance using wallpaper, it may be necessary to hire a carpenter to apply wood furring strips to rebuild the wall and make it even using another surface such as drywall.

Important: Bricks that have a sandy surface cannot be properly prepared for wallcoverings, therefore, it is not recommended to attempt this application.

Mildew Problems

Mildew is a fungus growth which flourishes or grows in a dark, moist environment such as bathrooms, shower stalls, basements, and closets. It may appear in many different colors such as pink, grey,

black, yellow, green, or purple. Frequently, mildew that is associated with wallpaper will be a grayish black or pinkish purple in color.

Mildew must be cleaned and disinfected before any new wallpaper can be applied, because if the mildew continues to grow underneath the wallpaper, it will show up as dark or pink discolorations on the surface.

There are several steps to aid in the protection against mildew:

(a) Wash the affected area with a solution of equal parts of household bleach and warm water and rinse with clean water. Allow the walls to dry.

(b) Spray the walls generously with a disinfectant or germicidal spray and allow to dry.

(c) Add 1 tablespoon of a liquid germicidal agent to each gallon of adhesive whenever extreme cases of mildew are present.

(d) Use a cellulose-based size and/or adhesive with a mildew protective agent to yield an extra added protection against the reoccurrence of mildew.

(e) Use a low-water-content adhesive such as clay-base pre-mixed, whenever applying a non-breathing wallcovering over an oil based wall surface.

(f) Apply an absorbent, lightweight liner paper prior to installing a non-breathable wallcovering over another non-breathable wallcovering or a hard laminate such as Formica to absorb any excess moisture from the adhesive.

Rusted Outside Corner Edges (Beads)

It is very rare to find an outside corner bead that has rusted on sheetrock (drywall) construction, however, if this problem occurs, it must be corrected or else the rust will bleed through the wallpaper primer/sealer and the decorative wallcovering. Listed below are a few steps that are neces-

sary to solve this problem.

(a) Sand the affected areas as smooth as possible with a 120-grit sandpaper.

(b) Prime the rusted areas with a high quality oil-based rust resistant primer and allow to dry.

(c) Re-prime the areas with a wallpaper acrylic primer/sealer prior to the installation of the decorative wallpaper.

Caution: Do not sand the rusted areas after the rust primer has been applied. If the primer is scratched or sanded the protection from rust would become void.

Designer Wallpapers

An inexpensive liner paper that is made of plain stock paper is usually required under expensive delicate wallpapers such as hand-screen prints, silks, or fabrics. These types of wallcoverings require a very uniform drying surface, as well as protection from existing wall conditions such as light and dark color contrast or high porosity factors. The cost of the liner paper and/or labor should not be an arguing factor when installing such expensive wallpapers. There is no choice. Liner paper must be used.

New Drywall (Sheetrock)

Since drywall is a gypsum composition that is sandwiched between layers of kraft paper, the exposed surface must be sealed prior to the installation of wallpaper. If the kraft paper is not properly prepared, it will shred and/or delaminate from the gypsum if the future removal of the wallpaper is ever attempted.

An oil-based enamel undercoat or sanding/sealer thinned with paint thinner (one quart of thinner per gallon of sealer) will serve as a great protective layer for the kraft paper surface of the drywall.

Since there are contrasting colors between the drywall and the mud used to repair the nails and seams, these areas must be completely coated with a pigmented primer/sealer prior to the application of a semi-transparent wallcovering.

It is important that this condition be checked beforehand, simply because it is too late to correct the problem after the new wallpaper has been installed.

Preparing Surface Damage

There are varying degrees of damage that can occur to the surface of drywall, especially when an existing wallpaper is being removed using a wallpaper remover solution and warm water. The following sections explains how to repair both minor and extreme cases of wall surface damage.

Minor Damage

It is not unusual to damage the very top exposed veneer layer of drywall (kraft paper), during the removal of some wallpapers. The damage will frequently be exposed as minor blisters or delamination of the first layer coming off the wall, It is important to repair these places prior to the installation of the new wallpaper, because if not, they will show up as blisters underneath the new wallpaper.

Caution: During the removal of any existing wallpaper, there are two important factors to consider.

(a) Do not over soak the existing wallpaper an excessive amount with a wallpaper remover solution, because it will penetrate the drywall's surface and cause extensive damage to it. Usually, about 15 - 20 minutes is plenty of time to allow the wallpaper remover solution to penetrate the existing wallpaper. **Note:** If the sheetrock wall becomes excessively wet, discontinue the wall preparation procedures until the wall has completely dried, and then start over.

(b) Never attempt to remove the wallpaper at a 90 degree angle to the wall surface. This would pull directly away from the wall and may cause unnecessary damage to the drywall. Always pull the existing wallpaper off the wall at a 10 degree angle!

Whenever the surface of the sheetrock wall has blistered or delaminated only very slightly, the damaged areas must be removed. The best way to expose (locate) all of the damaged areas is to wet the walls (only one section at a time) with a fine mist of warm water, using a garden sprayer or household spray bottle. This will cause the blisters or delaminated areas to swell and become very visible.

While the damaged areas are visible (still wet), cut them out, one at a time, using a sharp razor blade. Once the blistered or delaminated area has been cut around, it can be removed without causing the surface of the drywall to continue raveling while it is being removed. The razor cut creates a clean stopping point for the blister to be removed, otherwise the surface of the drywall would continue to peel (ravel).

Once all damaged areas have been removed, the walls should be allowed to dry and then primed with a wallpaper pigmented acrylic primer/sealer or an oil-based enamel undercoater (thinned down with paint thinner). After the primer has dried, the cut out areas will have become hardened.

Lightly sand the affected areas with 120-grit sandpaper and spackle them with a lightweight spackling that does not shrink.

Sand the spackled areas after they dry and re-prime them with the same primer/sealer previously used. The wall surface should now be smooth and ready for the new wallcovering to be installed.

Extreme Damage

If the outer layer of the drywall is extremely damaged, meaning the actual gypsum center of the drywall is exposed, then it must be sealed with an oil-based enamel undercoater. This will seal the exposed and frayed edges of the drywall veneer.

Once the primer has dried, the damaged areas must be spackled as best as possible. A liner paper may need to be applied to the repaired wall to further smooth out any indentions and visible flaws on the wall.

How to Repair a Hole in Sheetrock (Drywall)

Warning: There have been cases documented when live electrical wires are exposed behind the drywall where a hole exist. DO NOT reach in or stick metal objects or wet spackling into these holes without first inspecting it for live wires!

A hole in drywall should be repaired before installing any new wallcovering over it. The following twelve steps require only a minimum amount of spackling for the repair and in turn requires minimum drying time.

Step 1: Determine the actual thickness of the existing drywall. It may be ⅜″, ½″, or ⅝″ thick. A scrap piece of drywall will be needed, at least as big as the hole that has to be repaired, and it should be the same thickness as the existing drywall.

Step 2: Cut the new piece of drywall into either a square or rectangular shape, slightly larger than the hole. **(Fig.1)**

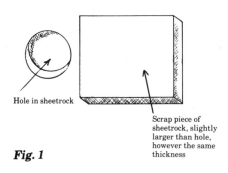

Hole in sheetrock

Scrap piece of sheetrock, slightly larger than hole, however the same thickness

Fig. 1

Step 3: Place the scrap piece of drywall over the hole and mark (scribe) with a pencil the exact outline of the piece. **(Fig.2)**

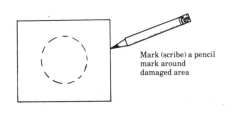

Mark (scribe) a pencil mark around damaged area

Fig. 2

WALL PREPARATION

Step 4: Remove the scrap (repair) piece of drywall and use a keyhole saw, utility knife, or jigsaw to cut through the drywall following the exact penciled outline. **(Fig. 3)**

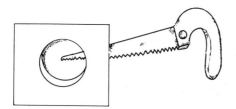

Fig. 3

Step 5: Remove the damaged drywall. The new hole should match the new repair piece of drywall. **(Fig. 4)**

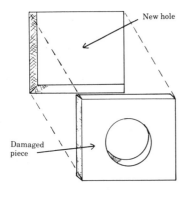

New hole

Damaged piece

Fig. 4

Step 6: Cut at least two pieces of wood to establish a foundation for anchoring the new repair piece into the new hole. This wood should be ¾″ thick by approximately 2″ to 3″ wide and should be about 8″ longer than the diameter of the hole.

Step 7: Insert the two pieces of wood (one at a time) into the new hole so that the ends extend at least 4″ past the top and bottom of the hole. Space them evenly apart to give a balanced foundation for the new repair piece of drywall. Use drywall screws to fasten the pieces of wood through the existing wall. An electric drill will be much easier than manually inserting the screws. **(Fig.5)**

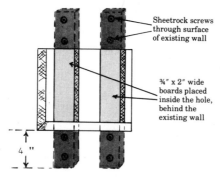

Sheetrock screws through surface of existing wall

¾″ x 2″ wide boards placed inside the hole, behind the existing wall

4 ″

Fig.5

Caution: Do not use a hammer or drywall nails to secure the boards. This will damage the drywall because it is not strong enough to withstand the force of the hammer around the repair area.

Step 8: Using drywall screws, secure the piece of drywall to the two pieces of wood. **(Fig.6)**

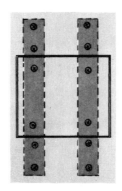

Repair piece of sheetrock in place and secured with sheetrock screws

Fig.6

Step 9: Apply a self-adhesive fibered mesh tape over the seams around the edges where the new repair piece of sheetrock was added. The mesh tape will prevent the seams of the drywall from cracking apart after the spackling has dried. **(Fig.7)**

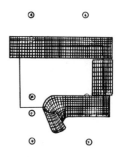

Fig.7

Step 10: Make sure the screw heads are recessed just below the surface of the drywall at least ⅛″. Spackle over these just as you would a nail head and spread spackling over the fiber tape evenly. Do not create a bulge. Extend the spackling out past the seams at least 6″ to 8″ to feather out the spackling with the wall.

Step 11: After the spackling is completely dry, sand it smooth using a 120 grit sandpaper. Be sure to sand in a circular motion so as not to create ridges in the spackling.

Step 12: Apply a wallpaper acrylic primer/ sealer and allow to dry. Now it is ready for the new wallpaper. **Hint:** When the hole to be fixed is too small to insert your hand, drill one of the drywall screws into the board for a handle. **(Fig.8)**

Fig.8

Painted Wall Surfaces

There will usually be paint on a wall if it is not new construction or has existing wallpaper. It is important to determine the type of paint and quality prior to installing new wallpaper.

Flat Oil

The first step to preparing any oil type surface is to etch the surface with a coarse sandpaper such as 50-grit. An acrylic wallpaper primer/sealer will serve as a good surface for the wallcovering to bond to, however, a starch sizing may be used only if a non-breathing wallcovering is being applied to the surface, otherwise a cellulose sizing is recommended.

The starch sizing may cause a mildew problem if it is trapped between two non-breathing surfaces.

Flat Latex

All flat latex wall paints must be tested for quality in order to determine the proper primer/sealer to apply. Once the quality of the latex paint has been determined, the proper preparation procedures should be followed.

Testing Paint Quality

Test: Rub the wall surface vigorously using a cloth moistened with warm water. If no color transfers from the paint to the cloth, the paint is of a good quality. Light to medium transfer of paint to the cloth will indicate a poor latex paint. Complete paint removal will indicate a defective paint or builder's flat (thinned down sheetrock mud, that was used as paint).

Good Flat Latex Paint

Good flat latex paint: Apply one coat of a high quality clear or pigmented wallpaper acrylic primer/sealer.

Poor Flat Latex Paint

Poor flat latex paint: Apply one coat of a high quality pigmented wallpaper acrylic primer/sealer.

Defective Flat Latex Paint Builder's Flat

Defective flat latex paint (builder's flat): Remove all loose paint with a strong solution of ammonia and warm water (2 parts ammonia mixed with 1 part water). Prime walls with a diluted oil-based enamel undercoater or sanding sealer. **Important:** Do not use the enamel undercoater full strength! If the enamel undercoater is used full strength it will not penetrate the defective paint, and the defective paint must be penetrated to form a sufficient bond to the wall surface.

Latex Enamel

Most all latex enamel painted surfaces will provide a very good foundation for installing wallcoverings; however, it is important that the paint has been allowed to dry (cure out) for a minimum of 14 to 21 days. It is also important to make sure the surface is clean of soaps, bath oils, cosmetics, etc., especially when the walls have been painted for a long period of time. If these contaminates are present they should be washed with a solution of equal parts of ammonia and water. However, it is advisable to apply an acrylic wallpaper primer/sealer prior to the installation of wallpaper in order to guarantee that no problems will occur.

Glossy Enamel

All glossy enamel paints are generally non-breathing (non porous), and therefore should be sanded with a coarse sandpaper (50-80 grit) to provide an etched surface for the wallpaper primer/sealer to bond to.

Apply a high quality wallpaper acrylic primer/sealer (either clear or pigmented) and allow to dry a minimum of 4 to 6 hours prior to the application of new wallpaper.

If a non-breathing wallpaper (such as fabric-backed vinyl) is being applied over the glossy painted surface, then an absorbent liner paper may be required to absorb any excess moisture from the new adhesive, which otherwise may cause a mildew problem to occur because of the amount of time it would take for the wallpaper to dry.

Metal Surfaces

All metal surfaces must be cleaned of all dirt and grease build-up with a solution of equal parts of ammonia and water. A high quality rust proof paint (oil-based is recommended) must be applied and allowed to dry. Next, apply a wallpaper pigmented acrylic primer/sealer and allow to dry 24 hours.

Painting Over Existing Wallpapers

Sometimes it is advisable to paint over an existing wallpaper rather than to remove it. Example: An individual wants to use only a border where a wallpaper is already existing. If the existing wallpaper is in good condition, it would be better to paint over it rather than to remove it, especially if the removal process would damage the wall.

Once the walls have been painted, the area where the border is to be applied must be primed with a wallpaper acrylic primer/sealer and allowed to dry.

There are times when it is possible to paint over heavily textured wallpapers such as grasscloth, stringcloth, or flock to produce a very even color tonal effect. In these cases, the existing wallpaper must be primed (sealed) with an oil-based stain killer primer/sealer. This will prevent any bleeding dyes (inks) on the existing wallpaper from penetrating the final paint application, which should be a good latex paint or an enamel paint.

Caution: A wallpaper primer/sealer is not a stain killer primer/sealer!

Sand-Painted Walls

Any wall surface painted with a sand finish paint must be sanded smooth before ever attempting to install new wallpaper over it. This may require a vibrating or belt sander and may also be very time consuming; however, if a satisfactory job is expected, it must be done.

Wallpaper will not properly bond when installed over a sand-painted finish simply because the wallpaper will adhere only to the outer surface tips of the sand finish. The seams will more than likely separate, and the wallpaper will eventually come loose or fall off.

Once the sand-painted walls have been sanded as smooth as possible, a high quality wallpaper acrylic primer/sealer must be applied and allowed to dry.

The selection of a heavily embossed wallpaper with a dull (matt) finish is recommended to camouflage the unsmoothed finish of the wall surface. A wallpaper selection with a shiny decorative surface will only emphasize every imperfection on a sand-painted wall.

Tongue & Groove Board Walls

Every wall surface made from individual boards will go through the process of thermo-expansion and contraction. This simply means that the boards will expand and contract with the temperature changes that take place within a structure, whether by natural or artificial means. Since this movement takes place, it is NOT advisable to install wallpaper over it. Even a heavy-weight liner paper will stretch and buckle during this movement.

The only solution to re-decorating these wall surfaces is to apply a layer of drywall (sheetrock) or plywood over them. The seams of either product must be finished as if they were being painted.

An oil-based enamel undercoater must be applied to plywood to help eliminate raising the grain. Then it must be sanded smooth prior to the application of wallpaper.

See section on New Drywall for the proper preparation procedures.

Ceramic Tile

The process for installing wallpaper over ceramic tile is very similar to installing over cement block walls or brick. The only difference is that ceramic tile is most often used in bathrooms and kitchens, and therefore must be completely cleansed of dirt, grease, or soap film prior to the application of the wallpaper acrylic primer/sealer.

Procedures will be the same as for cement block or brick walls.

Plywood Walls

If plywood is used as the wall surface, it must be primed with an oil-based primer/sealer prior to the application of wallpaper. This type of primer/sealer will help eliminate raising the grain of the wood. If the grain does raise after the primer has been applied, it should be sanded smooth with an 80-grit sandpaper.

Plaster Walls

Unpainted plaster must be at least 90 to 120 days old, then washed with a strong solution of vinegar to neutralize any alkaline areas. After this procedure is complete and the plaster wall is dry, a wallpaper acrylic primer/sealer should be applied and allowed to dry.

If the plaster is old it may have cracks (both large and small) present. If the cracks are large they must be scraped out with a sharp tool such as a screwdriver to remove any loose places. Once the crack has been cleaned, it should be repaired using a mesh repair tape embedded in spackling and then sanded once it has dried. The mesh tape will reinforce the spackling and help prevent the crack from reoccurring.

If the cracks in the plaster are only hairline size, then the use of spackling without the mesh tape would provide a sufficiently smooth surface.

It is advisable to apply a liner paper or fabric-backed vinyl over plaster walls that have a history of continuous cracking. Either of these wallpapers will support the plaster wall surface and help prevent cracking.

Pre-Sticking Papers

If a self-sticking paper has been applied to a wall surface such as contact paper, it is advisable to apply a wallpaper pigmented acrylic primer/sealer over the surface of it. After the primer has dried (usually 2 to 4 hours), any overlapped edges of the existing paper should be spackled. Once the spackling has dried it should be sanded and re-primed with the same primer/sealer.

The purpose for applying the wallpaper pigmented acrylic primer/sealer first is because the spackling will not usually bond to the slick surface of the contact paper without the primer/sealer.

If it is mandatory that the contact paper be removed, the existing adhesive on the wall surface must be removed. It should come off by washing it with a solution of paint thinner or lacquer thinner.

Caution: Only use these products in proper ventilation and avoid any type of open flame.

Once the walls have completely dried a wallpaper acrylic primer/sealer should be applied and allowed to dry prior to the wallpaper installation.

Hanging Over Existing Wallpaper

In order to install new wallpaper over existing wallpaper, it is critical that the existing wallpaper is very secure to the wall surface (especially around the seam areas) because the old wallpaper will become the foundation of the new. If any part of the existing wallpaper is loose and not repaired, then the new wallpaper can not be installed successfully.

With the exception of heavily embossed wallpapers or natural wallpapers such as grasscloth, reedcloth, stringcloths, or fabrics, new wallpaper can be installed over existing wallpaper--provided all the necessary preparation procedures are correctly followed as listed below:

(a) Spackle and sand every overlapped seam, even if it is barely noticeable. If the overlap is not eliminated it will show through the new wallpaper just as an old paint run will show through a new layer of paint.

(b) Re-secure every seam or pucker with a seam adhesive, otherwise they must be cut out with a razor blade and spackled.

(c) Check to see if the old inks on the existing wallpaper are bleeding inks, meaning they will penetrate through an ordinary wallpaper primer/sealer. Apply ammonia and water over the wallpaper to test. Colorfast inks will not change color. Others will turn a green-blue in color and will bleed through a standard acrylic primer/sealer. If this is the case, the existing wallpaper must be primed with a shellac or special pigmented stain killer primer/sealer, and then re-primed with an acrylic wallpaper primer/sealer. This is especially frequent with vinyl wallcoverings with metallic colors.

(d) Apply a high quality wallpaper acrylic primer/sealer over all existing wallpapers in order for the new wallpaper to properly bond to it.

(e) Be sure to check the new wallpaper for a semi-transparent quality which may allow problem wall conditions to show through. If so, the walls must be primed with a pigmented acrylic wallpaper primer/sealer.

(f) An absorbent liner paper should be applied if the existing wallpaper is a solid vinyl or non-breathing material. The liner will soak up the bulk of the moisture of the new adhesive, which otherwise could cause a mildew problem to occur. The use of a vinyl-over-vinyl adhesive would eliminate this step.

(g) When installing wallcovering over an existing vinyl wallcovering, it is important to check for loose plastercizers. If the surface of the wallcovering feels sticky, then it should be thoroughly washed with mineral spirits (paint thinner). After the mineral spirits have completely evaporated (dried), a high quality acrylic wallpaper primer/sealer should be applied and allowed to dry. Note the preceding step when installing a vinyl over an existing vinyl wallcovering.

(b) What type of wallpaper is on the wall?

(c) Is the existing wallpaper strippable?

(d) Is the wallpaper porous?

(e) Was the wall surface properly sealed to permit easy removal of the new wallpaper?

It is very rare that an individual will know the answers to these questions; therefore, the following tests may need to be performed to establish solutions that will provide the necessary information to yield a successful job.

Tests for Removing Wallpapers

In order to determine the strippability of wallcoverings, it is necessary to verify the wall surface and the type of wallcovering that was installed on it.

Test 1: Determining The Wall Surface

It is important to know the type of wall surface beneath the existing wallpaper. This information will be necessary to help determine the amount of moisture and/or tension that can be applied to the wall surface without causing unnecessary damage to occur.

The wall surface will usually be drywall (sheetrock or gypsum board) if the structure was built within the last forty years.

This type of wall surface is made of gypsum sandwiched between layers of facing paper (sometimes referred to as kraft paper). It is very sensitive to excessive moisture, therefore, extra care should be taken to avoid over wetting it during the removal of wallpaper. The surface of drywall will also delaminate if excessive pressure is applied, consequently, extra care should be taken not to rip or tear the surface during the removal of wallpaper.

Prior to drywall most wall surfaces were made of plaster. This type of wall surface

Removing Wallpapers

The process of removing old wallpaper can be a very challenging experience; however, it is always better to remove it-- if excessive damage does not occur to the wall surface during the procedure. There are many important factors that must be determined before removing the existing wallpaper. Some of them are as follows:

(a) On what type of wall surface was the wallpaper applied? (such as drywall, plaster, or wood?)

is made by smoothing plaster into the wood lathe which is nailed to studs in the wall. This type of wall surface is much harder than drywall and is not as sensitive to moisture. It is important, however, to avoid gouging any type wall during the removal of wallpaper.

Some wall surfaces are made of other materials such as Formica, glass, tile, or plywood. Whichever the case, it is important to avoid damaging to the surface of the wall so that very little repair is necessary.

Test 2: Determining Wallpaper Strippability

A couple of steps are necessary to determine the strippability of the existing wallpaper. First, use a scraper or putty knife to lift a small corner of the existing wallpaper away from the wall surface in an inconspicuous place such as behind a door or refrigerator.

Second, grasp the wallpaper with both hands and pull it at a 10 degree angle. Avoid pulling directly away from the wall surface at a 90 degree angle because this may cause unnecessary damage to the wall surface.

If the wallpaper strips off in its entirety without causing any excessive damage to the wall surface, then continue the same process until the chore is complete.

If the wallpaper does not completely dry strip, it (the existing wallpaper) will have to be saturated with water and wallpaper remover solution to dissolve the adhesive which is bonding it to the wall. See Test 3.

Test 3: Determining Wallpaper Porosity

If the existing wallpaper is not dry strippable, it must be tested to determined if it is porous or nonporous. This test can be done by saturating a small area (24" X 24") of the existing wallpaper with a solution of hot water and wallpaper remover solution.

Note: It is better to use a household spray bottle to perform this test. If it proves to be effective, use a garden sprayer to finish the job faster.

If the wallpaper is porous the solution will immediately soak into the wallpaper

and dissolve the old adhesive. The wallpaper remover solution should only be allowed to soak into the wallpaper for approximately 15 minutes. If it is allowed to penetrate an excess amount of time, it may cause unnecessary damage to the wall surface (especially drywall). Once the old wallpaper has been soaked, it can then be removed using a wallpaper scraper or broad knife provided the wall surface was properly prepared during the original installation.

If the wallpaper remover solution does not soak into the old wallpaper, it means the surface is nonporous. Nonporous types of wallpapers include those coated with a polyvinyl chloride (PVC) or an acrylic finish, or wallpapers that have been painted over. In either case the surface of the existing wallpaper will have to be etched (scored, scratched, or roughened) in order to make it porous so the wallpaper remover solution can penetrate to the adhesive and soften it for easy removal. This may be accomplished by using a coarse floor-sanding paper (4½ grit rating) or a tool devised specifically for etching the surface of wallpapers. Consult local wallcovering dealers. Once the test area is etched, spray it with a solution of hot water and a wallpaper remover solution to determine its strippability.

After the wallpaper has been saturated for 10 to 15 minutes, try to scrape it off using a small putty knife or a broad knife. If the wallpaper can be removed with a minimum amount of wall surface damage, proceed. Once the old wallpaper has been removed, the old adhesive should be removed by wetting with a wallpaper remover solution or non-phosphorus detergent and sponging clean.

Allow the wall surface to completely dry and apply the correct wallpaper primer/sealer prior to the installation of the new wallpaper. See chapter on Primer/Sealers and Sizings.

Existing wallpaper such as grasscloth, flock, stringcloth, heated vinyls, rushcloth, or hemp have a raised and uneven decorative surface and must be removed from the existing wall surface before any new wallpaper can be installed. Therefore, it may cause excessive damage to the wall surface if it were not properly prepared originally. If this happens, a liner paper may be required after the wallpaper has been removed and the walls have been

skim patched (patched with a thinned spackling) and covered with an oil-based wallpaper primer/sealer.

IMPORTANT:

If wall surface damage occurs during the removal of smooth surfaced wallpapers, DO NOT CONTINUE! It could be very costly to repair! There are many times that the wall preparation was NOT PERFORMED properly during the original installation, therefore, it will be impossible to remove the wallpaper without causing excessive damage. If this happens, it is better to install the new wallpaper over the existing by carefully following the steps listed in Hanging Over Existing Wallpapers.

It is advisable to use an embossed (raised) decorative surface wallcovering with a matt (dull) finish if the wall surface is not completely smooth. A wallpaper with a shiny decorative surface will only highlight every imperfection on the wall.

Removing Different Types of Wallpapers

This section will help identify the different types of wallcoverings that exist as well as offer the correct methods for their removal.

Commercial Vinyls

These are generally 48 to 54 inches in width and most often have a random or textured match. They are generally classified in three categories: Type 1, Type 2, and Type 3. Type 1 is the lightest and weighs between 7 and 13 ounces per square yard and will customarily contain a scrim (lightweight cloth backing) substrate. Type 2 is medium-duty and weighs between 14 and 21 ounces per square yard, and will commonly contain a drill or osnaburg substrate which is a heavier and coarser cloth backing. Type 3 is a heavy-duty wallcovering and will weigh 21 ounces or more per square yard and will usually have a drill backing which is a heavy-duty cloth backing.

All of these types of wallcoverings will ordinarily dry strip from the wall surface with a minimum of effort, however the angle of the removal process is critical. A corner should be pulled up with a scraper or broad knife, just enough to grasp it with your hands. Then pull the wallcovering off the wall at about a ten degree angle. This will eliminate pulling directly against the wall surface, which could, and probably would, cause extensive damage to the wall--particularly if it is sheetrock (drywall).

Some installers prefer to use a bread dough rolling pin to remove the wallcovering in which they start the loose part of the wallcovering onto the roller, near the ceiling, and actually roll the wallcovering off of the wall as it wraps around the rolling pin, naturally only a small strip at a time.

If extensive wall surface damage begins to occur, then the following steps must be performed: **(a)** All loose places must be re-secured, **(b)** an acrylic wallpaper primer/sealer should be applied, and **(c)** an absorbent layer of liner paper should be installed since the commercial wallpaper is totally non-breathable.

The liner paper would prevent putrefaction or the formation of mildew. Some installers only use a vinyl-to-vinyl adhesive to install over commercial vinyls and report reasonably good results.

Cork Veneer

This type of wallcovering has a texture with no definite pattern or arrangement. Real cork veneer is shaved from cork planks or blocks and is laminated to a substrate that may be colored or plain. Cork generally can be delaminated from its substrate (backing) by pulling away at a ten degree angle. If this is not effective, then it should be scored with a very coarse floor sanding paper (4½ grit rating) and then soaked with a full strength wallpaper remover solution.

The cork veneer may be removed (using a broad knife) after it has been saturated for about 15 minutes. If the substrate (backing) is secure to the wall surface it can usually be installed over; however, if it is not it must be removed using the latter method for removal. Note: It is generally not advisable to install any wallpaper directly over cork veneers because the final bond of the new wallpaper may be inadequate.

Felt or Suede

These wallcoverings resemble a leather-like finish with a napped surface resembling the leather made from the skin of a goat. The same method as the cork veneer is used to remove this type of wallcovering. Like the cork veneer, it is not advisable to install new wallcovering directly over the suede or felt cloth.

Flocked

These wallpapers are made from very fine cotton, silk, rayon, or nylon fibers that were applied to a slow-drying paint during its production. Sometimes high voltage electrodes are used to apply the cut fibers to the wallpaper which makes them stand up straight.

The substrate of the flock (either paper or scrim) will determine the correct procedure to use while removing the flock. If the substrate is paper, the flock will need to be wetted with a wallpaper remover solution or a wallpaper steamer machine. If it is necessary to score (scratch) the flock to allow the moisture to penetrate the decorative surface, it is advisable to moisten the flocked fibers prior to the etching process. This will help keep the fibers from contaminating the air.

Once the flocked wallpaper is saturated (about fifteen minutes) it can ordinarily be removed by using a broad knife. If the flocked wallpaper has a scrim backing, you're in luck. It should peel away from the wall surface in its entirety using the same method as with a Type 1 commercial wallcovering.

Foil

This type of wallcovering is constructed by laminating a thin sheet of aluminum foil onto a substrate of paper or scrim (a lightweight cloth backing). They sometimes have a polyester sheet in between the paper backing and the foil to prevent water in the adhesive from actually contacting the foil. Foils will not burn, but are fairly easy to tear. Most all foil can be scored with a rough sandpaper and removed by wetting with a wallpaper remover solution.

If it is necessary to install new wallpaper over the foil (to avoid extensive wall damage), the inks must be tested to see if they are colorfast. Wallcoverings with metallic colors that are not colorfast must be sealed with a pigmented shellac or stain killer primer/sealer because they will react with all acrylic primer/sealers and result in a bleeding stain. Any suspect ink may be tested with ammonia and water. Bleeding inks will turn green-blue while colorfast inks will not.

Grasscloth

This is a handcrafted product which is customarily made from a native vine (arrowroot) of Korea. Weavers use handmade looms which are strung vertically with cotton threads, referred to as the warp threading. The grass produces the weft (horizontal) threading and together they are called the netting. The netting is laminated to a paper backing (substrate) and then dyed to a specific color. Grasscloth contains natural shading effects that must be expected because of the handmade process--the real beauty of the product. Grasscloth can generally be removed by simply wetting the netting or decorative surface with warm water and a wallpaper remover solution. Once the netting is saturated, it will normally peel away from the paper substrate. The substrate must then be moistened and allowed to soak up the remover solution. After about 10 to 20 minutes, the paper backing should easily be removed using a broad knife or scraper. If it is not removable, it may be sanded after drying and used as a liner paper.

Hand-Printed Mural

This is a mural that is installed in individual paneled strips, either numbered or lettered in a sequence. It is hand printed (usually with a screening process) and resembles the structure of a solid sheet vinyl wallpaper. The decorative surface of this wallcovering will ordinarily peel away from the substrate by pulling it away at a 10 degree angle. The backing, which is commonly paper, will remain on the wall surface. It can be removed by wetting with a wallpaper remover solution and scraping with a broad knife after approximately fifteen minutes have elapsed. If the substrate (paper backing) cannot be removed, it may serve as a liner paper for a new wallcovering.

Heated or Raised Vinyl

This type of wallpaper will have a raised effect that is heat embossed by using a thermo-plastic material such as vinyl. Most raised vinyl wallcoverings will have a paper backing laminated to the decorative surface. During the removal process it can usually be separated from the paper backing by peeling at a 10 degree angle. Never pull directly away from the wall surface at a 90 degree angle simply for the reason that it could cause unnecessary damage, especially if the wall surface is sheetrock. Once the raised vinyl layer is removed, the paper backing could serve as a liner for new wallpaper. It is oftentimes fairly easy to remove the paper backing by wetting it with warm water and a wallpaper remover solution, waiting about 15 minutes, then scraping it off with a broad knife.

Hemp

This type of wallpaper is made from fibers of the hemp plant. Hemp wallpaper has a coarse fiber structure and closely resembles real grasscloth, but has a much finer weave. As in grasscloth, it will contain irregularities in color and pattern and the seams will be dominant. The same procedure that is used to remove grasscloth is also used for hemp.

Jute Weave

Jute weave is made by using jute, a strong coarse fiber that is used in making burlap. It is commonly produced in India and surrounding countries. Both the warp (vertical weave) and weft (horizontal weave) of this product may be made from jute or it can be combined with another type of natural fibered yarn. It is laminated to a paper backing much like grasscloth. The removal process of jute is the same as for grasscloth.

Liner Paper

Liner paper is a blank stock type of wallpaper. It comes in different weights such as light, medium, and heavy. It can be plain paper stock or a spun-type material. Most wallpapers can be installed over liner paper--assuming it is secure to the wall surface. If it is not, it will either dry strip in its entirety at a 10 degree angle or it will need to be wetted with a wallpaper remover solution and scraped off with a broad knife after it has been saturated for approximately 15 minutes.

Moiré

Moiré wallpaper has a watered silk effect. When the light reflection is at a certain angle, the moire will resemble a wood grain effect or texture. Moiré may be printed on paper or fabric. Most moire wallcovering will have a paper backing and will resemble the construction of a solid sheet vinyl, but will sometimes have a lightweight cloth backing (scrim). If the backing is paper, the decorative surface will peel away from the backing at a 10 degree angle which would help to eliminate excessive damage on the wall surface. The backing can be removed by wetting with warm water and a wallpaper remover solution for approximately 15 minutes and then scraped with a broad knife.

Mylar

Mylar is actually a trademark of DuPont for a particular brand of polyester film. This film is applied to the decorative print of wallpapers which may have a paper, woven, or non-woven substrate (backing).

Mylar wallpapers are often mistaken for foil wallpapers, which is very similar in appearance. Mylar is actually a polyester film that is metallized with aluminum or vinyl metallized sheeting. Mylar will not tear very easily, but, unlike foil, Mylar will burn.

Generally, Mylar will delaminate from its backing, or it will dry strip entirely from the wall surface. When the decorative surface will delaminate, it should be done so at a 10 degree angle to prevent damaging the wall surface. If a paper backing is remaining on the wall, it may be installed over, or may be removed using warm water and a wallpaper remover solution to wet it. After 15 minutes, remove it with a broad knife.

Paper Weave

This type of wallcovering is commonly made in Japan, and is very similar to real grasscloth. The weave, however, is actually paper that has been cut in thin strips which is twisted and spun into lengths of yarn (hanks). A manufacturer makes this paper yarn into a weave, and then it is laminated to a paper backing. These should not be classified or confused with the Korean grasscloths, reedcloths, or rushcloths. The removal process is the same as for grasscloth.

Photo Mural

This is a simulated photographic wallpaper that is enlarged. It is generally divided into quarter panels for purposes of the installation. This type of mural will usually portray nature scenes, mountains, sea shores, forests, woodlands, etc. They can usually be removed by delaminating the decorative surface from the backing and then removing the paper backing by wetting it with a wallpaper remover solution for about 5 to 10 minutes and scraping with a broad knife. If the decorative surface does not peel off, it will need to be scored with a floor sanding paper (4½ grit) and soaked with the wallpaper remover solution for about 15 minutes and scraped off with a broad knife.

Reedcloth

This wallcovering is a handcrafted wallpaper in which every individual reed is inserted into the cotton warp (vertical) threads of a handmade loom. The reeds will vary in thickness and color. This is the natural characteristic and should be expected. The production is very similar to that of grasscloth and the removal process is the same.

Rushcloth

This type of wallpaper is very similar to real grasscloth and is made basically the same way, except that rush, a juncaceous plant, is used instead of the arrowroot vine (see grasscloth). The rush is used for the weft (horizontal structure) of the netting (cotton and rush woven together). Rushcloth will contain a natural shading effect, such as that of grasscloth, and the removal process is the same as for grasscloth.

Silkscreen/ Hand-Screen Prints

Screen-printed wallpapers will have a paper substrate. They are printed either totally by hand, by hand and machine, or entirely by machine. A silk screen is used in the printing process. It is constructed just as a solid sheet vinyl and the removal process is the same as for solid sheet vinyl.

Solid Sheet Vinyl

This type of wallpaper has a paper substrate (backing) which is laminated to a solid vinyl decorative surface. It can be removed by peeling or pulling the decorative surface (the solid vinyl layer) from the wall at a 10 degree angle. This will prevent excessively damaging the wall surface itself. Once the vinyl layer is removed, the paper backing can be removed by wetting it with warm water and a wallpaper remover solution and allowing it to soak in for 10 to 15 minutes. Then it can be scraped off with a broad knife. If the paper backing is in good shape (no loose places), it can be installed over as a liner paper.

Standard Paper

This is wallpaper that has an inexpensive pulp (paper) substrate (backing) onto which the decorative print is directly applied. The decorative surface has a very thin vinyl coating and is not resistant to grease, excessive moisture, etc. Since the vinyl coating is very thin, the removal is relatively simple. The wall should be scored (etched) slightly with a coarse sandpaper and then sprayed with warm water mixed with wallpaper remover solution using a household garden sprayer. After the wallpaper has been saturated with the solution for 10 to 15 minutes, it can usually be removed using a broad knife.

Stringcloth

This type of wallpaper has very fine vertical threads that are laminated to a paper-type substrate (backing). It comes in a variety of shades and colors. Unlike grasscloth, the seams are not dominant. The vertical threads butt together at the seams so there are no mismatches. The removal process is the same as for grasscloth.

Vinyl-Coated

This type of wallpaper will have a paper substrate (backing) and the decorative surface is also paper with a liquid vinyl coating applied from the factory by means of a roller or by being sprayed. Frequently, vinyl coated (sprayed vinyl) wallpapers will be the pre-pasted type, which means the factory has applied a water remoisten-able adhesive to the backing.

If the wallpaper were immersed in water for the application, chances are it would dry strip from the wall--provided the wall had been properly sealed. There are, however, many times that the paper will not dry strip and will have to be scored with a heavy floor sanding paper (4 ½ grit), and be saturated with warm water and a wallpaper remover solution for approximately 15 minutes. Then it can be removed by scraping with a broad knife.

Wet Look

Wet look wallpaper has a high gloss finish that always appears to be wet. This type of finish may be applied to either paper or scrim (lightweight fabric) substrates (backings). The removal process is the same as for solid sheet vinyls or Type 1 commercial wallcoverings (lightweight scrim backing).

Adhesives

Two of the major decisions that a wallpaper installer must make are the selection of an adhesive and the appropriate viscosity (thickness) for its application. The substrate (backing) of the wallpaper and the wall surface to be covered will determine these decisions.

There have been many job failures documented where the proper adhesive was used for a particular wallpaper installation, but its application was too thick or too thin. Most all wallpapering failures that are associated with adhesives are due to the improper selection of the adhesive itself and the improper way in which it is mixed and applied.

Too much adhesive will only retard the drying process, which in many cases will cause the wallcovering to shrink, where otherwise it would not. This application could also create too much moisture between the wallcovering and the wall surface, and therefore cause a mildew problem to occur before the adhesive has completely dried. This is especially true when applying a non-breathing wallpaper over a non-breathable wall surface.

If there is too much adhesive applied during the application of delicate wallpapers such as linens, suedes, grasscloths, stringcloths, textiles, or fabrics, the adhesive and its moisture can penetrate the substrate and onto the decorative surface. This may result in a staining problem.

Whenever the adhesive is applied too thinly, it may cause the paper to dry out too quickly, therefore causing poor adhesion or edge curling. This may tempt the installer to apply too much pressure on the wallpaper while it is being installed. This can result in overworking the material and stretching or ripping it.

As you may have already perceived, the viscosity (thickness) of the adhesive is just as important (if not more) as selecting the proper adhesive in the first place.

It is important to understand that the adhesive must be compatible with the adherent if the adhesion (bond) is going to last. The adherent refers to the wall surface, primer/sealer, wallpaper substrate (backing), or any other surface to which the adhesive is bonding.

The strength of the adhesive is measured in ounces per traverse inch. This test is accomplished by adhering a prescribed wallpaper to a wall surface using a predetermined adhesive and viscosity. It is then allowed to dry completely. A one-inch-wide strip is used by some manufacturers of adhesives to effect this test. After the strip has completely dried, it is pulled away. During the pulling (removing) process, the amount of weight (in ounces) that is required to pull it away is measured and recorded.

The average amount of weighted pressure determines the adhesive's ounce-per-traverse-inch score. As a rule, the wall surface or the wallpaper will be destroyed if it requires more than 16 ounces to remove it. A minimum of six ounces pressure is required to assume a satisfactory adhesion. Different types of adhesives (either thin or thick viscosities) and different wall surfaces (either porous or non-porous) make the readings change substantially.

There are many different types of adhesives on the market today. They are ever changing, so the installer should keep up-to-date on any distinct changes and the effect they may have on a specific substrate (backing of the wallpaper).

Regardless of the type of adhesive being used, it is imperative to keep the decorative surface of the wallcovering clean during the installation. Most all problems that deal with ink flaking, ink smearing, hazy smears, etc., are commonly caused by the decorative surface of the wallpaper being contaminated with a residue of adhesive.

Some wallcoverings such as foils and Mylars will require immediate drying with a soft cloth after it is rinsed with a sponge and clean water. This will prevent the decorative surface from spotting, such as a glass spots.

Some wallcoverings such as stringcloths, grasscloths, linens, fabrics, textiles, etc., must always be protected against adhesives getting on the decorative surface. This could cause permanent stain damage. There have been many cases where just clean water has caused staining simply because of the moisture coming in contact with the surface. These types of delicate wallcoverings usually require the expertise of a professional installer.

Listed below are several types of adhesives along with their purpose and make-up.

Starch-Based

Starch adhesives are made essentially from wheat, potato, tapioca, corn, and sago. Starches are natural polymers. They are also low in cost as well as abundant in quantity. The most common starch used is wheat starch. Most all of the pre-mixed products on the market today are originally derived from wheat starches.

Starches are very easily dissolved in water and are fairly easy to clean. They are chemically similar to cellulose since they are both derived from plants. Both give very good adhesion to cotton and paper substrates (backings of wallpapers). Special preservatives must be incorporated in starch adhesives in order to prevent putrefaction (decay) or mildew problems.

Glue

Animal glue is an impure protein gelatin made from collagen, a protein ingredient from animal hides, tissues, bones, hooves, tendons, cartilage, etc., and is highly organic. These types of adhesives provide a strong bond in a short period of time.

Paste

These are adhesives made from starches and dextrin, a gummy substance. Dextrin acts as a binder. Borax is used to adjust or modify starch adhesive viscosity (thickness) and tackiness. Starches with borax will bond faster and also give more initial tack (holding power on the wall surface).

Cellulose

These are adhesives made primarily from structural elements of plants, especially cotton, wood pulp, or fibers. When cellulose is mixed with glycerine (a syrupy liquid) and water, it is often referred to as Methyl Cellulose. Most cellulose pastes are usually non-staining, have good slip (movement), will remain moist longer, and will not sour as fast as starches (under the same conditions). Cellulose adhesives will re-wet and strip off the wall faster and easier than the starch-type adhesives.

Clay-Based Pre-mixed

These adhesives are basically the same as starches with clay added as solids. These provide greater tack during the wallpaper installation. The clay itself does not add to the adhesion, however it acts as an absorbent sponge to the moisture within the adhesive.

It provides greater viscosity and makes drying and setting-up time much faster during the wallpaper installation. Sometimes the clay-based adhesive is mixed with an acrylic resin (vinyl-to-vinyl adhesive) and is thinned down to a paint consistency and applied to the wall surface as a pre-sizing. The clay causes the wallpaper's adhesive to set up even faster,

while at the same time the acrylic resins add an extra amount of adhesion. This will also help decrease the shrinkage problem that is common with some wallpapers. This is especially useful when installing wallpaper around small outside-corner-returns such as recessed windows and door frames or soffit corners.

It is imperative that a clay-based adhesive be used whenever a non-breathing wallpaper is being applied to a totally non-breathing wall surface. Otherwise, another type of adhesive may require a longer drying time which in turn will sour or even mildew before it is dry. Sometimes an absorbent liner paper may be used in place of the clay-based adhesive to serve the same purpose as the drying agent.

Two of the major drawbacks of using a clay-based adhesive are:

(1) It is messy to work with and must be cleaned very well during the wallpaper installation process.

(2) If the adhesive wrinkles are not completely smoothed out during the wallpaper installation, they may never totally dissipate (dry out) simply because of the solids incorporated within the clay itself.

Clear Pre-mixed

When the clear pre-mixed adhesives came on the scene, every paperhanger thought it was the answer to all wallpaper adhesion and staining problems. However, this was not the case. There is no such thing as a clear pre-mixed adhesive. If it is smeared across a wallcovering's decorative surface or on glass, it will invariably dry to a haze. Therefore, the chore of keeping it off the decorative surfaces of wallcoverings is still necessary.

Admittedly, the so called clear pre-mixed adhesives are not nearly as messy as the clay-based adhesives, because they are much easier to clean. A clear pre-mixed adhesive is basically a wheat paste that has been cooked with steam or acid. Since wheat starch is a good adhesive and cleans

up fairly easily with water, it has taken the place of most clay-based adhesive applications.

If the clear pre-mixed adhesive is applied too heavily during the application of the wallpaper, it will generally dissipate (dry out), and stretch tightly to the wall surface. This is another advantage to using it as opposed to the clay-based type.

It is not recommended to use clear pre-mixed adhesives whenever wallpaper is installed over an oil-based primer/sealer, because it generally requires twice as much time to set up and dry as opposed to the clay-based adhesive. During this drying-out period, the wallpaper may shrink. If the wallpaper is a breathable type, this should not be a problem; however, if the wallpaper is non-breathable, it will probably develop a problem because of the time required for the adhesive to dry.

Vinyl Over Vinyl

These types of adhesives commonly contain an acrylic resin that will bond to just about any surface. They contain very little moisture and are used to bond vinyl wallcoverings over vinyl wallcoverings without the use of a special primer/sealer. Because of the low moisture content, there is very little or no risk of a mildew problem, unless extra water has been added prior to the application.

Vinyl-over-vinyl adhesives are used rather extensively for installing borders directly over existing wallcoverings because of the bonding power it has without the use of an additional primer/sealer. It is important, however, that the border be checked for a semi-transparent quality before this is done. If the existing wallpaper is even slightly visible through the border, a pigmented acrylic primer/sealer should be applied to the existing wallpaper. Allow it to dry before applying the border. Another option used to avoid the problem of transparency is to inlay the border instead of installing it over the existing wallpaper. See chapter on Borders.

Pre-Paste (Water Re-moistenable)

This type of adhesive is applied to the substrate (backing) of light-weight wallpapers at the factory by means of a roller or sprayed application. Some manufacturers still use the starch dusting process, whereby a liquid is applied to the substrate and the starch dust bonds to it while it is still wet. Once the pre-paste has been applied, it is transferred to a heating chamber and dried before it is rolled for packaging.

Sometimes the wallpaper contracts during this process which causes it to curl during the installation. This problem can usually be eliminated by reverse-rolling the roll or pulling it across the table-top at a 45 degree angle (referred to as drawing the wallpaper). This breaks the dried adhesive into tiny squares and allows the wallpaper to lay flat on the work-table rather than curl.

The pre-pasted adhesive must be activated before it can be applied to the wall surface. This is usually done by submerging the strip into a wallpaper water tray. Pre-pasted adhesives will contain an insoluablizer to make the adhesive dissolve when it is submerged into water. If too much insoluablizer is added, the adhesive will almost immediately wash off into the water. If this is a problem, add about one table-spoon of vinegar to a water tray. This will retard (slow down) the insoluablizing process and allow the wallpaper to still be used.

If the insoluablizer is weak or does not appear to be added to the pre-pasted adhesive; the adhesive will not properly activate. If this is the case, adding one tablespoon of ammonia to the water tray will help it to dissolve.

All pre-pasted wallpapers will commonly expand one to two percent after it is wet, therefore it is important to allow the wallpaper to relax (remain folded while wet) for a minimum of five to ten minutes before it is installed. If the wallpaper is installed too soon after it is wetted, it will continue to expand on the wall surface which will cause vertical blisters to form. If this happens, remove the wallpaper and allow it to relax for a longer period of time. Hint: Place the booked (folded and rolled) strips of wallpaper into a plastic trash bag (such as bread in its wrapper) to contain the moisture until ready to install. This will help keep it from drying out too soon! This technique is especially useful when the adhesive volatile factor (evaporation rate) is high such as on new construction in summer months.

There are times when pre-pasted wallpapers **will not** contain enough adhesive to adhere properly to the wall surface. This is especially true when a porous wall condition is present.

Many professionals prefer to re-activate the water-remoistenable adhesive by re-pasting it. **It is imperative that the installer dilute the additional adhesive with 50% more water than normally required.** If the extra adhesive is applied too heavy, it will retard (slow down) the drying process, which in turn may cause a major shrinking problem. It is just as important to make sure that the entire backing is pasted, otherwise, the pre-paste will not properly activate, and the wallpaper may never properly expand.

It is better for individuals that cannot properly use a pasting brush or roller to use a water tray. It is important, however, to submerge the wallpaper for only about 10 seconds and slowly pull it completely out of the water and fold it (book it). While the paper is relaxing, an additional watered-down adhesive may be applied directly to the wall surface with a brush or roller.

Caution: Never apply a dry strip of pre-pasted wallpaper to the wall into a wet adhesive. The paper will have no choice but to fully expand on the wall, which would result in a complete disaster of expansion wrinkles!

Unless you are an experienced professional installer; it is not wise to use a clay-based adhesive for re-activating pre-pasted wallpapers, because the solids within the adhesive may clog the pores on the substrate (backing) of the wallpaper.

Warning: When additional adhesives are being applied to pre-pasted wallpapers, it is important not to create an over-abundance of adhesive because it can only retard the drying process and cause a problem. If the extra adhesive (even though it is diluted) is applied with a long-nap roller cover (½″ nap or larger), it will only add to the adhesive because the mixture can not be spread to a thin viscosity; therefore, a long-nap roller cover is not recommended for applying adhesives--especially to pre-pasted wallpapers.

However, if the extra adhesive is applied with a pasting brush or short-nap roller cover (¼″ to ⅜″ nap), the entire mixture can be spread to an even consistency which can then be regulated (applied heavy or thin) according to the wall surface conditions that prevail and the type of wallpaper being installed.

Most manufacturers of pre-pasted wallpapers strongly suggest not re-pasting the wallpaper because of these adverse reactions. Chemically, most all the adhesives are compatible, however, as it was stated at the outset, the viscosity (thickness) and the application of the adhesive are just as important as the adhesive selection itself.

Pattern Matches

There are five basic kinds of pattern matches associated with installing wallpaper. One of the first major rules when installing wallpaper is to be able to properly identify the pattern match and possibly any recurring pattern motifs that may be present within each individual strip. This information will enable precise engineering (determining seam placement) as well as enable the technique of pattern segmentation to be employed whenever necessary. See chapter on Engineering and Pattern Segmentation.

The five basic pattern matches are explained and illustrated in this chapter with the proper procedures to identify and install them in a way that will be aesthetically pleasing.

Random Match

This refers to any definite pattern or design which has no match or vertical repeat that can be identified. The best example of these is stripes. **(Fig.1)**

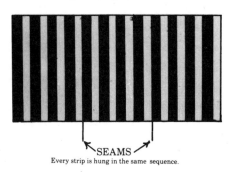

Every strip is hung in the same sequence.

Fig.1

Every strip, however, must be installed in the same direction vertically to prevent two identical edges from meeting at the seam, such as two stripes of the same color, as illustrated in **Fig.2.**

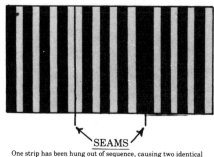

One strip has been hung out of sequence, causing two identical stripes at two different seams to be placed together.

Fig.2

Since a stripe does not have a **vertical repeat,** it can be cut at the specified length of the wall, without any extra for matching, however, the allowance of 2 to 3 inches at the top and bottom are still required for trimming once the strip is in position on the wall.

Stripes generally will have duplicated **horizontal** repeats which should be identified and considered during the engineering and installation process. See chapter on Engineering and Pattern Segmentation.

Random Textures

Random textured patterns have no definite pattern or design to be matched vertically or horizontally. They do not have a specified rightside-up or an upside-down.

When installing random textures, every other strip should be reversed. This means every other strip is turned upside-down during the installation process. Be sure to unroll each bolt the same direction and cut all the strips from the same end of each bolt. This will prevent getting confused, or cutting a bolt from the wrong end. As you cut each strip, indicate which end is the top by placing a small arrow on the back side where the allowance for trimming will be. **(Fig.3)** Sometimes it is quicker just to notch one corner of the strip for the purpose of indicating the top of the strip.

RANDOM TEXTURES

A small arrow has been placed in the upper corner indicating the up end of the strip.

Fig.3

The reason for reversing every other strip is that during the actual printing process, the ink may have been applied slightly heavier on one side than the other. This is usually undetectable just by looking at the roll; but when two strips are placed side by side on the wall, the lighter edge will be very obvious when installed against the darker edge.

We are told in life, **never assume anything.** This saying definitely holds true when installing random textures. Always reverse every other strip. **Never assume** that random textures were printed evenly. Therefore always reverse every other strip so they will not shade.

Note: When some wallpapers are wet with adhesive, shading will not be evident until the wallpaper completely dries. Then it is too late to correct the problem. If the wallpaper were not shaded originally, it will not affect the outcome to reverse the strips anyway. It is better to be safe than sorry!

See **Figs.4 & 5** for examples of the correct and incorrect methods for installing random textures.

NON-REVERSED TEXTURE

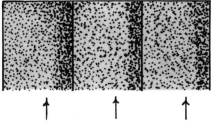

Each strip has been hung in the same direction. A shading effect has resulted.

Fig.4

REVERSED TEXTURE

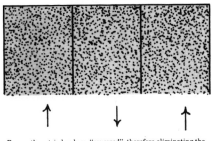

Every other strip has been "reversed", therefore eliminating the shading.

Fig.5

Grasscloth and stringcloth wallpapers are considered random textures and should be reversed during the installation, with the exception of those with background pattern designs that have to be matched.

Important: Most all grasscloth will present a natural shading effect because of its handmade process. The seams of grasscloth will be dominant because the horizontal weave will not match up from one strip to another. This is suggested to be the beauty of the product. When grasscloth is being installed, careful consideration should be given to the seam placement because of the dominant effect the seams will have on the wall. It is recommended to establish the seam placement of the grasscloth to provide a balanced effect on any major focal walls. It is possible to manually trim each strip to obtain strips that will be evenly spaced on the wall.

Straight Across

This is a pattern or design that will either match up or line up in a straight-across horizontal sequence, therefore every individual strip will have the same pattern or design at the ceiling line.

In order to determine if a pattern arrangement is a straight-across match, first identify a definite pattern design on the right or left side of the wallpaper strip that has been divided. Then establish the exact position of a particular point of that design, such as the tip edge of a flower. **(Fig.6)**

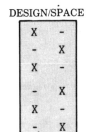

Right side of pattern.

Fig.6

Next, identify the exact position of the specified point of design on the opposite edge of the wallpaper, which would be the tip edge of the same flower. **(Fig.7)**

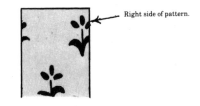

Left side of pattern.

Fig.7

The use of a framing square will help determine if both sides of the divided pattern are aligned straight across from each other. If they are, the pattern is considered a straight-across match. **(Fig.8)**

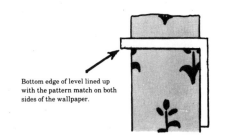

Bottom edge of level lined up with the pattern match on both sides of the wallpaper.

Fig.8

Sometimes a straight-across match will have to be determined by identifying a sequence, rather than a divided design. Often a design will repeat itself horizontally, as well as vertically, within the same strip. When this happens, the duplicated pattern design will create a strip segment. This means that a design...space repeat will appear within the strip. **(Fig.9)**

DESIGN/SPACE

X	-
-	X
X	-
-	X
X	-
-	X
X	-

Fig.9

Anytime this happens, every strip must be the same at the ceiling line or else two duplicated designs will appear together. **(Figs.10 & 11)**

CORRECT SEQUENCE

X	-	X	-
-	X	-	X
X	-	X	-
-	X	-	X
X	-	X	-
-	X	-	X

Fig.10

INCORRECT SEQUENCE

X	-	-	X	-	X
-	X	X	-	X	-
X	-	-	X	-	X
-	X	X	-	X	-
X	-	-	X	-	X
-	X	X	-	X	-

Fig.11

Rule: When a strip begins with a design and ends with a space horizontally across the same strip, the match will always be a straight-across match because the successive strip must begin with the same design to continue the pattern sequence. **(Fig.12)**

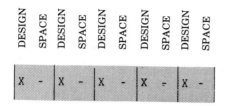

Fig.12

Conventional Half-Drop

This is a pattern or design that will either match up or line up in a diagonal sequence, rather than in a horizontal sequence. This will result in every other strip's having the same design at the ceiling line.

By following the same procedure as illustrated in the straight-across match, you must first identify a definite divided design and then a specific point of that design on the right-hand side of the wallpaper strip. **(Fig.13)**

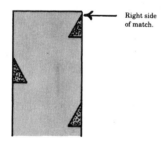

Right side of match.

Fig.13

Next, proceed down the same edge of the strip vertically and identify the exact pattern design. This is referred to as a vertical pattern repeat. **(Fig.14)** Note: Every single wallpaper pattern will always have a vertical repeat, except for random patterns and textures.

Once the distance of the vertical repeat has been established, make a note of the

exact measurement. In **Fig.14** a 25″ vertical repeat is illustrated.

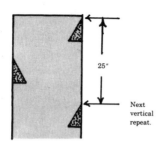

25″

Next vertical repeat.

Fig.14

Next, identify the divided design on the opposite side of the strip and the exact point of design. **(Fig.15)**

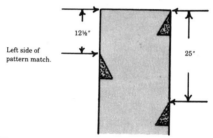

12½″

Left side of pattern match.

25″

Fig.15

Make a note at where this point is. If this point of design is exactly one half the distance down from the right hand measurement, then the pattern is a conventional half-drop match. This is normally the case whenever the match is **not** straight across. **(Fig.16)**

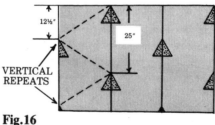

12½″

25″

VERTICAL REPEATS

Fig.16

When a divided pattern is not present, a half-drop match sequence may still be applicable. By determining any duplicated pattern segments, such as design...space, you may find the segments appear in single/double form or double/triple form. In any case, the sequence will still result in every other strip's being the same at the ceiling line. **(Fig.17)**

Space/design/space sequence

Fig.17

This means that one strip may have two designs at the ceiling line and the next strip will have three designs at the ceiling line. Another example: One strip may have four designs at the ceiling line and the next strip will have five designs at the ceiling line.

Once the seam placement has been engineered either on one wall or the entire room, indicate with a letter which strip will be placed between every seam. Develop a system for identifying the top of the half-drop match patterned strips, since every other piece is the same. This will eliminate accidentally installing two of the same identical strips back to back and also will also aid in pre-cutting all the strips for the room. For example, if the **left** edge of the matching design will be at the ceiling line, label that strip L. If the matching design on the **right** side of the paper is at the ceiling line, label it R. **(Fig.18)**

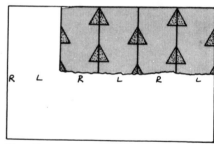

R   L   R   L   R   L

When making strip indications on the wall. Use the pencil lightly, to prevent show-through. Left/right sequence.

Fig.18

Another example: If the pattern sequence required only a **single** design at the ceiling line, label that strip S. If the pattern sequence requires two of the same designs at the ceiling line, label that strip D for **double**. **(Fig.19)**

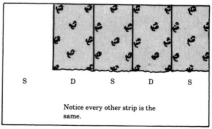

S   D   S   D   S

Notice every other strip is the same.

Double/single sequence.

Fig.19

This system can go on and on--T for triple, Q for quadruple, etc. Even when hanging random textures, they should be indicated by using either S for straight, R for reverse, or ↑ for straight, ↓ for reverse, to indicate the reversing technique required to minimize shading.

These indications should be very lightly penciled in on both the wall and the top edge of the wallpaper strip within the allowance. Note on the matching sequences in **Figs. 20, 21, & 22** that no matter which of the matches you view, every other strip is the same at the ceiling line, regardless of the actual match or sequence.

LEFT/RIGHT sequence.

Fig. 20

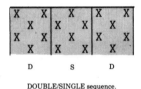

DOUBLE/SINGLE sequence.

Fig. 21

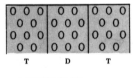

TRIPLE/DOUBLE sequence.

Fig. 22

Multiple-drop

The multiple-drop match has a very unusual pattern match and/or sequence. The pattern match must be identified before the engineering or cutting process begins. You may suspect a multiple-drop match when neither a straight-across nor half-drop match can be determined.

One advantage of a multiple drop match is the limited amount of times a design will meet at the ceiling line. This helps eliminate the possibility of detecting an unlevel ceiling line or a print that is on the bias.

Multiple-drop matches are the rarest breed of matches and the most difficult to analyze. A multiple-drop match design can drop in sequence as many as 20 times or strips, before it will repeat itself at the ceiling line or other horizontal obstacle.

First you must choose a divided pattern design on one side of the wallpaper, and draw a horizontal line across the strip of wallpaper using a framing square. **(Fig. 23)**

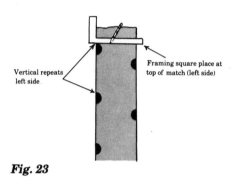

Vertical repeats left side

Framing square place at top of match (left side)

Fig. 23

Then measure the distance down from the horizontal line on the opposite side of the strip to where the other half of the design will match. **(Fig. 24)**

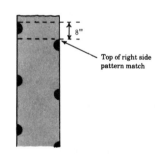

8"

Top of right side pattern match

Fig. 24

Divide this distance of the full vertical repeat and this will determine if you have a ⅓, ¼, ⅕, etc., multiple-drop match.

In **Fig. 25** the pattern design is neither a straight-across nor a standard half-drop match. The pattern in this case drops 8", or one-third of the vertical pattern repeat. This means the pattern will drop 8" on each consecutive strip until the design will return to the ceiling line:

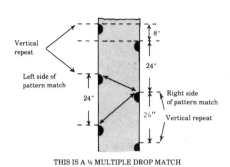

Vertical repeat

8"

24"

Left side of pattern match

Right side of pattern match

24"

Vertical repeat

24"

THIS IS A ⅓ MULTIPLE DROP MATCH

Fig. 25

In **Fig. 26** the one-third multiple illustrates the diagonal pattern sequence from one strip to another. The divided pattern on the right side of strip #1 drops 8" from the ceiling line. This is one-third of the vertical repeat from the left side (24"). This means that each consecutive strip will drop an additional 8" until the pattern is again repeated at the ceiling line. In this case and on every one-third multiple drop match, the pattern will repeat itself every fourth strip at the ceiling line.

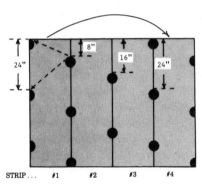

24"

8"

16"

24"

STRIP . . .   #1   #2   #3   #4

Strip #4 is identical to strip #1. Every 4th strip is identical to the 1st strip, therefore this is a ⅓rd multiple drop match.

Fig. 26

Fig. 27 depicts a one-fourth multiple-drop match with a 24" vertical repeat on the left edge of strip #1. The divided design drops only 6" from the ceiling on the right side of strip #1. Since 24 divided by 6 equals 4, this match is a one-fourth multiple-drop match. Every consecutive strip thereafter will drop 6" until it repeats itself at the ceiling line, which in this case, would be every fifth strip as indicated in the illustration. The same would apply to every one-fourth multiple-drop match.

PATTERN MATCHES

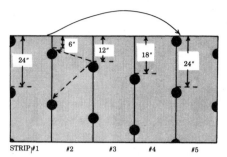

Every 5th strip is identical, therefore, this is a ¼ multiple drop match.

Fig.27

Up to this point, all of the illustrations have indicated a multiple-drop match in whole inch increments. There will be times, however, when the situation will become more complex. It may be required to convert inches into eighths, fourths, halves, etc., to determine the exact multiple-drop match that is involved.

In Fig.28 the vertical repeat on the left side of the strip is 3½ inches and the matching design on the right-hand side drops only ⅞ inch from the ceiling line. In this example, 3½ inches will need to be converted into eights in order to determine the multiple-drop match. Once this is established the multiple drop will become evident.

In Fig.29 a ¼ multiple-drop match is indicated with a sequence as opposed to a divided pattern. Notice the vertical repeat is 24 inches and the top of the second strip is 6 inches down from the original pattern. Each consecutive strip will drop an additional 6 inches until the original pattern sequence is repeated at the ceiling line.

Before installing any multiple-drop match pattern, remember that each strip must be matched in the proper sequence, and from the proper direction. In other words, strip 2 must be installed to the right of strip 1, and strip 4 must be installed to left of strip 1, and so on.

The conventional half-drop match strips can be installed in either direction because every other strip is the same.

Refer to the chapter on Engineering and Pattern Segmentation for further information.

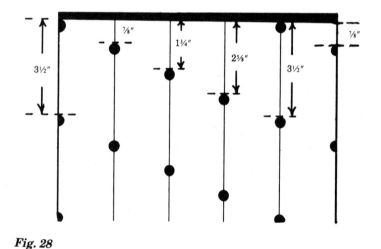

Fig. 28

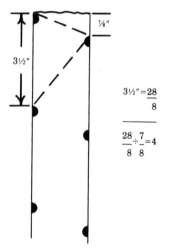

$$3\frac{1}{2}'' = \frac{28}{8}$$

$$\frac{28}{8} \div \frac{7}{8} = 4$$

Fig.29

Seams and Seaming Techniques

There are many types of seams and seaming techniques involved in the art of installing wallpaper. An installer must be creative when different situations arise and must be able to employ the proper technique in order to produce a satisfactory job. Aside from the aesthetical pattern placement and/or the positioning of patterns, the seams become a very important aspect to the consumer's eyes.

There are times when everything you do will seem to be a dead end to success. This is especially true when the wallpaper shrinks after you have supposedly formed a perfectly fitted or joined seam.

The main thing to remember during the installation is never overwork the wallpaper. This results in stretching the extensibility factors of the wallpaper beyond its normal relaxed or expanded structure. This one item alone is probably the major cause of seaming problems. If a seam is only a hairline apart, a gentle tap from the opposite side of the paper from the seam will usually suffice, but do not apply pressure at the seam.

Sometimes a **swatching (or velcroing) technique** can be used. This is accomplished by diluting a mixture of clay-based adhesive with at least 50% more water and applying the mixture (very thinly) on the wall surface only where the wallpaper seams will be, and the edges along the ceiling line, door frames, around windows, etc. This diluted adhesive should be applied a few hours prior the installation of the wallpaper.

Note: Do not use a roller to apply the thinned clay-based adhesive because it may cause a textured effect to show through the new wallpaper.

Careful engineering of the seam placement must be done before the seam swatching technique can be employed. The clay-based adhesive must be dry prior to the installation of the wallpaper in order to be effective. It acts as a blotter when the wallpaper is installed, forcing the adhesive at the seaming area to dry first. Once the seaming area is dry, it will not separate.

Another technique is the **squeegee technique.** Simply pull a broad knife or plastic wallpaper smoother vertically down the seaming area after the wallpaper strip is in place on the wall. This forces the bulk of the adhesive away from the seam and allows it to dry faster than the center of the strip. Another important thing to remember is to look back and check the seams within approximately 5 to 10 minutes after it has been installed.

Important: Once the wallpaper has completely set up, it is practically impossible to correct any problems!

Creating a perfectly fitted seam should be the goal of every paperhanger during an installation. The seam should not be noticeable at a glance; however, with some types of wallcoverings it is impossible to completely hide them.

It is important to understand various problems associated with unattractive seams. There are many times the seams of the wallpaper are fitted perfectly together; however, there appears to be a white gap (space) still visible--especially on dark colored wallpapers. This is because the manufacturer trimmed the selvage from the wallpaper using a trimming device that was either dull or adjusted at the wrong angle. When this happens, a V or slanted cut on the edges of the substrate (backing of the wallpaper) will expose a white edge. This is a manufacturing defect and if the problem is very noticeable the wallpaper should be returned for credit.

However, there are many times this problem can be disguised by applying artist water colors (mixed to the color of the wallpaper's background) into the seams to dye the white edges of the substrate to blend with the background. The colorant should be mixed very thinly and applied vertically into the seam. After ap-proximately 5 to 10 seconds the excess colorant should be wiped off horizontally to the seam using a slightly damp sponge. This will prevent removing the colorant out of the seam. It is usually advisable to dry the seam area with a soft cloth immediately after it has been wiped with a sponge.

> **Caution: The preceding technique of dying (coloring) seams should be tested on a scrap piece of wall-covering prior to its application on the finished installation. Some colorants will permanently stain or ruin the decorative surface of the wallcovering. This technique is intended to salvage a job that has already been done. It does not mean the manufacturer is not at fault.**

Other major problems which are associated with unattractive seams are usually caused by the following reasons:

(a) The adhesive was improperly applied prior to the installation, therefore the wallpaper did not adhere properly to the wall surface.

(b) The adhesive volatile factor was high, meaning it evaporated very fast during the installation and the adhesive dissipation process. This is a very common problem especially on new construction during hot summer months.

(c) There was too much pressure applied horizontally at the seaming area by the installer in an attempt to join two strips of wallpaper together. This pressure will many times stretch the wallpaper beyond its normal extensibility limits; therefore, the wallpaper will tend to shrink back to its original width.

(d) The wallpaper returned slightly to its original width because of the shrinkage of the substrate.

Several main points to remember when installing wallpaper are:

(a) Make absolutely sure that all necessary wall preparation procedures are done correctly including the application of the primer/sealer. There have been many problems documented that are associated with poor adhesion and seam curling of the wallpaper simply because the wall preparation was not performed properly. Professional installers should always be responsible for making sure these procedures are done whether they are doing the preparation themselves or having someone else do it for them--such as a homeowner or painting contractor.

(b) Never try to join strip of wallpaper to an adjacent strip by forcing it together after it has been pressed to the wall surface. If there is a space (gap) between the strips, simply remove the strip being installed and reinstall it. Always begin the installation of every strip by joining the seam first-- then smooth out the remainder of the strip. Avoid pulling the seam apart while smoothing the wallpaper to the wall surface.

(c) Always allow the wallpaper to relax (remain in a booked form) until it has fully expanded. This usually requires 5 to 10 minutes.

(d) Always adjust the adhesive viscosity (referring to the thickness that the adhesive is mixed and applied) to best adhere the wallcovering to the wall surface. The porosity of the substrate (backing) of the wallpaper and the wall surface will determine this adjustment.

The following types of seams which are illustrated are the most common methods used in the industry and will vary with each individual installer according to the wallcovering and wall conditions that exist on each individual job.

Butt Seam

The butt seam is probably the most common type of seam used in wallpapering. Two strips join without any overlap. Once the paper is joined together it should be gently rolled or secured with either an oval or flat seam roller. **(Note: Do not roll a heavily embossed wallpaper because it may flatten or burnish the seam-- creating a shiny streak.)** The seams should be rolled as soon as the wallpaper strips are in the correct position, then re-checked after approximately 10 minutes of setting-up time. **(Fig.1)**

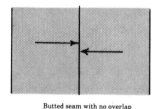

Butted seam with no overlap

Fig.1

Wire Seam

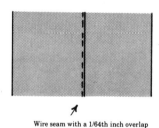

Wire seam with a 1/64th inch overlap

Fig.2

The wire seam (also called a ridge seam) is created by overlapping the edge of one strip very slightly over an adjoining strip. This type of seam is sometimes used when either scalloped (wavy) edges are present or when an uneven wall surface is being covered. A wire seam can be undesirable if the available lighting conditions are high. If a wire seam is necessary, the overlap should face opposite the dominant entrance of the room.

The installer should start the wallpaper installation on the opposite side of the room and work toward the main entrance to achieve the proper effect of wire seaming. This is referred to as "back lapping". **(Fig.2)**

Spring-loaded Seam

This is a seam created after a wire (ridge) seam has set-up approximately 3 to 5 minutes. It is pulled gently apart, using the palms of the hands. Allow the seam to spring flush together while gently securing it with an an oval seam roller. This creates a natural spring reaction which provides a very smooth and tight butt seam. **(Fig.3)**

Begin with a wire seam with about 1/64" overlap

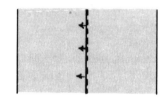

Pull back gently with fingertips and roll with oval seam roller

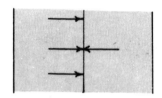

Springs back to a smooth butted seam

Fig.3

Note: The original overlap should never be more than about $\frac{1}{64}$". Any more than this could result in a puckered seam. The spring-loading technique is useful when installing solid sheet vinyls or wallpapers with very slightly scalloped edges.

Double-cut Seam

The double-cut seam is a result of overlapping one strip over the top of another and cutting through both layers with a single cut (usually with a razor blade). The excess end of each strip is removed and the two new edges can be joined together to form a perfectly joined butt seam. This technique is used with the pattern segmentation technique and often to create the final seam for the kill point (where the final strips of the room meet). **(Fig.4)** Note: It is often necessary to place a scrap piece of wallpaper (or wax paper) under the double cut to protect the wall surface during the cutting process. This is referred to as padding the double cut.

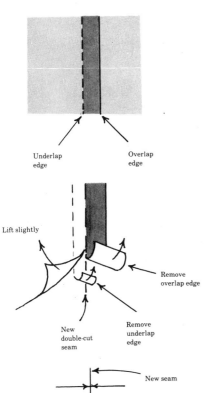

Fig.4

Cross Seam

Cross seams are formed when a liner paper is installed horizontally and the finished decorative wallpaper is installed vertically. The seams will cross to form a lattice arrangement which creates a secure bond. **(Fig.5)**

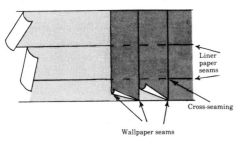

Fig.5

Mitered Seam

The mitered seam is actually a double-cutting technique that is a result of mitering the corners of borders that are installed around door and window frames, along sloped ceiling lines, etc., or under the corners of soffit edges. Mitered seams can also be used for special effect projects such as a circus tent effect on a ceiling. **(Fig.6)**

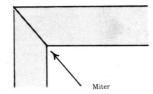

Fig.6

Vertical Seam

The vertical seam is perpendicular to the plane of the horizon, or is upright plumb. Most wallpaper seams are vertical seams. **(Fig.7)**

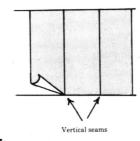

Fig.7

Horizontal Seam

A horizontal seam is at a right angle to the vertical seam. Most liner papers are installed horizontally so the seams will cross the vertical seams of the finished wallpaper to insure a greater bond. **(Fig.8)**

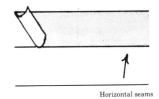

Fig.8

Wrap & Overlap Seam

This is a seam used to realign crooked outside corners. The strip is spliced on the corner's edge. The remainder of the divided strip is backed up and re-aligned to plumb on the adjoining wall. This will result in the strip's edge wrapping around the corner. The strip that is on the first wall will be lifted and overlap the wrapped edge of the remaining section. This overlap should be secured with a vinyl-to-vinyl adhesive. **(Fig.9)**

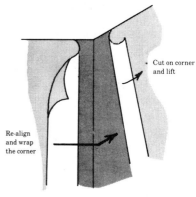

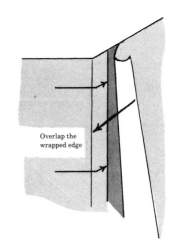

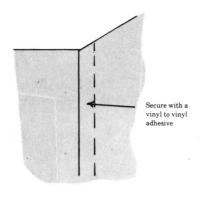

Secure with a
vinyl to vinyl
adhesive

Fig.9

Masked Slipsheeted Seam

This type of seam is created by cutting through two overlapping strips; however, the underlying strip is protected with either wax paper or masking tape. These protective tools are used to prevent any adhesive from getting on the surface of a previously installed strip of wallpaper during the double-cutting process. This is especially useful when installing suede, stringcloth, or any other easily stained wallpaper or heavily textured wallpaper. (Fig.10)

Caution: Do not use masking tape if the decorative surface can be easily pulled off. Examples: stringcloth, grasscloth, etc.

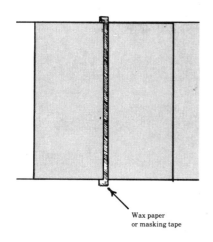

Wax paper
or masking tape

Fig.10

Overlap Seam

This is a seam that is formed when one edge of a wallpaper strip overlaps another. This is very seldom used except when correcting outside corners, archways, soffits, etc. Over-lapped seams should always be secured with a vinyl-to-vinyl adhesive. (Or better yet, use a double-cutting technique to eliminate the overlap entirely.) (Fig.11)

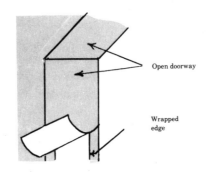

Open doorway

Wrapped
edge

Fig.11

Padded Double-Cut Seam

This is a standard double-cut seam that is padded with wax paper or scrap wallpaper before the two layers are cut. This is accomplished by applying a scrap piece of the allowance trimming, wax paper, or scrap vinyl directly on the wall surface underneath the cutting area to protect it. When the double-cut is employed, the pad will help prevent the razor from cutting through the primer/sealer and/or the surface of the wall--which could result in wall damage and/or seam shrinkage. (Fig.12)

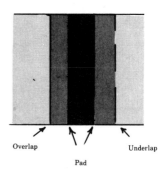

Overlap   Underlap

Pad

Fig.12

Summary: It is impossible for manufacturers of wallcoverings to list every technique to provide a satisfactory job. This is mainly because of the many different wall conditions that exist and the many different types of adhesives available. There are many variables associated with wallpapering and the seaming process that simply cannot be listed; therefore, trial and error may be the only way to perform successful seaming techniques.

It is important that professional installers learn different techniques to employ--especially when problems occur when seaming wallpaper strips together.

It has always been stated that experience is the best teacher; however, experience usually obtained by trial and error are useless unless the knowledge is retained for future reference. The experience of knowing how to perform a certain technique and identifying a potential problem ahead of time should be the goals of every professional wallpaper installer.

Engineering

Seam Placement

The process of engineering is the technique of pre-determining the actual seam placement of the wallpaper prior to the installation. This process, when properly planned, will become the single most important step towards producing an easier job of installing the wallpaper.

There are, however, different factors to be considered before the engineering process should begin. Some examples are: the aesthetical pattern placement of the wallpaper, all focal points and/or accent walls, border placement, the arrangement of door and/or window frames, etc. Any of these factors could affect the actual seam and/or pattern placement, therefore, they would become the dominant source of information for the starting points, ending points, or kill point of the room.

The engineering process should generally begin in the area of the room that will present the most difficult situations during the wallpaper installation. Once these areas or circumstances have been engineered, the seam placement can be established in two different directions working from the problem area back to the kill point, or ending point. By determining where every seam will be before the wallpaper installation begins--unnecessary seams can be prevented in undesirable places such as two inches or less beside a window, door, or corner. Therefore, the amount of wallpaper required to complete a job can be minimized.

It is advisable for a right-handed wallpaper installer to plan on installing the wallpaper working from the right to the left. A left-handed wallpaper installer should plan on working from the left to the right. Once the first strip has been installed, the second strip can be adjoined using the natural hand of the installer by using this procedure. This will eliminate working backwards, although it is sometimes necessary to do so, depending on the particular engineering requirements.

There are times when pattern placement will be more important than seam placement. Whenever this is the case, the pattern motif (recurring subject matter) on the wallpaper should be placed where it will appear aesthetically pleasing at a first glance. Consideration should still be taken to combine pattern placement and seam placement whenever possible.

It is important to measure the expanded width of the wallpaper before the process of engineering begins. Most all wallpaper will expand one to two percent after it has been pasted or submerged into water; however, some wallpapers do not expand at all. If the seam placement is determined prior to knowing the expanded width, all the effort of engineering may be in vain once the installation of the wallpaper begins.

To establish the expanded width of the wallpaper, apply the proper adhesive onto the back of a small scrap piece of the wallpaper to be installed, or submerge it into a water tray if it is prepasted for only about 10 seconds. In either case, book it (fold pasted sides together), and allow it to relax

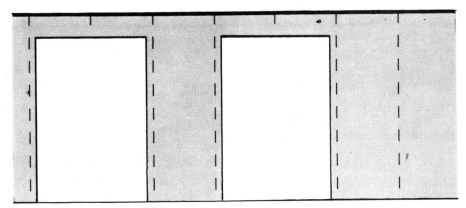

Fig. 1

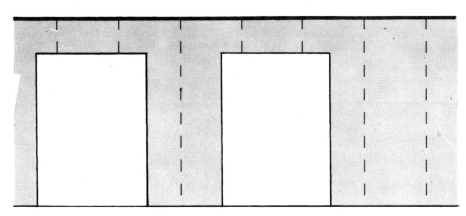

Fig. 2

5 to 10 minutes. Unfold the pasted piece of wallpaper and re-measure it for its expanded width.

It is not unusual for the wallpaper to expand anywhere from ¼ to a full inch in width. The new measurement will represent the actual width of the wallpaper once it is installed, so this measurement should be used during the engineering process.

Try to avoid having any seam fall less than 2 inches beside any obstacle such as a door frame or corner. Sometimes this cannot be avoided, but in most cases it can.

In **Fig.1** notice that a routine unplanned seam placement would result in several small vertical strips as well as unnecessary seams.

Notice that a very small strip was required beside both doors, which forced three strips to be installed between them instead of two. Unless the small strips beside the doors were spliced in, there would be a tremendous amount of wallpaper wasted on this wall during the installation.

If the normal deduction of ½ single roll had been allowed for each of these two doors during the original estimate, it would have jeopardized having enough wallpaper to complete the job. This would result in the unnecessary waste of one full roll.

In **Fig.2** the seam placement (engineering) was planned more carefully. Notice that the wall in **Fig.2** is the same as the wall in **Fig.1.** By engineering (predetermining) the seam placement, there are no small strips to be filled in and there are only two strips instead of three between the doors. Also a small strip was used over each door, further minimizing waste.

Be careful not to waste any more wallpaper than absolutely necessary during the installation. A flaw may be noticed in a roll of wallpaper at the last moment. If a portion of the wallpaper is carelessly wasted earlier in the installation, it could result in an unfinished job.

Remember: Engineering (determining careful seam placement) will save a tremendous amount of time and prevent problems during the installation process, as well as insure the maximum amount of yield from the wallpaper quantity.

Pattern Segmentation

Pattern segmentation is the technique of changing seam placement without altering the pattern sequence (motif) of the wallpaper. In order to perform this process, it is absolutely necessary that the installer is able to recognize and identify every pattern motif that is repeated horizontally across a strip of a wallpaper. This information must be known prior to the engineering process in order to be effective.

When there are duplicated horizontal pattern repeats within a single strip of wallpaper, the installer may overlap one design over a duplicated design and double-cut through the overlap. This will produce a strip narrower than the normal width without breaking the pattern sequence. This allows the luxury of changing the seam placement to avoid an undesirable situation.

Pattern segmentation is used to add or remove a small strip segment over doors, windows, etc. In **Fig.3** notice that the pattern appears three times across the 21″ wide strip of wallpaper. This would enable the installer to add either a 7″ or 14″ segment over a door or window by overlapping one design on top of the other, and double-cutting through the two layers.

In **Fig.4** notice that the normal seam placement indicated at the lower part of the wall would have resulted in narrow strips as well as an unnecessary seam between the doors. By utilizing the technique of pattern segmentation and adding a 7″ segment over each door, the seam placement was changed without changing the pattern sequence. This eliminated the seam between the doors while at the same time, eliminated all the narrow vertical strips. Notice how every full-length strip is utilized to its fullest potential, therefore, the amount of waste is minimal.

There are times when a change of seam placement can be established with a drop-match pattern as shown in **Fig.5.** When a double-single sequence (half-drop match), for example, is being used, the seam placement can be changed by overlapping and double-cutting through two consecutive doubles or two consecutive singles; or overlapping and double-cutting a double with a single, to produce a smaller segment.

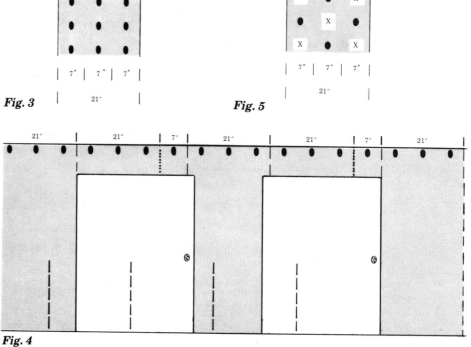

Fig. 3

Fig. 5

Fig. 4

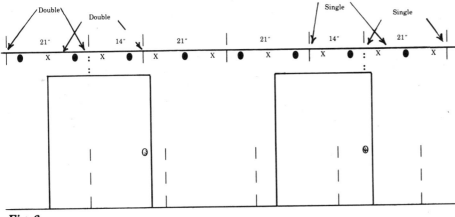

Fig. 6

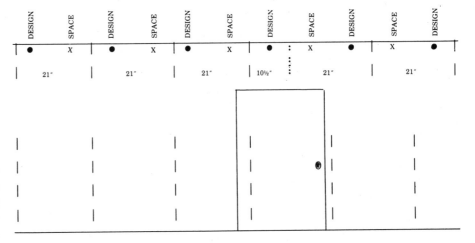

Fig. 8

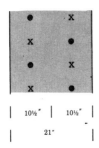

Fig. 7

not be ignored. Use them!

After determining where every seam will be, indicate (on the wall) the pattern sequence to be used at the ceiling line of each individual strip. Make these indications on the wall using a very light pencil mark. (Dark pencil and ink pen marks may show through the wallpaper.) A mark should be used for each strip using a system that identifies the pattern at the ceiling line. See chapter on Pattern Matches for pattern identification symbols.

When pattern segmentation is to be employed during the installation, it should be

In **Fig.6** compare the original seam placement at the bottom of the wall with the change of seam placement (segments) at the top. Notice how careful engineering (using pattern segmentation) minimized the number of seams and narrow vertical strips that would have occured. The seam placement can be changed even with the drop-match pattern.

At times, it will become necessary to reverse the original pattern placement at the ceiling line when cutting and installing strips for the purpose of using pattern segmentation with a straight-across match. This will allow one pattern to be overlapped by a duplicated pattern.

When a straight-across match is being installed; every strip will have the same pattern design placed at the top. This will always be true until a duplicated pattern segment has been added.

In **Fig.7** the horizontal pattern is duplicated only once within the strip, therefore a 10½″ segment can be used for pattern segmentation.

In **Fig.8** compare the original seam placement at the bottom of the wall with the new seam placement at the top. By adding a 10½″ segment over the door, the small vertical strip at the right of the door was eliminated. Notice that the pattern

was started at the left side of the wall at the ceiling line, using a design...space, design...space sequence. Once the segment was added over the door, each strip began with a space...design sequence rather than a design...space sequence at the ceiling line. Even though the seam placement was changed, the continuous pattern sequence at the ceiling line was never broken. **Important: Never change pattern sequence during the engineering process, but by all means take advantage of inserting or removing pattern segments (pattern segmentation) when needed to eliminate an undesirable situation.**

Remember, some wallpaper designs do not have horizontal pattern repeats within an individual strip, therefore, extra time should be spent during the engineering process to prevent an undesireable seam placement. When there are duplicated horizontal pattern motifs present within a strip of wallpaper, pattern segmentation can be utilized. These horizontal pattern repeats are a luxury to the paperhanger and should

indicated on the wall since it may require two of the same segments placed together for double-cutting. Do not forget to note these changes during the strip-cutting process at the work table.

When adding in or removing a pattern segment directly in line with another, indicate the change of seam placement (segmentation) on the wall by using the symbol C.

Important reminder: Do not write with a dark pencil or marker on the wall, because of the possibility of the marks bleeding or showing through the wallpaper.

Fig.9 shows an example of how one might mark pattern segments identifications on the wall.

Once the engineering process is complete, the installer will then have the option of starting at any of the predetermined seam placements in the room. It is possible to start in the middle of the room and work from there in two different

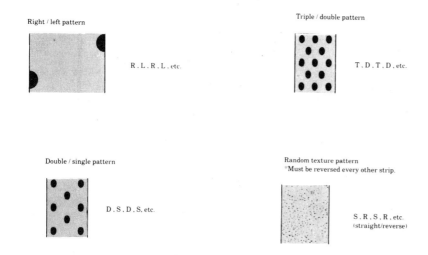

Right / left pattern

R . L . R . L . etc.

Triple / double pattern

T . D . T . D . etc.

Double / single pattern

D . S . D . S . etc.

Random texture pattern
*Must be reversed every other strip.

S . R . S . R . etc.
(straight/reverse)

When you use pattern segmentation, this must be indicated also, this will require two of the same segments double-cut together. Do not forget to allow for these changes when cutting several strips ahead of yourself. R , L , (R , R), L , R , etc.

Fig. 9

directions, back to the kill point (the ending point). The kill point should always occur in the most inconspicuous place, usually over an entrance door, or in the back corner of a bathtub or shower. Normally, the kill point will always result in a mismatch.

Important: Just because the installation begins in the middle of the room doesn't mean it has to end there. The wallpaper will have to be installed in two different directions in order to meet back at the kill point.

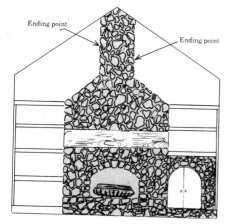

Ending point

Ending point

Fig. 10

When the wallpaper does not meet back together during the installation, for reasons such as fireplaces, accent walls, cabinets, etc., there will not be a kill point (mismatch). The wallpaper simply ends at an obstacle, which is referred to as an ending point. **(Fig.10)**

Aesthetical Pattern Placement

Aesthetical pattern placement is the technique of placing a particular pattern or design at a specific point on a wall so that it will look pleasing to the eye at first glance. Particular areas may include ceiling lines, chair-rails, door and window headers, soffits, dados, etc. The beauty of the placement may be either vertical or horizontal or the pattern is balanced between the ceiling line and the chair-rail or other parallels. **(Fig.11)**

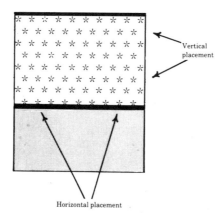

Vertical placement

Horizontal placement

Fig. 11

The horizontal pattern placement is sometimes critical to produce a pleasing job. The pattern may be centered between the two corners of a wall or between two other parallels. Sometime the horizontal placement balance can be established on only one wall, therefore, it should be the focal wall.

There are many times that a particular aesthetical pattern or sequence is not evident or readily noticed such as a variegated design of flowers and stripes. In these cases, the importance of engineering a specific alignment of patterns is not a factor to be concerned with.

It is very important, however, to determine the aesthetical pattern placement when borders are being used in conjunction with a companion wallpaper. This procedure is fully detailed in the chapter on Borders.

The main points to remember about aesthetical pattern placement is to balance it (the pattern) vertically and horizontally on the wall to deliver the most pleasing effect possible. Otherwise, the installation may not satisfy professional requirements.

Focal Walls

When installing wallpaper on a focal wall with a dominant pattern arrangement, be sure to consider the horizontal as well as vertical pattern placement at the ceiling line.

The pattern should be balanced between the corners, doors, windows, etc. In these cases, pattern balance is more important than seam placement.

Notice that **Fig.12** is better balanced than **Fig.13** at the ceiling line.

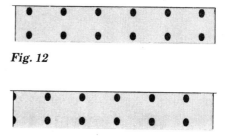

Fig. 12

Fig. 13

When hanging a focal wall, keep the wall balanced by centering either the seam placement and/or pattern placement. The focal area may be between two corners, two doors, two windows, over a fireplace, etc. Whatever the situation, it is important to engineer the focal areas so that seams and/or patterns are centered.

If the focal wall has a large picture window, it is important to center the wallpaper pattern and/or seam around it. **(Fig.14)**

When the focal wall is the only wall being installed the seam placement position will become important if the seams are obvious such as with grasscloth. If this is the case, engineer the seam placement to provide equal strips (in width) on each end of the wall. Notice in **Fig.16 & 17** that a dominant seam placement, using grasscloth, would look more balanced in **Fig.16** than in **Fig.17.** Note: It is possible to manually trim each individual strip (provided it is a texture such as grasscloth) to equal widths to provide a perfect balanced effect on the wall.

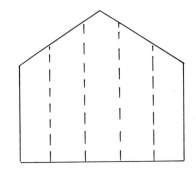

Fig. 16

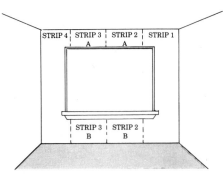

Fig. 14

When a companion wallpaper is being installed on three walls (for example) and the focal wall is being installed with a different pattern, the focal wall should be installed first, leaving approximately ¼″ overlap at the corners where they (the focal wall and companion walls) meet. **(Fig.15)**

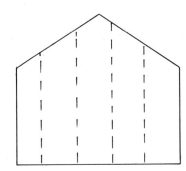

Fig. 17

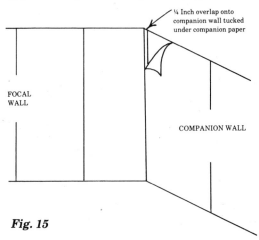

¼ Inch overlap onto companion wall tucked under companion paper

FOCAL WALL

COMPANION WALL

Fig. 15

Once the companion wallpaper is installed, the final strips that adjoin the focal wall should overlap the ¼″ that was wrapped from the focal wall. However, the companion wallpaper allowance at the focal wall should be creased exactly in the corner with a trim guide and cut with scissors to prevent cutting through the ¼″ overlap that was originally wrapped from the focal wall.

Safety and the Work Area

Safety should be the number one priority whenever installing wallpaper. A checklist of different factors should always be taken into consideration on every job to prevent injury to any individual that is present or to any property that is related to the job.

Safety considerations should always be given to other people who may be present on the job site. Small children and pets should always be supervised and kept clear of the work area.

The following diagram displays an organized work area.

Safety tips should include, but are not limited to, the following:

■ The work area should never be set up in a high traffic area such as an entrance foyer or hall especially when other workers are present.

■ Allow as much room as needed to be operative without being crowded. Sometimes this may require rearranging some furniture.

■ Cover the floor surface under the work table and the surrounding furniture with either clean drop cloths, old bed sheets, or plastic. This will protect the items from adhesive, dust, or whatever. Be sure to use a slip-resistant (rubber-backed) drop cloth when working on slick floors such as hardwoods or vinyls.

■ Arrange a work table or surface that is not easily tipped over. Set the table at a comfortable height to avoid constant bending of the back during the table technique procedures.

■ Place the adhesive on a small stand or stool that will not easily tip over. This should be placed at the right side of a right-handed installer, or the left side of a left-handed installer.

■ Have the measuring tools (yardstick, measuring tape, folding ruler, etc.) convenient to eliminate having to constantly search for them during the room engineering and strip cutting process. Some installers prefer to make measuring indications on the work table.

■ Position the pasting brush or roller close to the adhesive bucket (tray) for easy access.

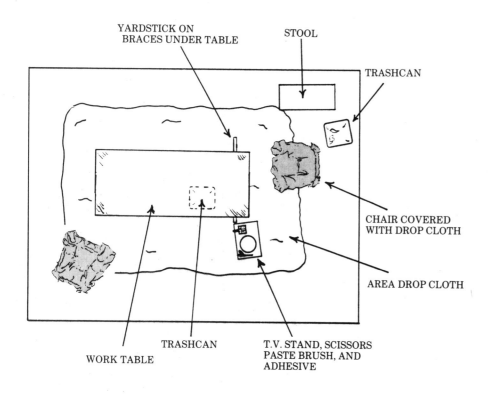

YARDSTICK ON BRACES UNDER TABLE

STOOL

TRASHCAN

CHAIR COVERED WITH DROP CLOTH

AREA DROP CLOTH

WORK TABLE

TRASHCAN

T.V. STAND, SCISSORS PASTE BRUSH, AND ADHESIVE

■ After engineering a room or wall, place the work stool, ladder, or scaffolding in the proper position for the first strip to be installed. Make sure that any standing device does not interfere with the wall surface. If it is necessary to lean a ladder against a wall, use foam pad or soft pillow to protect the wall surface.

■ Place a trash container at the work table and at the wall where the actual installation is occurring. It is very important to discard all wet scrap wallpaper trimmings and old razor blades in a trash container. A person could slip on a wet scrap piece of wallpaper that was discarded on the floor. Even a dry scrap piece could trip or throw someone on a slick floor or carpet. **Do not** allow anyone to ramble through the trash. It is very easy to get cut on the debris in the trash container.

■ When a walk plank or other scaffolding tool is needed, be sure to secure it by using rubber elastic straps.

■ Use a dolly or special appliance rollers to slide appliances such as refrigerators, washers, or dryers away from the wall surface to be covered.

■ Never leave a tool belt with razors or other dangerous tools just lying around. Curious children (and adults) pick them up without realizing how harmful they can be in untrained hands.

■ Never leave extra adhesives or primer/sealers open. Pets may get into them and cause damage to themselves or to the surrounding area.

■ Do not allow anyone to pass under ladders or other work platforms while you are working on them. They could accidentally knock your support or you may accidentally drop a tool on them. Ask them to wait for you to move.

■ When existing wallpaper is being removed, keep it off the floor surface. Use rubber-backed drop cloths to protect them. Sometimes, especially when old wallpaper is sprayed with a chemical remover or dishwashing detergent, old dyes in the wallpaper may be loosened and stain the floor, or old adhesives from the backing could cause stains to form.

■ Keep a supply of very lightweight plastic or bed sheets on hand to lay over dishes or china that may have been removed from a china cabinet. This will protect the items from dust or hard-to-clean residues.

■ Be sure to disconnect any supply of electrical current before removing or replacing an electrical fixture. Even a slight shock can cause you to get hurt or make you drop the fixture if it catches you off guard. A current tester is a very valuable, yet inexpensive, tool to test for electricity. Keep one on hand to determine whether electricity is present before you touch exposed wires. **Do not take chances!** Keep a supply of various wire caps and electrical tape available in case you need to replace existing ones.

■ Be sure to turn off the water outlet faucets before removing a toilet or wall-hung fixture. If a cut-off valve is not present, either turn off the main water cut-off or **do not remove the fixture.**

Summary

Always be safe and especially mindful of the safety of others when you set up your work area. The old saying still applies: "An ounce of prevention is worth a pound of cure."

Verifying Quality Control and Hanging the First Strip

A wallpaper installer can eliminate a lot of unnecessary wasted time and trouble if he/she will employ some basic table techniques. Most all minor problems caused by the manufacturing process of the wallpaper can generally be worked around, provided it is detected early enough and prior to the actual installation.

Example: Suppose an installer is inspecting the wallpaper for problems and notices an ink smear down one side of a double roll. That roll may still be used if the strips are placed so the bad side will be cut out within door openings. The installer may have to replace one side of the strip over the door, by using the double-cutting technique; however, that is better than throwing away the entire double roll, and possibly not finishing the job.

This is just one example of the many problems that can be solved through definite and pre-planned table techniques. The following steps can be used as a guide for table techniques.

Step 1: Reverse-roll each roll to inspect for flaws and to uncurl the window shade effect, caused by the packaging process. **(Fig.1)**

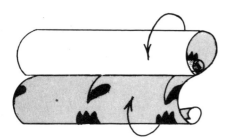

Fig. 1

Use the following as a checklist to find any flaws that may exist:

■ Verify that all rolls have the same pattern number and dye-lot number (run number). Record these for future reference.

■ Check for patterns that may be printed on the bias or out of square with the edges of the wallpaper.
■ Make sure the pattern outlines are not out of register or out of line with their colors.
■ Scan the wallpaper for any partial pattern that may be missing.
■ Make sure that the inks are not flaking from the decorative surface of the wallpaper.
■ Scan the wallpaper for any ink that may be splotched or blotted on the surface.
■ Make sure the wallpaper surface's vinyl coating is consistent and that the vinyl coating was not smeared (especially on the edges) by the rollers of the printing press.

Note: The preceding are discussed in detail in the chapter on Problem Solving & Trouble-Shooting.

Step 2: If you are a professional, be sure to advise the customer of an existing flaw. Even if it is minor, be sure to get final approval before installing it. If the flaw is major and is not acceptable, **do not hang the material.** If everything is **acceptable** or can be worked around, then proceed to install the wallpaper.

Step 3: Knead or apply pressure with the palms while pressing the re-rolled paper back and forth. This technique will help eliminate the window shade effect even more. **(Fig.2)**

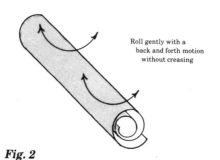

Roll gently with a back and forth motion without creasing

Fig. 2

Step 4: Un-roll the entire roll at the base of the work table so that the top end of the wallpaper (design side up) will feed to the top of the work table surface. Make sure the wallpaper is able to feed to the top of the work table from an accordion folded fashion on the floor, such as a computer paper feeds into a computer. **(Fig.3)**

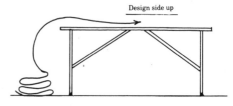

Design side up

Fig. 3

Step 5: Determine the seam placement from the starting point and choose the direction you will be installing. It is better to work counterclockwise if you are right-handed, and is easier to work clockwise if you are left-handed. These procedures will enable you to align each strip with your dominant and natural hand, and eliminate working backwards. Be sure to select the most inconspicuous place for the kill point (final mismatch and ending place). You may begin in the middle of the room if you prefer, and work in both different directions, always working towards the kill point or final ending point.

Step 6: Before cutting the first strip, establish a vertical plumb guideline. This is achieved by making a small pencil mark near the ceiling line, approximately $1/8''$ to the left or right side of where the first strip will be installed. Next, make a plumb line using a carpenter's spirit level and pencil, or a chalk line and plumb line.
Note: Make a habit of using light-colored chalk or pencil. Ink pens, dark pencils, and dark-colored chalk will bleed through

all semi-transparent wallcoverings. **(Figs.4&5)**

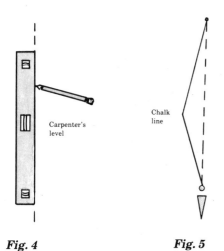

Fig. 4   *Fig. 5*

In either case, be sure to keep the line at least ⅛″ away from the actual seam, to prevent the pencil mark or chalk line from penetrating the seam once the second strip is adjoined to the first.

Step 7: Identify a dominant pattern design on the wallpaper and consider the aesthetical pattern placement that will be placed at the ceiling line. It may be important to consider the pattern placement along a chair-rail, under or over a border, etc. In any case, be sure to select a specific pattern design and do not mistake it for a similar design during the strip cutting process. **(Fig.6)**

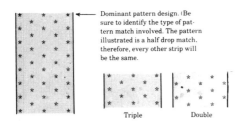

Fig. 6

Step 8: Measure the length of the first strip to be installed using a yardstick. Develop a system for using the yardstick both at the wall and at the work table. Example: If a strip is 62″ long, measure it as 1 yard 26 inches with the yardstick. If the strip is 93″ long, measure it as 2 yards and 21 inches, Remember, a yardstick will read in a reverse direction by flipping it over. This

will eliminate putting the yardstick end to end or turning it around during the measuring process. **(Fig.7)**

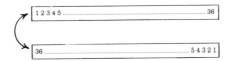

Fig. 7

Note: Some professional installers prefer to mark the measurements on the top surface of their wallpaper table. This will enable them to cut the strips without the use of a yard-stick.

Step 9: Cut the first strip according to the wall measurement. Be sure to allow at least a couple of inches for trimming at the top and at the bottom of each strip. This is referred to as the allowance and will be trimmed off once the strip is in the correct position on the wall.
Important: Always measure the length of the strip from the pattern design; **not** from the allowance cut. If you measure from the allowance cut it will become a bad habit, and sooner or later a mistake will be made and the wallpaper strip will be cut too short. **(Fig.8)**

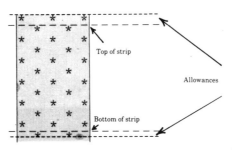

Fig. 8

Step 10: Once a strip has been cut it should be rolled up, starting at the bottom of the strip and rolling it towards the top of the strip. The top of the pattern should always be the loose end of the roll. If a drop-match pattern is being installed, be sure to place the odd strips in two separate areas (stacks). Once all the strips are cut, the next procedure is pasting.
Note: If the wallpaper is pre-pasted, see chapter on Installation Techniques (section on Pre-Pasted Wallpapers). Other-

wise use the following illustrated steps for unpasted wallpapers. The same technique may be used for applying an additional diluted adhesive onto the substrate (backing) of pre-pasted wallpapers if it becomes necessary.

Step 1: Place the strip face down on the work table making sure the top of the strip is at the right-hand end of the table if you are right-handed and vice versa if you are left-handed.

Step 2: Place the adhesive bucket and brush (or short-nap roller) on a stand such as a TV tray at the same end of the table as the top of the strip. See chapter on Safety and the Work Area.

Step 3: Prime the brush by dipping it into the adhesive and tapping it lightly from side to side of the bucket. This will fill the bristles with adhesive. **(Fig.9)**

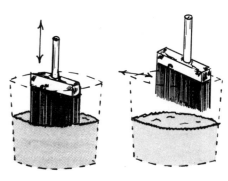

Fig. 9

Step 4: Apply the adhesive to the back of the wallpaper using a figure 8 motion, covering the backing evenly and smoothly. Give special attention to the edges, going off the edges, without coming directly back onto the table in the same stroke. **(Fig.10)**

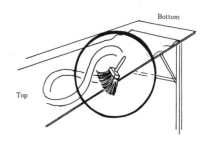

Fig. 10

Step 5: Once the top section of the strip is pasted, it is booked (folded paste side to paste), and immediately rolled up in a loose newspaper roll fashion. Important: Do not crease the wallpaper at the folds. **(Fig.11)**

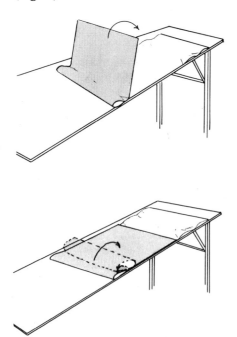

Fig. 11

Step 6: The remainder of the strip is then pulled onto the table surface, and the pasting is completed. Book the bottom half, paste to paste, until it overlaps the end of the first fold approximately ½ ". **(Fig.12)**

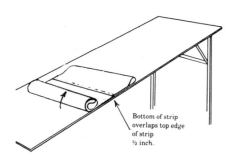

Bottom of strip overlaps top edge of strip ½ inch.

Fig. 12

Step 7: Finish rolling the strip up as it was started in Step 5. **Note:** Some installers prefer to make large folds as opposed to rolling the paper up in the newspaper fashion. The top fold is generally larger than the bottom to indicate which end is top. The advantage to rolling the strip as opposed to making large folds is:

(a) the rolling effect will prevent curling of the edges during the expanding process

(b) the rolling effect will help prevent the wallpaper from drying out too soon after it has been pasted and prior to the installation.

Step 8: After the strip is pasted, it should be allowed to relax in the rolled (folded) position for approximately 5 to 10 minutes. This allows the paper to expand and the adhesive to penetrate into the substrate (backing). This process will eliminate the possibility of expansion wrinkles occurring after the strip is in position on the wall. **Note:** There are some wallpapers that are required to be installed immediately after the adhesive application. If it is allowed to relax (sit) too long, it may cause the wallpaper backing to delaminate from the decorative surface and/or cause the folds to stick together. These types of wallpapers are generally very expensive and an experienced professional wallpaper installer should do the installation.

Step 9: If you are pasting several strips ahead, place them in a systematic order, so the first piece that will be installed is the first piece that was pasted, and continue in the proper sequence. This may be followed by placing each pasted strip on a table or TV tray, with the loose fold of the rolled strip always facing or indicating the first or the next successive piece to be installed. Note: Keep the work table clean of adhesive at all times and clean all tools often. Clean the paste brush after each day's use. Pick up all scrap wallpaper as you work, and dispose of it in the trash can to eliminate the possibility of an accident. Wallpaper left on the floor will be slippery and hazardous, whether it has adhesive on it or not. **Important!** Throw all razor blades into a trash can and avoid reaching into it. Professionals, be sure to remind customers and children to stay clear of the trash containers for their safety. Trimmings and razor blades left lying on the floor are dangerous and are hard to clean up--especially after the adhesive dries.

The time has finally come to install the first strip after several strips have been pasted and allowed to relax. Use the following steps as a guide:

Step 1: Set a ladder or step stool in position (if applicable) and unroll the booked and rolled strip towards you, as if you were addressing a king with a scroll and announcement. **(Fig.13)**

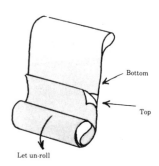

Bottom

Top

Let un-roll

Fig. 13

Step 2: The top of the strip should be facing you at the fold. Gently grasp the strip at the areas where the bottom and top meet. **(Fig.14)**

Hold fold while grasping top corners between thumbs and index fingers

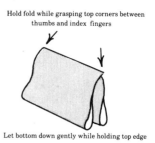

Let bottom down gently while holding top edge

Fig. 14

Step 3: Unfold the top section only and position it near the wall aligning the edge of the wallpaper to the guideline. Note: To prevent stretching, be sure to leave the bottom of the strip folded until the top is in position. **(Fig.15)**

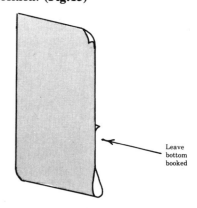

Leave bottom booked

Fig. 15

Step 4: Apply the strip to the wall and align the proper edge with the guideline. Always remember to leave a ⅛ " space between the edge of the strip and the vertical guideline to prevent the chalk or pencil mark from penetrating the seam. Also, check the pattern placement at the ceiling line. Smooth down only the guideline edge of the wallpaper using a professional smoothing brush or plastic wallpaper smoother and apply gentle pressure using vertical strokes. Pull the opposite side of the strip away from the wall gently, and start smoothing out the paper from the center of the guideline edge towards the opposite seam, allowing the paper to be smoothed without getting air trapped underneath the strip. **See (Fig.16) Note:** The bottom half of the strip will still be folded at this point.

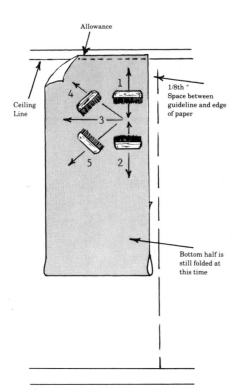

Fig. 16

Proceed to the bottom of the strip. Unfold and smooth out using the illustrated sequence of strokes. **(Fig.17)**

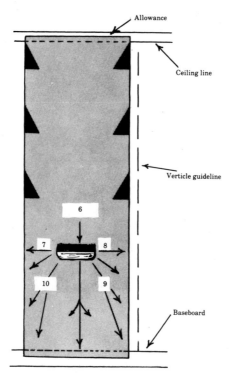

Fig. 17

Once the first strip is installed and aligned properly, proceed with the second strip following the same procedure. Paste, book, and roll. Allow the proper relaxing time of 5-10 minutes. Match and align the design pattern as you join the seams of the two strips together. Align the adjoining seams with one hand while the other hand holds the opposite edge off the wall. **(Fig.18)**

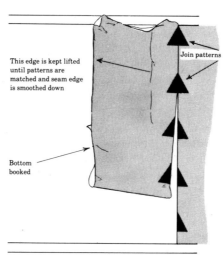

Fig. 18

This process will prevent the strip from sticking to the wall prematurely or in the wrong place. If this happens, you will be tempted to force-slide the strip, which could result in overworking (stretching) the wallpaper. This would cause a slightly gapped seam to appear after the wallpaper has dried because the wallpaper would shrink. **Never** force a seam to align with another by sliding it over after it is stuck to the wall. You should gently remove the entire strip and start over by aligning the adjoining edge first. This will help eliminate the separating seam problem.

Now that the seam is closed, use the same smoothing stroke sequence for the top half as you would in the first strip. The bottom half requires a little different sequence, as is illustrated. **(Fig.19)**

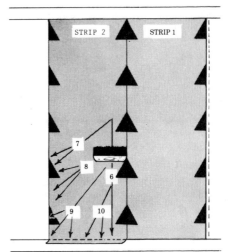

Fig. 19

Note: Always brush away from the seam once you start installing additional strips. This eliminates the possibility of forcing excess air pockets back into the previously installed strip. Proceed using the same sequence as STRIP 2 on all remaining strips.

Installation Techniques

Trimming Allowance Edges

The secret to obtaining a neat, precise trim around edges is keeping an ample supply of new sharp razor blades available and changing them frequently. Never risk the chance of a rip or tear by trying to over use a razor blade. When hanging very delicate or soft wallpapers, or when rough edges have to be trimmed, it may be necessary to change a blade after every single cut to insure a perfect trim without tears.

A trim guide should always be used in conjunction with the razor knife to hold the wallpaper secure along the edges. A small 3″ slanted scraper/putty knife or broad knife may be used. Always position the trim guide beside the wallpaper--leaving the allowance selvage exposed. (**Fig.1**)

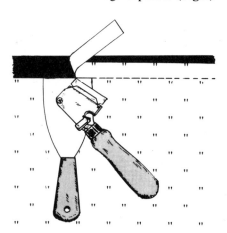

Fig.1

This will avoid cutting the wallpaper surface should a slip occur. If the wallpaper is not trimmed neatly, it may still be re-trimmed. In extremely tight places such as behind door frames or in tight inside corners, it may be necessary to crease the wallpaper using a trim guide where the trim should be. (**Fig.2**)

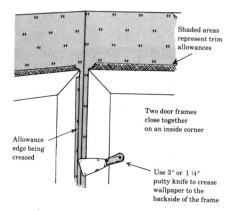

Shaded areas represent trim allowances

Two door frames close together on an inside corner

Allowance edge being creased

Use 3″ or 1¼″ putty knife to crease wallpaper to the backside of the frame

Fig. 2

Since it is practically impossible to get a razor knife in these positions, the wallpaper can be pulled away and cut with scissors along the crease. (**Fig.3**)

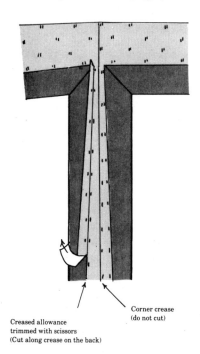

Creased allowance trimmed with scissors (Cut along crease on the back)

Corner crease (do not cut)

Fig. 3

Then the wallpaper can be tucked into these small areas.

Note: It is better to allow a little extra (maybe a ¼″) to wrap around the back side of the door or window frame in tight areas. This overlap cannot be seen, but, if it is cut short it may be noticeable.

When trimming the allowance edges away from the ceiling line, it may be necessary to use the creasing technique to prevent cutting through the thin sheetrock tape in the absence of crown molding. This is done by simply creasing along the ceiling line a couple of times with the edge of the trim guide. (**Fig.4**)

(Creasing technique)

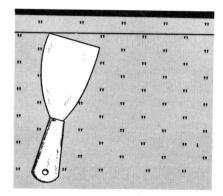

Fig. 4

Pull the strip away from the ceiling and using scissors, trim along the crease line and discard the allowance.

Note: The crease is more visible from the backside of the paper rather than the front decorative side. (**Fig.5**)

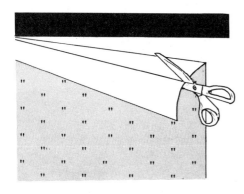

Fig. 5

Important: Do not try to trim off the allowance edges until all relief cuts have been made. If excessive pressure is still present, it may result in an unnecessary rip or tear or an unsatisfactory trim.

Door Frames

When working around a door or window frame, the important factors to remember are: Make all necessary relief cuts at the proper angles, and make sure the small section over the door or window does not become accidentally tilted off plumb.

In **Fig.6** notice the proper smoothing strokes to use when installing around doors.

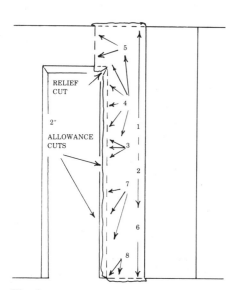

Fig.6

Notice that most of the strip that overlapped the door has been cut away except the 2″ allowance for trimming. This eliminates excess adhesive from getting on the surface of the door. Also notice the relief cut at the top corner of the door frame. Fig.7 illustrates the proper angle to make this relief cut. Once the strip has been smoothed out up to sequence 4 (in Fig.6), lift the left-hand side of the strip up and away from over the door and make the relief cut at a 45 degree angle, which should be a mirror image of the 45 degree mitered cut on the door frame. **(Fig.7)**

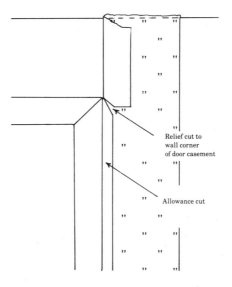

Relief cut to wall corner of door casement

Allowance cut

Fig.7

Important: Make sure the relief cut is made all the way to the back corner of the door frame next to the wall. If the cut is made only to the front of the corner of the frame, the relief cut will be in the wrong place and could result in a rip or tear at the corner. Place a finger at the corner of the relief cut on the wall before positioning the small section of the strip over the door frame. This is important to avoid ripping or tearing.

Once the first strip is installed around the door, proceed to hang the small header (section over the door). Be sure to keep the aesthetical pattern placement level with the ceiling line. Notice the smoothing strokes on the header strip in **Fig.8.**

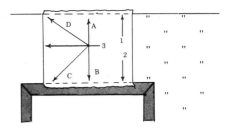

Fig.8

Once the header is installed, the last strip can be installed around the door frame. First establish a new vertical plumb line. Use a small expanded spacer near the ceiling line to determine the proper distance to make the plumb line, allowing ¼″ past the actual seam placement so the plumb line will not fall on the seam. **(Fig.9)**

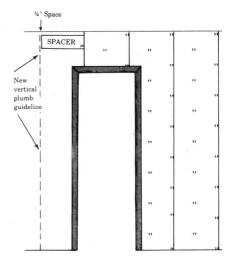

¼″ Space

SPACER

New vertical plumb guideline

Fig.9

Match the adjoining seams over the door and then make another relief cut. This one, however, will be the opposite angle from the cut on the other side of the door frame. Lift up on the entire strip at the top of the door frame and press it gently to the actual door frame to temporarily hold the pressure off the strip. Use your fingers to feel the corner where the mitered relief cut will be. Then use a razor knife to start the relief cut. This should only be a 3″ to 6″ cut. Then finish the relief cut with scissors. **(Fig.10)**

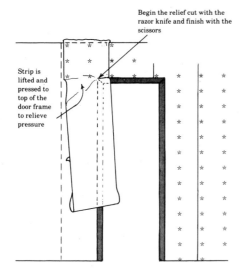

Begin the relief cut with the razor knife and finish with the scissors

Strip is lifted and pressed to top of the door frame to relieve pressure

Fig.10

Important: Do not cut the face side of the door frame with the razor knife. Use the scissors to finish the relief cut. Hold a finger at the corner of the relief cut to prevent a rip or tear. Gently unfold the remainder of the strip, lowering the left side down from the top of the door frame. Next, align the left edge of the strip with the new vertical plumb line. **(Fig.11)**

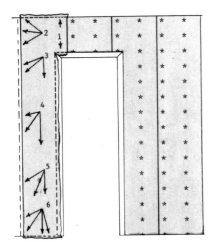

Fig.11

Note: If there is an excess amount of wallpaper overhanging the door frame and the door, cut all but approximately 2″ away as soon as possible to prevent adhesive from getting on them. This 2″ allowance is left on for more accurate final trimming. Once the strip is properly smoothed out, the allowance edges can be accurately trimmed from around the door.

See **Fig.11** for proper smoothing strokes on the last strip around the door.

Multiple-Mitered Relief Cuts

The main technique involved with odd-sized window frames is establishing the correct relief cut angles at every mitered corner. Always make sure the relief cuts **do not** slice a section of wallpaper strip that will remain on the wall as a finished product. See the following illustrations of different relief cut angles. **(Figs.12,13,&14)**

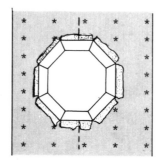

Fig.12

Fig.13

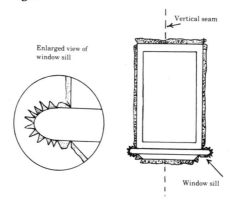

Enlarged view of window sill

Vertical seam

Window sill

Fig.14

Nearly all the wallpaper inside the window frames have been cut away, leaving approximately 2″ to 3″ for allowance. This prevents any excess adhesive from getting on the window frame as well as removing excess paper so the final trim will be easier and more accurate.

Note: The speckled areas of the illustrations represent the allowance cuts (approximately 2″ to 3″). The dotted lines represent the preferred seam placement. The mitered corner relief cuts should be made after the allowance cuts. This allows for more accurate cuts at the miters.

Caution: Do not cut past the mitered corner. When a relief cut leaves only a small piece attached, be careful that the weight of the remaining strip does **not** tear at the relief cut. **(Fig.15)**

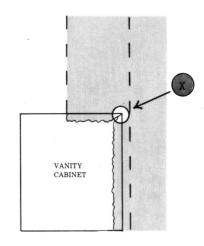

VANITY CABINET

Fig.15

When this relief cut is made, the weight of the vanity section of the strip should be carefully attended. If not, the remaining couple of inches that will be applied beside the cabinet will be easily ripped or torn.

Inside Corners

When hanging an inside corner strip, a vertical plumb guideline should be established on the adjoining wall before beginning to install the corner strip. Most paperhangers pre-cut the corner strips prior to hanging, rather than hanging the full strip. However, using the following method will give the best looking corner and a minimal if any mismatch. Sometimes, however, it will be necessary to pre-cut a corner strip if an obstacle prevents the normal procedure. These exceptions may include tight corner vanities, commodes, or the like.

Step 1: Determine whether the corner is square. This is done by using expanded spacers at the top, middle, and bottom of the wall. Join the spacers to the edge of the last piece installed, and wrap them inside the corner. **(Fig.16)**

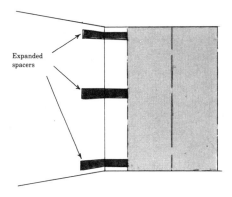

Fig. 16

Step 2: Once the expanded spacers are in place, hold a level or plumb line beside the exposed ends of the spacers to determine which one is closest to the corner. **(Fig.17)**

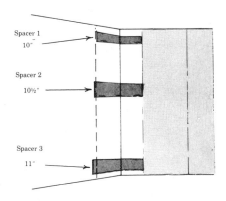

Fig.17

Step 3: In **Fig.17** SPACER 1 is 10″, SPACER 2 is 10 ½″, and SPACER 3 is 11″ from the inside corner. This indicates the need to establish another plumb line ¼″ past the edge of the shortest spacer.

Make a small (light-colored) pencil mark at this point. Remove the expanded spacers and establish a vertically plumb guideline. (Use a light colored chalk line or pencil to prevent show through).

Once the new plumb line is established, proceed to hang the inside corner strip. Align and match the adjoining strip and smooth toward the corner. Tuck the paper into the corner as you would beside a door frame, then cut the entire strip from the top to the bottom, using a razor knife and a trim guide. If the corner is weak in structure, a crease should be made with the trim guide and should be cut with scissors.

Separate the strip into A and B; SIDE A will be the side adjoining the last strip and SIDE B will be the remaining half. **(Fig.18)**

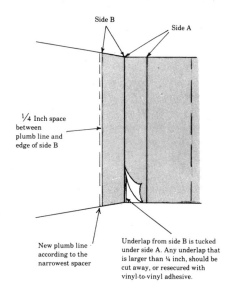

Fig. 18

Step 4: Realign SIDE B with the new vertical guideline, and allow it to overlap SIDE A approximately ⅛″ at the narrowest place in the corner. This will be at spacer 1 in the illustrated case. Also match the cut patterns of SIDES A and B as close as possible where the ⅛″ overlap occurs. **(Fig.18)**

Once this is done, concentrate on the new plumb line. SIDE B should now be plumb. You will notice that the overlap in the corner will get larger as you realign the strip. This is because the corner is not square. To prevent this overlap from showing, lift the corner of SIDE A away from the wall. **(Fig.18)** Tuck the corner edge of SIDE B under SIDE A. Any

under-lap larger than ¼″ on SIDE B should either be cut away or re-glued to the edge of SIDE A with a vinyl-to-vinyl adhesive.

If the corner is out of square, a slight mismatch will occur. There is no way to avoid the mismatch. However, by cutting the strip directly in the corner rather than pre-cutting the strip, you will eliminate as much mismatch as possible. This is because you are cutting the wallpaper strip at the same angle as the corner.

Important Reminder: Establish the new plumb line ¼″ past the actual edge of SIDE B to prevent the plumb guideline from being directly on the seam. Also, consider the transparency of light colored wallpapers when creating guidelines. It is better to form a habit of only using light-colored chalk or light-colored pencils.

Never round a corner, because after the wallpaper dries, it will pull away from the inside corner and leave a void between the wallpaper and the corner or may wrinkle during the settling of the structure.

Outside Corners

There are two specific factors to remember when installing an outside corner. First, an outside corner is commonly a focal point; therefore, any dominant pattern within the outside corner strip should line up or appear to be parallel with the corner. Second, an outside corner should never be cut directly on the corner **unless** it is so far out of square that a wrap and overlap technique is the only possible way to correct the problem. If the strip is cut directly on the corner, it will expose the edges which are susceptible to being pulled away. This will also cause a mismatch at a focal point.

There are different methods or techniques that can be engineered to make an outside corner look good. In the first example, assume the outside corner is perfectly square. All that is required is the proper smoothing techniques and cutting (snipping) the allowance at the top of the strip and the bottom of the strip (precisely on the corner) to provide a relief cut. This will enable the strip to round the corner. **(Fig.19)**

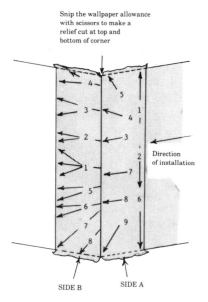

Snip the wallpaper allowance with scissors to make a relief cut at top and bottom of corner

Direction of installation

SIDE B SIDE A

Fig. 19

Follow the smoothing stroke sequences as illustrated in **Fig.19** on SIDE A. Once the relief cuts have been made at the top and bottom, proceed with the smoothing techniques illustrated on SIDE B. Notice the smoothing strokes begin on SIDE B about middle way the strip, working away from the corner at all times. Be sure to keep the corner edge tight and smooth at all times to prevent puckers from forming as the strip is installed around the corner.

Note: If the corner is perfectly square, the pattern designs on the wallpaper should align plumb with the corner.

Now assume the outside corner is off plumb, but no more than ½″. This ½″ can be absorbed within 6 to 12 inches of the outside corner strip either before the outside corner's edge or after the outside corner. This is accomplished by using the **shredding technique.**

The shredding technique is cutting the wallpaper vertically within a single strip beside a stripe or within the background between a row of pattern motifs. Once the splice has been made, the wallpaper will be divided into two sections. The first section will adjoin the previous strip as normal. The remainder of the wallpaper strip can then be slightly overlapped over the first to be re-aligned with the corner's edge, door frame, or other obstacle,

without distorting the first section of the strip.

This technique will allow the wallpaper to be installed plumb, while at the same time a pattern can be re-adjusted beside a door or corner to make it appear aesthetically pleasing and parallel to the obstacle. The overlap should always take place within the background of the pattern and within 6 - 12 inches of the obstacle so that once the overlap has been double-cut the missing background will probably never be noticed.

Important: If the pattern is not aligned with an obstacle, it will definitely be obvious and unattractive.

Since a corner is a major focal point, the pattern within the outside corner strip should be lined up as near perfect as possible. If the corner appears straight, this will eliminate all questions, such as…Is the corner crooked? or… Is the wallpaper crooked? If the corner's edge and the wallpaper pattern **look** or appear straight, then who cares whether it is crooked? See **Fig.20** for an illustration on where to shred in order to make an adjustment.

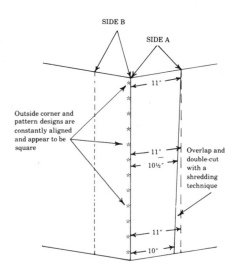

SIDE B
SIDE A

Outside corner and pattern designs are constantly aligned and appear to be square

11″
11″
10½″
Overlap and double-cut with a shredding technique
11″
10″

Fig. 20

It depends on the type of pattern as to where the shredding will take place. Any adjustment should be absorbed between designs and within the background or beside stripes. This is only one example. The actual shredding and double-cutting could take place within the strip or around the corner, depending on the actual pattern situation.

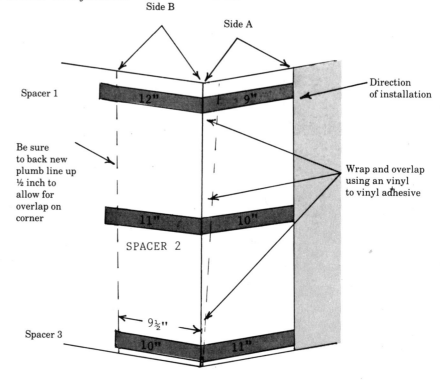

Side B Side A

Spacer 1 12″ 9″

Direction of installation

Be sure to back new plumb line up ½ inch to allow for overlap on corner

11″ 10″

SPACER 2

Wrap and overlap using an vinyl to vinyl adhesive

9½″

Spacer 3 10″ 11″

NOTE: If the new plumb line had been established with spacer 1 in this case, this would result in a 2″ gap at the bottom, rather than a 2″ overlap at the top of the strip.

Fig. 21

Important: The shredding technique creates a fake image that the outside corner or obstacle and the wallpaper pattern are perfectly plumb, when in reality they are both crooked. An individual's eyes will notice a misalignment on an outside corner much faster than a misalignment of the wall itself.

* * *

When an outside corner is more than ½″ off plumb, the problem must be corrected directly on the corner's edge. If the corner is this crooked, there will not be any question of whether the wallpaper is crooked or the corner is off plumb. It will be obvious that the wall corner is out of plumb.

The technique needed to correct this problem is the **wrap-and-overlap method.** This is accomplished by using the same basic steps as described for the **inside corner.**

Before installing the actual corner strip, you must establish a vertical plumb guideline around the corner on the adjoining wall. Use at least three expanded spacers to pre-determine the position of the new plumb line around the corner. **(Fig.21)**

The spacers will indicate where the narrowest distance to the corner will be once the outside corner strip has been installed. In **Fig.21** notice that SPACER 3, is the shortest of the three, once they have rounded the corner. Unlike the inside corner, the new plumb line should be ½″ closer to the corner (rather than ¼″ away from the inside corner). This will allow at least ½″ overlap to occur at the corner--making it easier to secure with vinyl-to-vinyl adhesive later. Proceed to install the outside corner using the same smoothing strokes as a normal straight corner. Then use a new razor knife (blade) to cut the entire strip from top to bottom directly on the outside corner. Realign SIDE B according to the new plumb line on the adjacent wall. This should result in an excess of ½″ to extend past the corner where the wallpaper strip was divided.

Notice in **Fig.21** a 2″ overlap will occur at the top of the corner, with a ½″ overlap at the bottom of the corner. This is because this corner is approximately 2″ out of square. Next, lift the corner edge of SIDE A and wrap the corner edge of SIDE B around the outside corner and underneath the corner edge of SIDE A. SIDE A will

then overlap the wrapped portion of SIDE B. Use a vinyl-to-vinyl adhesive to secure this overlap or it may come loose after the paper has dried.

If the wallpaper is ending on an outside corner it should never be cut exactly on the corner's edge. The exposed edge should be cut ⅛″ short of the corner to prevent the edge from fraying or coming loose.

Note: Sometimes it is advisable to use a protective outside-corner molding made of either clear plastic or wood to protect the edges of the wallpaper from coming loose. A wood outside-corner molding, either painted or stained, would eliminate the obvious mismatch that will occur on extremely crooked corners.

Whenever there are two different or companion wallpaper patterns adjoining on an outside corner, there are a few basic steps that should be employed in order to avoid having exposed edges.

Step 1: In **Fig.22,** STRIPS 1-4 have been installed with STRIP 4 wrapping the outside corner approximately 3″ to 4″. This is a minimum amount because there must be enough overlap to insure the corner does not lift or pucker after it has dried.

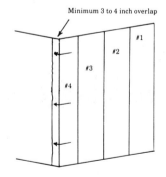

Fig. 22

Step 2: Use a lightweight non-shrinking spackling to spackle over the exposed edge of STRIP 4. Once this is dry, it should be sanded very smoothly, using a 100 to 120-grit sandpaper. **(Fig.23)**

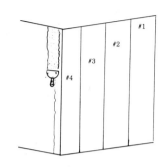

Fig. 23

Step 3: Establish a small pencil mark the distance of the new designed wallpaper's expanded width. Twenty-one inches is used in the example. The new plumb guideline should be 21⅜″ from the corner. The reason the plumb guide-line should always be ¼″ past the edge of the wallpaper is to prevent chalk or pencil lead from penetrating the seam. The other ⅛″ allowance is to prevent the new strip's corner edge from being exposed directly on the outside corner. This will prevent it from being pulled away when normal traffic passes by. **(Fig.24)**

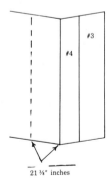

Fig. 24

Step 4: Proceed to hang STRIPS 5, 6, and 7, being careful to align the left edge of STRIP 5 with the new guideline. **(Fig.25)** If the outside corner is out of square, STRIP 5 would need to be backed up to compensate for the problem and the right-hand side would need to be cut ⅛″ short of the corner. **(Fig.26)**

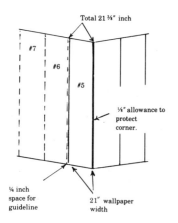

Total 21 ¼ inch

#7

#6

#5

⅛″ allowance to protect corner.

¼ inch space for guideline

21″ wallpaper width

Fig. 25

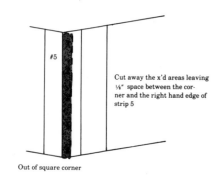

#5

Cut away the x'd areas leaving ⅛″ space between the corner and the right hand edge of strip 5

Out of square corner

Fig. 26

Step 5: The overlap of STRIP 5 over STRIP 4 should be secured with a vinyl-to-vinyl seam adhesive to prevent lifting up from normal traffic. **(Fig.27)**

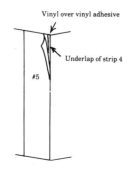

Vinyl over vinyl adhesive

Underlap of strip 4

#5

Fig. 27

Parallels and Guidelines

General Use

One of the facts that a wallpaper installer has to face sooner or later is that most homes or buildings are **not** perfectly level, either horizontally or vertically. This may be due to the construction itself or settling of the structure after construction. It is very important that the paperhanger installs the wallpaper in a manner that will compliment both the wallpaper and the structure. This can be achieved through advanced horizontal and vertical guidelining techniques. These techniques are described on the following pages. Study them carefully and learn where and when to apply the techniques.

Horizontal guidelines are used to to make patterns appear parallel with the ceiling, chair rail, counter-tops, etc., even though they are not level. Vertical guidelines are used to make patterns appear parallel with door frames, cabinets, windows, etc. even though they are not plumb.

Notice in **Fig.28** that a horizontal guideline was established 5″ down from the ceiling. Since the distance from the ceiling to the chair-rail is 3′ 25″ at both ends of the wall, the horizontal guideline can be used to install the wallpaper so that it will appear level with an unlevel ceiling and chair-rail.

When actually installing the wallpaper, a horizontal pattern sequence should be aligned with the guideline so that the pattern will, in turn, run parallel with the ceiling line even though neither is level.

It is also very important to use this technique when borders are being installed, since borders have to run parallel with the ceiling, chair-rail, etc. The wallpaper pattern should be aligned with the border.

Unlevel Ceilings and Chair-Rails

Step 1: Make sure the bias of the print is square with the edge of the wallpaper. See chapter on Problem Solving & Trouble Shooting (Printing on the Bias).

Step 2: Measure down an equal distance from the ceiling line at both ends of the wall. In **Fig.29,** 5″ was used.

Step 3: Use a framing square to draw a vertical guideline at a right angle to the horizontal guideline.

Step 4: Install the wallpaper according to the new vertical guideline and not with a level plumb line. The true vertical plumb line would cause the pattern to run unparallel with the ceiling and chair-rail as shown in **Fig.30,** whereas if the paper were installed by the tilted guideline in **Fig.31,** the wallpaper would run parallel with the ceiling and the chair-rail.

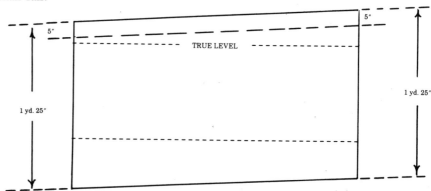

5″

5″

TRUE LEVEL

1 yd. 25″

1 yd. 25″

NOTE: This example is exaggerated!

Fig. 28

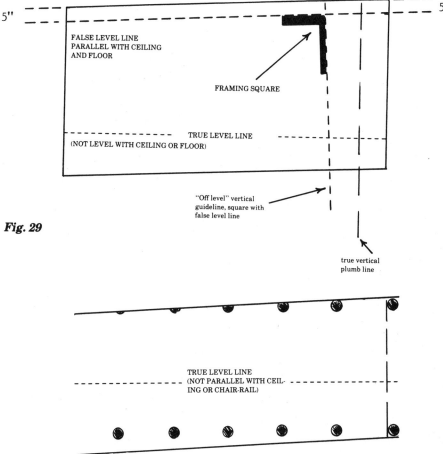

Fig. 29

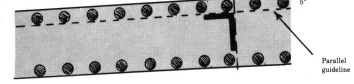

Fig. 30

The wallpaper is installed by a true level guideline. As you see, the pattern begins to disappear at the ceiling and gain pattern at the chair-railing because the wall is not level. Figure 31 looks much more aesthetically pleasing than Figure 30.

The wallpaper is installed by the guideline in order to appear level with the ceiling and chair-rail. An optical illusion occurs and the pattern looks level with everything. Success!

Fig. 31

Level ceiling with an unlevel chair-rail

Fig. 32

Unlevel ceiling with a level chair-rail

Fig.33

Always consider where and what kind of print is being installed before using guidelines. For example, when installing a floral pattern with an all-over print, a guideline would not be necessary unless a dominant design were to be positioned at the ceiling line. Plaids should always be installed using a horizontal guideline and never using the level, except when pre-determining the guideline itself.

When situations arise as illustrated in the following examples, install the paper with the truest of the two. **(Figs.32&33)**

When there is not a chair-rail being used, install the wallpaper in alignment with the ceiling line, because the focal point is always up.

If the ceiling and chair-rail are both dominantly unlevel in different directions, install the wallpaper true to level. Then the wallpaper pattern would at least be balanced.

Vertical guidelines are necessary when a carpenter's level can not be used in tight places or when re-matching strips of wallpaper around obstacles such as windows. In **Fig.34** the wallpaper strip rounded the corner and ended up in the middle of the window. Since it is impossible to draw a plumb line using a level through a window; a temporary vertical plumb guideline is established just past the window. 40″ was measured back to the seam from the temporary guideline to re-establish SIDE B back to plumb.

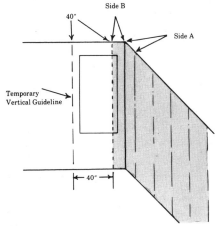

Fig. 34

This guideline may be placed at any random point, as long as it is past the obstacle.

In **Fig.35** guidelining is used to insure the seams joining over the window and below the window match without leaving a gap or overlap. Expanded spacers are used to determine exact position of the guideline. The guideline should be plumb if the last strip before the window were installed plumb. If the last strip were leaning to the right or left, then the vertical guideline should be exactly parallel with it.

The vertical guideline should always extend past the seam about ¼″ to prevent a pencil mark or chalk line from penetrating the seam.

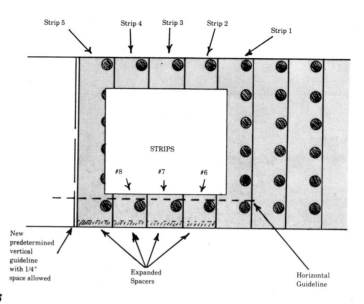

Fig. 36

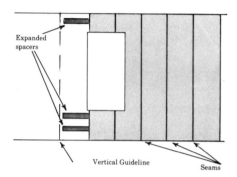

Fig. 35

The strip past the window or obstacle should always be parallel with the strip before the window or obstacle; however, the previous strip may not always be plumb.

The wallpaper strips would align perfectly if the window were not there in the first place. There are many times, however, that the wallpaper will not align as it should around an obstacle. The reason is because the strip prior to the obstacle is probably not perfectly plumb and the installer tries to correct the problem by establishing the strip to a plumb position following the obstacle. This will always result in a gap or overlap occurring under the obstacle or over it. Needless to say, a mismatch will also occur.

When installing around multiple size windows, both horizontal and vertical guidelines are used. **(Fig.36)** Expanded spacers are used in place of STRIPS 5, 6, 7, and 8 to predetermine the vertical guideline at the left edge of STRIP 5 at the floor and ceiling height. Be sure to allow ¼″ for the space between the guideline and STRIP 5.

The horizontal guideline at the bottom of the window allows several strips to be installed matching each other without leaning up or down.

Install STRIPS 1-5 before hanging under the window. Once STRIP 5 has been installed according to the new vertical guideline, snap a horizontal guideline from a specific point of a design in STRIP 1 across to an identical matching design in STRIP 5. Follow this guideline to install and align STRIPS 6, 7, and 8. **Do not** trim the allowance edges on STRIP 5 until all strips have been finalized in position. A minor adjustment can still be made on STRIP 5 if it has not been trimmed at this particular point. **Important: Once a strip has been trimmed it cannot be moved or adjusted on the wall.**

In **Fig.37** the left edge of SIDE B on the inside corner strip overlapped the window frame. Since it is impossible to use a level or a chalk line through the window frame a temporary vertical plumb guideline must be established just past the window. This temporary guideline can be established at any random point past the window or obstacle. The position of the new guideline can be established by using expanded spacers around the corner to simulate the corner strip.

Once the expanded spacers are in place a new vertical guideline can be established by measuring from the temporary guideline which is past the window. In this illustration, 27″ was the distance between the

temporary guideline and the new plumb line for SIDE B of the corner strip.

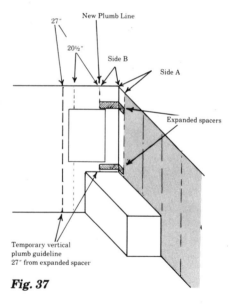

Fig. 37

Note: If two expanded spacers had been used side by side to round the corner the temporary guideline past the window would already be in the correct position for the strip to be installed after the corner strip. This would save a step in establishing another guideline. If this method is used be sure to allow a ¼″ space between the expanded spacer and the vertical guideline so the line does not fall on the seam.

Checking Levels

Using a 2′, 4′, 6′, or any other size level is a continuous part of installing wallpaper correctly. These are used constantly for determining vertical plumb guidelines as well as horizontal guidelines.

It is important to remember, however, that levels are used as **guidelines only.** Even though the wallpaper may be installed perfectly level or plumb, if the final appearance does **not** look aesthetically pleasing to the eye it usually will not be satisfactory. The bottom line rule of every job is to make the wallpaper pattern and/or wall appear to be straight even if in reality neither the wall surface, door frame, ceiling line, chair-rail, crown molding, etc., nor the wallpaper is really straight. Remember, you don't want any questions such as... Is the wallpaper installed crooked? or...Is the house built crooked? Make them look as good as possible!

Referring to the levels, it is important to keep them checked for accuracy. It is not advisable to install wallpaper or check wall conditions against an untrue level. The basic steps to check levels for accuracy are listed below.

Step 1: Establish a chalked vertical plumb line of at least 7′ to 8′ long on a flat wall surface, using a chalk line and plumb bob tool. **(Fig.38)**

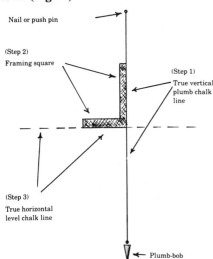

Nail or push pin

(Step 2)
Framing square

(Step 1)
True vertical plumb chalk line

(Step 3)
True horizontal level chalk line

Plumb-bob

Fig. 38

Step 2: Once a true vertical plumb line is established, use a carpenter's framing square to establish horizontal line through the vertical line. **(Fig.38)**

Step 3: Align the level against either the vertical or horizontal lines and compare the level vials for accuracy. If the level has more than one vial, it is possible for one to be accurate while the other may be off. In this case, a symbol can be used to indicate which of the two is accurate by marking the level at the vials with either * or x.

It is important to read the level vials accurately. When the level is true horizontally or vertically, the small floating bubble will be **exactly centered** between the lines of the vial. **(Fig.39)**

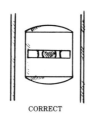

CORRECT

Fig. 39

If the small bubble is to the left or right, even slightly, it is not truly level. **(Fig.40)**

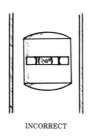

INCORRECT

Fig. 40

Remember to check levels often for accuracy.

It is possible for them to loose their accuracy either from dropping them on the job or knocking them around during transportation.

Concave/Convex Walls

When a job involves concave or convex walls, the engineering procedure becomes a continuous process. Very seldom will a circular wall such as a helix (spiral) staircase be perfectly equal in circumference; therefore each strip, or every other strip, will require an individual vertical guideline. The reason for this is because the wall will not have an exact curve at all wall height positions and an adjustment will need to be made. If a curved wall is very uneven, an overall pattern or heavily embossed texture should be used to compensate for the problem. A wallpaper with a high extensibility (stretchable) factor will also be desired. Most of the time, the wallpaper seams will require a very slight ridge (wire) seaming technique to allow the wallpaper to adjust to the wall without causing any major gaps to occur.

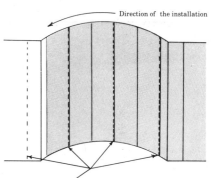

Direction of the installation

New guidelines are established at least every other strip to keep the vertical alignment as true as possible.

Another factor to consider about circular walls is the ability to establish a true horizontal sequence during the installation process. If you are a professional it is a good idea to discuss these variables with the client or customer to make sure everyone involved understands what the present conditions may cause on the final appearance.

Safety is another important factor to consider when concave or convex walls are to be installed, especially if they involve a helix stairway. Generally, special equipment will be needed to establish a level work surface to be used during the installation. If the installer, whether professional or do-it-yourselfer, does not have the proper equipment the job should be not be undertaken or it should be given to another professional with the proper equipment.

Remember: Safety should always have top priority in every circumstance.

Soffits

Applying wallpaper over soffits requires only a few basic techniques. They are described in the following steps:

Step 1: Determine the aesthetical pattern placement that will be used for the specified soffit profile. Once this has been determined, pre-cut the needed strips at the proper length and be sure to allow for the underside section of the soffit.

Step 2: Start installing the wallpaper using the same method as with any other wall. The only exception will be the underside section and the profile corner edge. Use the following smoothing stroke techniques to achieve this. **(Fig.41)**

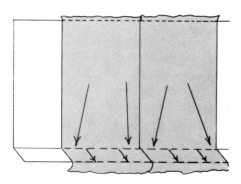

Fig. 41

Step 3: Do not make the allowance cuts until at least three strips are installed in the correct position. Once the strips are installed in a satisfactory manner, the trimming can be completed. **Important: A strip cannot be adjusted once the allowance edges have been trimmed. Do not forfeit the luxury of making this and any other adjustment by trimming the allowance edges too soon!**

Step 4: When the outside corner of the soffit is being installed, the same procedures that are used for any outside corner will be followed with the exception of the underside.

Step 5: Once the outside corner strip has been wrapped around the soffit profile, snip (cut) the bottom of the allowance cut to the outside corner section. **(Fig.42)**

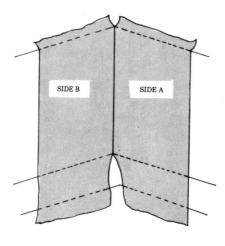

Fig. 42

Step 6: Next, smooth the bottom section of the first half (SIDE A) of the strip to the underside of the soffit following the strokes as indicated. **(Fig.43)**

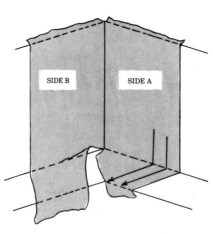

Fig. 43

Step 7: Smooth out the second half (SIDE B) of the strip on the underside section of the soffit. This will create an overlap at the mitered section of the underside. Then trim off the allowances. **(Fig.44)**

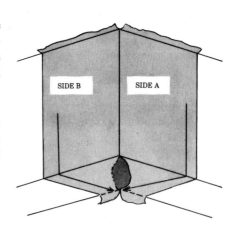

Fig. 44

Step 8: Use a new razor blade to double-cut through the overlap. This will form a 45 degree mitered cut on the underside of the soffit as indicated. The double-cut is made from the cabinet corner to the intersected corner of the soffit. **(Fig.45)**

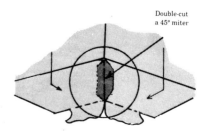

Double-cut
a 45° miter

Fig. 45

Step 9: Remove the excess pieces from the double-cut and join the remaining ends together to form a perfectly fitted seam. Use an oval seam roller to secure the seam. **(Fig.46)** This mitered cut will most likely result in a mismatch but is frequently unavoidable since the paper is wrapped from two different directions.

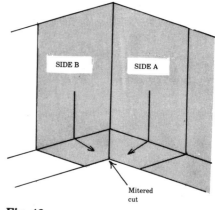

Mitered cut

Fig. 46

Step 10: When an inside corner of a soffit is being installed, a simple cut from the bottom edge of the soffit down to the allowance cut will allow the undersides to be smoothed out in two different directions. **(Fig.47)**

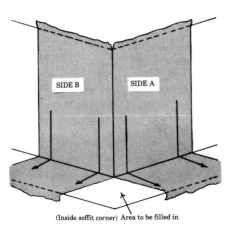

(Inside soffit corner) Area to be filled in

Fig. 47

Step 11: Once this is done a hollow square place on the underside in the corner will be left void. Fill in with a scrap piece that will closely match the adjoining sides, or follow steps 12a-12b. **(Fig.48)**

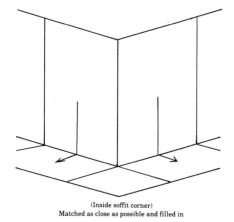

(Inside soffit corner)
Matched as close as possible and filled in

Fig. 48

Step 12a: Smooth SIDE A into the corner and allow sufficient paper to go completely to the bottom edge of the soffit underside of SIDE B, cutting away all excess and making a relief cut as shown. **(Fig.49)**

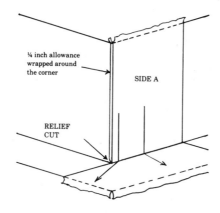

¼ inch allowance wrapped around the corner

SIDE A

RELIEF CUT

Fig. 49

Step 12b: Use the pattern segmentation technique, or cut another identical strip as the one installed in the corner. Allow enough paper to wrap around and on the underside of SIDE A as shown, and trim all allowances away. The darker shaded area illustrates the SIDE B section. **(Fig.50)**

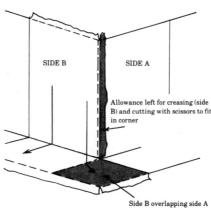

SIDE B   SIDE A

Allowance left for creasing (side B) and cutting with scissors to fit in corner

Side B overlapping side A

Fig. 50

Step 12c: Form a crease using a trim guide or broadknife in the inside corner where SIDE B and SIDE A intersect. Use a pair of scissors to make this cut. A razor blade will probably cut into the corner and should not be used. **(Fig.51)**

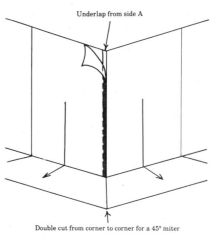

Underlap from side A

Double cut from corner to corner for a 45° miter

Fig. 51

Step 12d: Double-cut at a 45° angle from the inside of the corner underside of the soffit, and remove the excess. Roll lightly with an oval seam roller to secure the seam. This mitered cut will most likely result in a mismatch. **(Fig.51a)**

Fig.51a

Note: When the underside of the soffit is larger than the profile, the mitered corner on the underside may possibly be matched to form a mirror image. The pattern motif must be centered directly into the inside corner of the profile to perform this technique, therefore may require starting in this location in order to make the mitered soffit underside very attractive. **Fig.51b** illustrates the result of the pre-planned miter.

Fig.51b

The Complete Guide to Wallpapering **71**

Recessed Windows

Any recessed type situation--whether it be a window, door, etc.--will involve a few basic techniques. A step-by-step outline of these techniques is explained in this section for a recessed window and/or an open door casement. Use the illustrations to identify each strip or strip segment that will be discussed.

A right-handed installer is being assumed for the purpose of this illustration, therefore the strips will be installed from the right to the left in a counterclockwise direction around the room. This will allow the installer to align each adjoining strip using the natural hand.

Step 1: STRIP 1 in the illustration has been installed ¼″ to the left of a vertical plumb guideline, and the allowance edges have been trimmed away. **(Fig.52)**

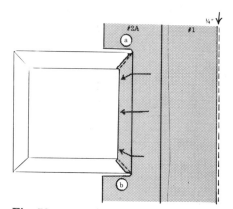

Fig. 52

Step 2: STRIP 2 will match STRIP 1 at the seam; however, the left edge must be wrapped around the outside corner or the right-hand side of the recessed window. Therefore, two relief cuts have been made at the angles described at points A and B. **(Fig.52)** These relief cuts allow the left side of STRIP 2a to be wrapped around the inside section of the window.

When the relief cuts of A and B are made, this automatically cuts into the part that is over and under the window (the headers). There is no way, however, that the single STRIP 2a could wrap both the top and side sections of the recessed

window at one time. These will have to be done in two separate strips.

Step 3: Cut the remaining left-hand side of 2a away since it can no longer be used. See cuts C and D. **(Fig.53)**

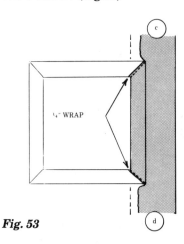

Fig. 53

Step 4: In order to wrap the top and bottom headers of the recessed sections, two more strips will have to be cut that will overlap the entire remaining portion of 2a. (These will be labeled 2b and 2c.) For STRIP 2b, the length should be long enough to wrap under the top header. For STRIP 2c, the strip likewise should be long enough to wrap the over-side of the bottom header.

Before installing STRIPS 2b and 2c be sure to cut away all but approximately 2″ of the right-hand section of each of them. The extra two inches is enough to overlap STRIP 2a and allow for double-cutting. **(Fig.54)**

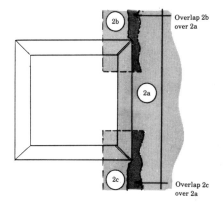

Fig. 54

Step 5: Make the correct relief cuts at angles C and D of STRIPS 2b and 2C. **(Fig.55)**

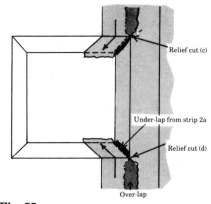

Fig. 55

These two relief cuts will allow the bottom of 2b to wrap the underside of the top header while at the same time overlapping the remaining edge of 2a for double-cutting. The same applies for STRIP 2c at the bottom.

Step 6: Trim out the allowance cuts next to the window itself and in the inside corners of the recessed areas. **Note:** Be sure to leave a ¼″ underlap around the inside corners when trimming the allowances for STRIP 2a **(Fig.55)**

Step 7: After the pattern is aligned perfectly, proceed to double-cut through the overlapped section to form a seam between 2a and 2b. Next double-cut to form a seam between 2a and 2c at the bottom. **(Fig.56)**

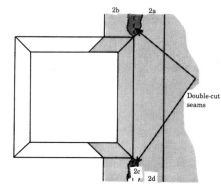

Fig. 56

Step 8: Cut, paste, and install STRIPS 3 and 4, but do not trim the allowances. **(Fig.57)**

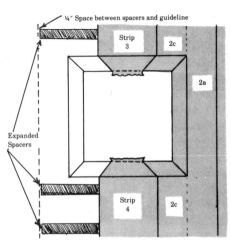

Fig. 57

Step 9: Apply three expanded spacers at the points listed in **Fig.57** and make a temporary guideline exactly in line with the spacers. Leave a ¼" space past them. This will insure that the chalk or pencil lead will not penetrate the seam. Remove the spacers.

Step 10: Paste STRIPS 5b and 5c, and then 5a. Once they have relaxed, apply 5b first and allow to underlap the upper header. Be sure to make relief cuts at the mitered corners. **Do not** trim allowances. **(Fig.58)**

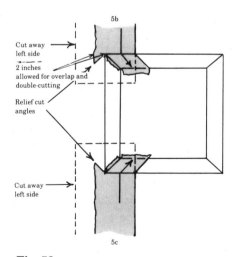

Fig. 58

Step 11: Cut away all but 2″ left of the window, from 5b and 5c. **(Fig.58)**

Step 12: Install STRIP 5a in line with the new guideline, allowing it to overlap 5b and 5c completely. Make all cuts indicated by dotted lines. Remove the two areas marked X and allow the right side of 5a to wrap the inside of the recessed casement. **(Fig.59)**

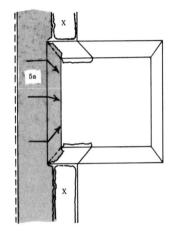

Fig. 59

Step 13: Double-cut through the overlap of STRIPS 5a and 5b to form a seam, and also the overlaps at the bottom of STRIPS 5a and 5c. Remove the excess pieces and trim all remaining allowance cuts. **Note:** If a minor adjustment was needed under or over the window to obtain an exact match, it should have easily been accomplished since all allowance cuts of 3, 4, and 5a, 5b and 5c were left untrimmed. **Fig.60** is an illustration of the finished seams, double-cuts, and proper wraps. The dotted lines represent the double-cut seams.

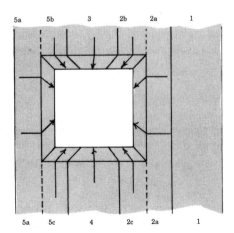

Fig. 60

If an open door casement is being installed, use the basic techniques described for the recessed window using the sequence shown in **Fig.61**.

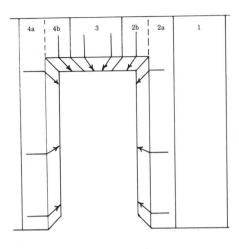

Fig. 61

Archways

When an archway or open doorway with a dome top is involved, careful engineering of seam placement should be employed. See **Fig.62** for preferred seam placement.

Notice in **Fig.63** that SEAMS 2 and 3 were positioned to extend far enough into the dome so that STRIPS 1 and 3 would completely wrap the inside of the arch. This will prevent having a seam close to the corners of the arch as well as within the archway itself.

Fig.64 illustrates the strip placement and relief cuts that are necessary to install wallpaper around the archway obstacle.

In **Fig.63,** points A and B indicate where the horizontal relief cuts were made so the strips could be wrapped into the archway as would an outside corner. This will allow the pattern to continue matching inside the archway up to the relief cut. Notice that the inside of the arch up to the dome section can only be matched from one side of the opening or the other. It will not match both rooms including the header on the opposite side of the archway, therefore it is important to consider the side of the archway that is the most frequently entered.

The domed section of the arch should have little notched relief cuts which will permit the allowance cut of about one inch to wrap the under side of the arch. **(Fig.64)**

A small strip (the thickness of the arch) will need to be placed inside the dome. It is recommended that the two inside strips of the arched opening are each matched with the small strip on each side of the archway. Once they have been matched to the sides, they will join at the center of the dome to form a kill point. The overlap where the two strips meet should be double-cut to provide a smooth butted seam. **(Fig.65)**

If only one room of the archway opening is being installed with wallpaper, the inside section of the arched door opening should be cut smooth along the inside edge of the arch. It is advisable to cut the wallpaper at least ⅛″ away from the edges to prevent fraying during the normal passing of traffic.

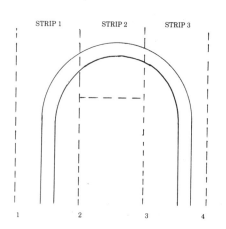

Fig. 62

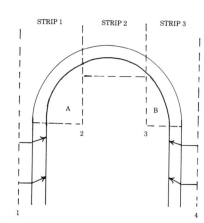

Fig. 63

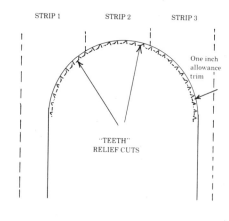

Fig. 64

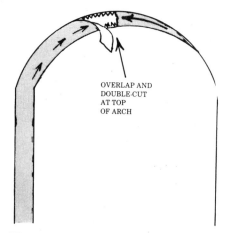

Fig. 65

Dormers

When an attic room or sloped ceiling wall is being installed, there are special techniques that should be employed to successfully do the job. Follow the step-by-step procedures that are outlined below.

Step 1: The illustration assumes a right-handed installer is working from the right to the left. The wall at the end of the attic room will be installed before approaching the sloped ceiling wall. Notice STRIPS 2 and 3 in **Fig.66** are allowed to overlap the sloped ceiling wall approximately ½″ where they intersect.

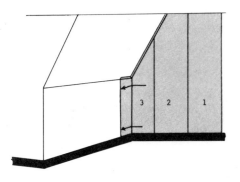

Fig. 66

Step 2: There are two methods to establish a vertical guideline for the first sloped ceiling strip. The first method involves a simple measuring technique as illustrated in **Fig.67**.

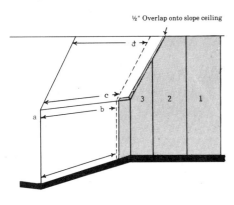

Fig. 67

Measure and record the distance between points **a** and **b**. This represents the span or distance from the outside corner's edge of the knee wall to the exposed edge of the inside corner strip.

Subtract ¼″ from the measurement and transfer it onto the sloped ceiling at points **c** and **d.**

Snap a chalk guideline from points c and d and this will serve as the guideline that will be exactly parallel with the sloped ceiling outside corner edge. The ¼″ is allowed to prevent the chalk line from penetrating the seam. This guideline will prove to be important, especially if a striped design is being used. The outside corners of the sloped ceiling as well as the knee wall are always very high focal points; therefore, the pattern, especially stripes, should be exactly parallel with the corners whenever possible.

In the second method, a vertical guideline for the first strip on the sloped ceiling can be established by using a horizontal line that is parallel with the ceiling line. **Note:** This method should be used even if a dormer does not exist on the sloped wall. **(Fig.68)**

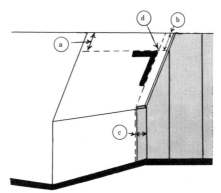

Fig. 68

Start by measuring down from the ceiling at points **a** and **b,** at any random measurement as long as they are the same. (example 10″)

Snap a chalk line at these two points. The horizontal guideline should be parallel with the ceiling line. If the ceiling line is slightly curved (wavy), the guideline would average out to be parallel with it from one end of the wall to the other.

Measure ¼″ past the edge of the inside corner strip at point **c** on the knee wall and transfer this measurement onto the sloped ceiling at point **d** on the horizontal chalk line.

Use a framing square as illustrated in **Fig.68** to draw the vertical guideline. This line will be a true 90° angle to the horizontal chalk line. It is important that the new vertical guideline on the sloped wall matches up with the guideline on the knee wall. The vertical guideline on the sloped wall must still be at a right angle to the horizontal guideline.

Step 3: Proceed to install the first sloped ceiling strip according to the guidelines. Be sure to secure the overlaps from the corner strips with a vinyl-to-vinyl adhesive. **(Fig.69)**

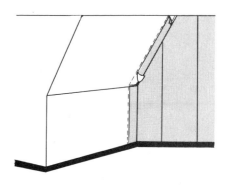

Fig. 69

Step 4: Next, install the remaining sloped ceiling strips to the outside corner, allowing each one to overlap the knee wall ½″. The corner strip should overlap the outside corner ½″ also. These overlaps are indicated in **Fig.70.**

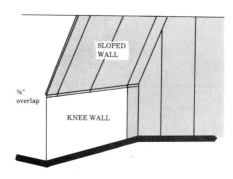

Fig. 70

Step 5: Install all the knee wall strips and allow them to overlap the sloped wall strips in the horizontal corner between them. Always secure every overlap with vinyl-to-vinyl adhesive. Allow the last knee wall strip (the outside corner strip) to wrap around the corner ½″. **(Figs.71 & 72)**

Step 6: Apply an expanded spacer at the seam of the last full knee wall strip that was installed and wrap the outside corner. Then establish a mark ¼″ past the spacer. **(Fig.73)** Establish a vertical plumb guideline at this point and install a full length strip as indicated. If a pattern is involved, it should match the knee wall strip exactly

in the corner. Trim the full length strip exactly, even on the outside corners of the sloped and knee walls. Secure the overlaps with vinyl-to-vinyl adhesive.

If a dormer is involved, proceed toward and around the window and reverse all techniques when installing on the walls opposite the dormer.

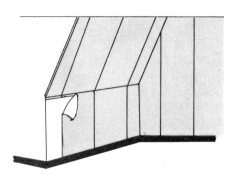

Fig. 71

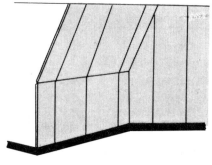

Fig. 72

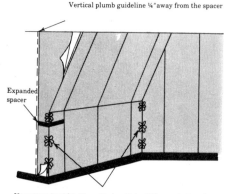

Vertical plumb guideline ¼″ away from the spacer

Expanded spacer

If a pattern is within the wallpaper, it should be matched on the outside corners and the inside corners.

Fig. 73

Wall Sink

In a room where a wall-hung sink is involved, usually a bathroom, special care should be taken during the seam engineering process. The seams should be arranged to equally divide the fixture in half if possible. This will allow for easier and more accurate relief cuts to be made during the installation of each wallpaper strip involved with the obstacle. **(Fig.74)**

Fig.74 represents the relief cuts that need to be made when installing wallpaper around a sink and pipes.

Note: Slide the pipe collars away from the wall. This will allow the relief cuts around the pipes to be tucked in behind the collars. Notice the "pie-sliced" relief cuts around the pipes and the vertical seam placement dividing the sink in equal halves.

Be very careful **not** to make the relief cuts at the wrong angles, particularly at the lower edges of the sink itself.

If the sink has been removed, it is better to allow the wallpaper to dry 24 hours before remounting it. Extra care should be taken so the sink does not scratch or tear the new wallpaper. It is advisable to have assistance when replacing the wall-hung sink.

Remember: Determining the seam placement is the first major step in conquering wall-hung sinks.

It is always better to remove the sink itself if possible. First, be sure to turn the hot and cold water faucets to the off position--usually clockwise. **(Fig.75)**

Use a small adjustable or open-end wrench to loosen the nuts that attach the water supply pipes to the faucet. **(Fig.76)**

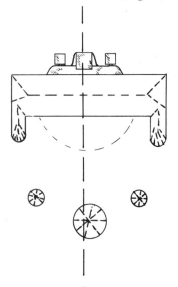

Fig. 74

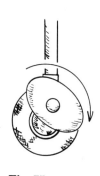
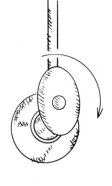

Fig. 75

Fig. 76

Next, loosen the drain pipe connection of the sink and free it from the drain pipe on the wall. **(Fig.77)**

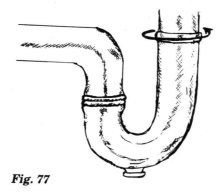

Fig. 77

Once all the connections have been disconnected, carefully lift the sink upward. A wall-mounted bracket is all that is left supporting the sink at this point. Pre-arrange a safe place to store the sink until it is ready for re-installing. Be careful not to bend the supply pipes when resting the sink on the floor. It is better to rest the wall side of the sink on the floor.

Permanently-Mounted Fixtures

There are many times when a "make-do" situation will arise during the task of wallpapering. Permanently-mounted towel bars are only one such example. This section deals with a couple of techniques to install wallpaper around these types of obstacles since they cannot be removed without causing damage to them or the wall surface.

The basic skills of determining the seam placement or engineering will play a very important part in any difficult situation. In order to prevent a large horizontal seam when installing wallpaper around a permanent towel rack, the seam placement should be as close to the mounting brackets as possible. **(Fig.78)**

In this illustration, the seam between STRIPS 1 and 2 intersect the towel bar's left mounting bracket. The seam of STRIPS 2 and 3 fell only a couple of inches from the right mounting bracket.

STRIP 1 can be installed in the usual manner, only needing a couple of relief cuts to work around the left mounting bracket.

STRIP 2 can be installed by sliding the strip between the two mounting brackets and behind the towel bar and using a couple of small relief cuts to work around the left mounting bracket.

STRIP 3 must be cut in order to match STRIP 2, and work around the right mounting bracket. As a general rule this splice should be directly behind the towel bar. There it would be less visible. Sometimes a pattern may have a strong vertical embossed design and it would be better to

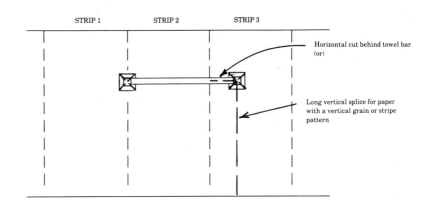

Fig. 78

slice the wallpaper vertically from the right mounting bracket to the bottom of the strip. This would prevent cutting across the natural grain of the pattern. **(Fig.78)**

If the seam placement has to be somewhere middle-way the towel bar, the wallpaper should always be spliced verti-

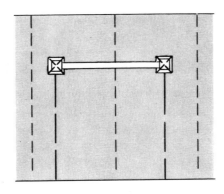

Fig. 79

cally through each bracket to the bottom of the strip, and relief cuts made at the proper angles. This will add an additional vertical seam. However, if a new razor blade is used to make the splice, the seam should not be very noticeable. **(Fig.79)**

Important: A vertical splice is always easier to re-join than a horizontal splice. Also, the vertical seam will be less likely to separate during the drying process. A horizontal seam will commonly tend to separate because of the weight of the lower section pulling down from the upper section.

Remember: The key to any difficult situation is careful seam engineering. A few minutes spent on engineering will eliminate a tremendous amount of time and problems during the installation!

Ceilings

There are two basic factors to remember when engineering the seam placement on a ceiling. First is pattern direction and second is pattern balance.

Determine the proper direction that the pattern should be installed. The pattern should be facing you when you are facing the focal wall and look up.

Determine the aesthetical pattern placement for balance. (See Chapter on **Engineering & Pattern Segmentation** section on Pattern and Seam Placement of a Focal Wall). If there is no pattern to be concerned with (such as in a solid texture), the seam placement should divide obstacles such as light fixtures during the engineering. Of course, any light fixtures, heating vents, smoke/fire alarms, etc., should be removed if possible, and replaced to make the installation of wallpaper on the ceiling easier. Once the wallpaper is installed, replace the fixtures. **Caution:** Be sure to reverse every other strip when installing textures to prevent shading.

Before installing wallpaper on a ceiling, a guideline must be established. Once the seam placement has been determined, choose the position of the first strip. Then follow the next steps:

Step 1: Scribe a pencil mark approximately ¼″ outside the first seam location at two separate points at opposite ends of the ceiling.

Step 2: Snap a chalk guideline from one end of the ceiling to the other at these two points. This is where the first strip will be installed. **(Fig.80)**

Remember: Check for transparency of colored chalk when installing semi-transparent wallpaper selections and apply the chalk line ¼″ from the actual seam.

Engineering and proper preliminary steps should include: establishing a guideline; determining seam placement and pattern placement; determining the proper direction of the pattern; deciding whether the wall will have wallpaper adjoining the ceiling; and determining the focal wall to be matched. Scaffolding or two stools, two work benches, or two ladders will be

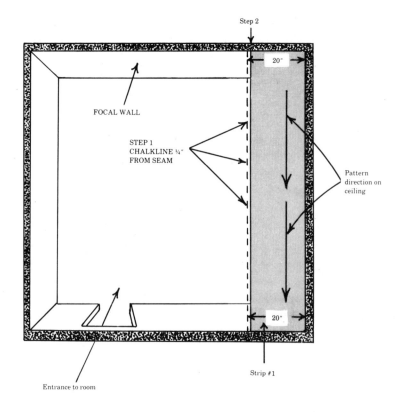

Fig. 80

required to be set up with an aluminum or wood extension plank bridged between them.

Important: Do not overextend or reach beyond the scaffolding during the installation. It is imperative to keep your balance. Establish a tool belt of some kind to hold the necessary tools--especially the smoothing brush--so they can be reached without leaving the scaffolding or walk plank.

When cutting the strips for the ceiling, be sure to add at least 3″ for the allowance cuts both at the top and bottom of the strip. Since the strips that are being installed are longer than normal, it will be necessary to book each strip after pasting, using the accordion folding technique. Be sure to make these folds no further than 18″ to 24″ apart.

After the first strip has been pasted, accordion folded, and allowed to relax, it is ready to be installed on the ceiling. It is advisable to have an assistant available to aid in the installation. It is not practical for one person to safely install ceiling strips, especially if the strips are over 8 feet long. The assistant can hold the accordion-folded strip across his/her left arm, with the top of the strip exposed.

The assistant should always stand on the floor--**not on the scaffold.** The assistant will also hold a push broom (or other similar tool) that is long enough to reach the ceiling without having to extend beyond shoulder height. **(Fig.81)**

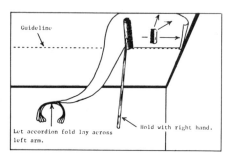

Fig. 81

The accordion-folded strip will then feed off the other arm of the assistant, across the top of the broom. The installer should align the strip with the chalk guideline previously made on the ceiling. Once the installer has the strip started in position, the assistant gently presses the broom against the ceiling, holding the wallpaper in place until the installer is ready to move farther across the ceiling or rest his arms. As the strip is installed, the assistant slides the broom farther along the ceiling guide-line, therefore allowing the paper to feed off the accordion fold.

Note: The same smoothing strokes used to apply the first strip onto an upright wall surface should be used on the first strip on a ceiling. **(Fig.81)**

When planning to install wallpaper on adjoining walls in conjunction with ceilings, be sure to allow a ½″ overlap from the ceiling strips onto the walls when trimming along the edges. Be sure to snip the wallpaper in the corners with scissors to prevent it from gathering or "bunch-ing".

Important: Only one wall can be matched to the ceiling, and this should be the focal wall.

Establish a vertical plumb line on the wall so that the seams on the ceiling will be in line with the seams on the focal wall. **(Fig.82)**

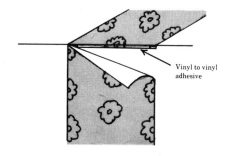

Fig. 83

and ceiling with a vinyl-to-vinyl adhe-sive.) **(Fig.83)**

When hanging a ceiling with an extreme number of obstacles (such as wall par-titions, fluorescent light fixtures, recessed areas, etc.) it may be necessary to work from the bottom of the sheet, rather than from the top, or splice the entire strip where the obstacle(s) may be. **(Fig.84)**

In **Fig.84,** notice the direction of the in-stallation of each strip. STRIP 2 was in-stalled from the bottom to the top in order to split the partition at the top end of the wall. STRIP 5 was split before the installa-tion to aid in going around two end par-titions.

See chapter on Estimating to determine the quantity required for ceilings.

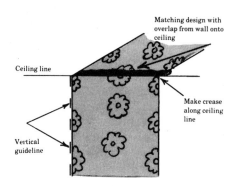

Fig. 82

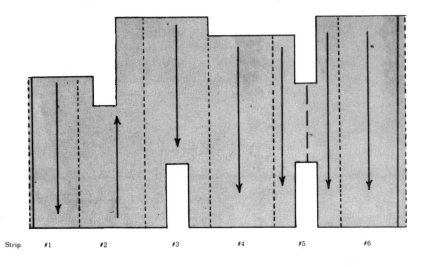

Fig. 84

Correctly match the pattern designs on the wall strip with the ceiling strip and allow approximately 1″ or 2″ overlap on the ceiling. Crease the overlap with the trim guide where the ceiling and wall join.

It is advisable to position the pattern on the wall so as not to divide it in the corner where the wall and ceiling intersect. Pull the top of the wall strip away from the wall and cut through the crease using a pair of scissors. **Do not** use a razor knife to make this cut because you will most likely cut through the ½″ overlap from the ceiling. (If a vinyl wallpaper is being installed, be sure to secure the overlap from the wall

Murals

Murals generally are packaged as indi-vidual panels. They join together in a num-bered or lettered sequence to form a pic-ture or scene setting. Before ordering a mural, these questions should be answered in order to eliminate potential problems:

■ Is the mural picture large enough to cover the wall without looking lost or too small?

■ Is the picture so large that it will over-power the wall?

■ Does the mural have extra back-ground filler paper? If not, how much extra should be ordered to fill out ex-cess wall space on each side of the pic-ture?

■ Is the mural continuous (interlock-ing), meaning the first and last panel will join and the pattern designs will match? If so, how many extra panels will be required to complete the entire length of the wall?

■ Will there be any particular details, such as furniture size, ceiling heights, or chair-railing, that could have an adverse effect on the mural picture itself?

See chapter on **Estimating** (Mural Section) for further details on how to estimate for murals.

When installing murals, there is a limited number of different panels or strips which must be installed in the proper sequence in order to display the picture properly. Murals must be positioned both vertically and horizontally according to the wall size and room setting.

Step 1: Decide which panel or panels have the highest point of design and the lowest point of design. **(Fig.85)**

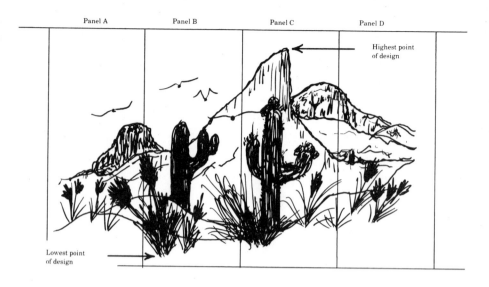

Fig. 85

These two points may be on the same panel or strip, but more than likely they will be on separate panels. In either case, this information is vital in order to determine the vertical picture placement.

Consideration should be given to any furniture which will be placed in front of the mural, so that once the mural is installed, a chair, couch, buffet, etc., will not cover the picture. The mural picture should appear to "float" or suspend into the furniture.

Sometimes a small black and white picture is included with the mural package to give you information on the high and low points of design.

When you have no information about furniture or chair-rail placement, you should place the center of the mural at approximately eye level or a little higher. **(Fig.86)**

Step 2: Measure the width of the wall to be covered, and divide by 2, to predetermine the center.

Step 3: Make a plumb line very lightly to prevent "show through" approximately 1" - 2" left of center. This will establish a vertical guideline for the first strip, that will not be directly on the seam.

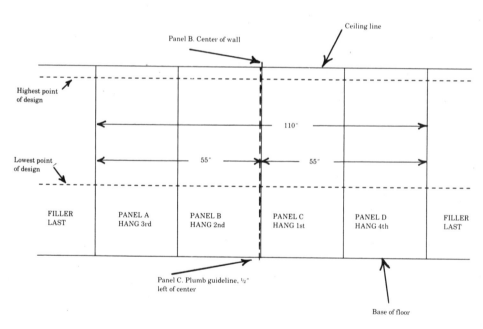

Fig. 86

Note: A spacer may be used from a scrap piece from the top or bottom of a mural panel to pre-determine the expanded width. Continue with Step 4 and finish the wall.

Step 4: Begin installing the panel just to the right of center (PANEL C). Then install PANEL B to the left of center. Next install the remaining mural strips PANELS A and D.

Step 5: Finish the wall with the background (filler) paper. A double or triple roll is sometimes furnished with the mural. This will depend on the individual manufacturer of the mural.

Step 6: If the mural contains an **odd** number of panels, the middle panel must be centered on the wall first. Measure the width of an expanded panel, divide it by 2, and offset a vertical plumb line that distance plus ½″ from the center of the wall to the left edge of the center panel. **(Fig.87)**

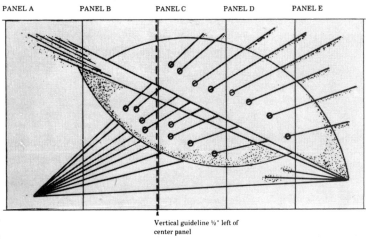

PANEL A   PANEL B   PANEL C   PANEL D   PANEL E

Vertical guideline ½″ left of center panel

Fig. 87

Photo Murals

Photo murals are the same as regular murals with the exception that they are usually divided in quarter panels. Photo murals look more like an actual photograph that has been enlarged.

Most manufacturers suggest that you start with the center lower panels first and then install the upper half of the mural second. This procedure is not recommended unless there are two professional installers working together. It is almost impossible for one person to join or match the top half with the bottom half. It is advisable to install the panels in the sequence shown in **Fig.88.**

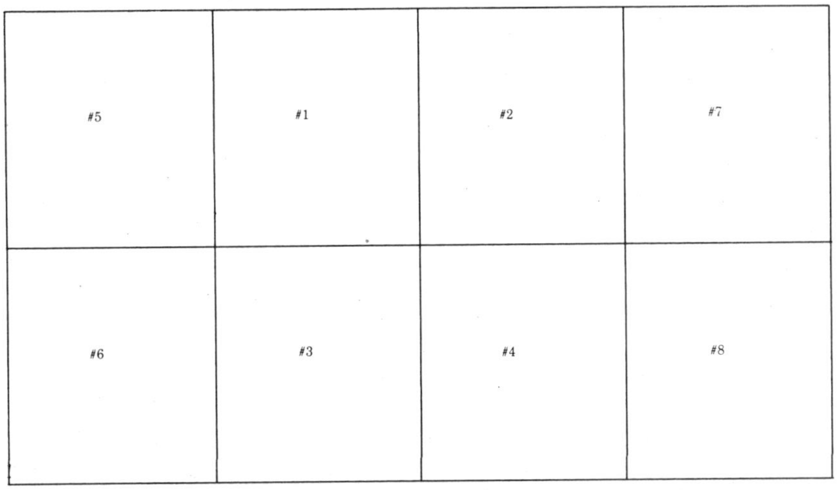

#5	#1	#2	#7
#6	#3	#4	#8

Fig.88

Do not over soak or overwork photo mural panels. They become very limber and tender, and will tear very easily during the installation. Also, be very careful when wiping the seams or front surface of the photo mural, because the color and print may wipe off.

Handle them with extreme care and allow plenty of time for accuracy to install these types of murals. It is best to paste only one panel at a time.

Note: Some photo murals are made to be overlapped at the seaming areas. This is because it is difficult to install every panel perfectly square with one another. If the overlaps are undesirable, they may be double-cut and removed as the mural is being installed.

It is highly recommended that the exposed edges of each strip be lifted away from the wall until the adjoining strip is ready to be aligned with it. If the adhesive has dried along the lifted edges; they may be moistened by using a household spray bottle with lukewarm water. The double-cut must be performed immediately after two consecutive panels are joined. **Important: This double-cutting technique should only be attempted by an experienced wallpaper installer, otherwise follow the manufacturer's instructions.**

Liner Papers

Liner paper can be very useful in preparing many different wall surfaces to make the finished product a much better one. These may include installing over prefinished paneling or concrete block walls. Liners may be used to make a damaged surface a smooth surface, such as where extensive wall damage resulted from the removal of existing wallpaper. It may be used to provide a sound and consistent foundation for a very expensive designer wallpaper.

Whatever the situation, the actual hanging techniques used to install liner papers are explained and illustrated here.

Step 1: Be sure that all walls have been properly prepared, meaning that a good quality wallpaper primer/sealer has been applied to the wall surface and allowed to dry the proper amount of time. Be sure that all necessary spackling and repairs are done.

Step 2: Cut the liner paper the desired length. The liner paper should always be measured and installed horizontally on the wall surface. This will allow the decorative wallpaper to provide a cross-seamed effect when it is installed vertically. **(Fig.89)**

Step 3: Apply the manufacturer's recommended adhesive on the back of the liner or on the wall surface.

Step 4: If the adhesive has been applied to the back of the liner, the liner should be folded in an accordion fashion with folds no larger than 2' to 3' long. This will allow easier handling of long strips during the application.

Step 5: Set up the proper work stool, ladder, or walk plank in position for the first strip, starting along the ceiling line. This will allow easier adjoining of succeeding strips.

Step 6: Start installing the liner on the wall and use very strong horizontal smoothing strokes in the direction toward the beginning end of the strip. **(Fig.90)**

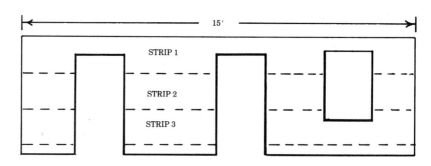

Fig. 89

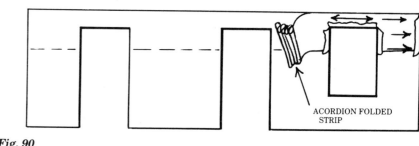

Fig. 90

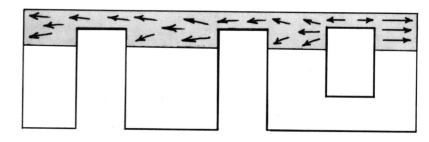

Fig. 91

Step 7: The next smoothing strokes and all following strokes should be pressed toward the end of the strip. **(Fig.91)**

Always keep the liner as tight as possible during the installation process. This will allow it to bridge or stretch over hollow areas such as prefinished paneling grooves. If it is smoothed out vertically and not kept tight, it may be pressed or sink into the vertical grooves. If any places shrink into the grooves of the paneling; it will need to be filled in with spackling before the final decorative wallpaper can be applied.

Note: It is sometimes better not to spackle the grooves of pre-finished paneling or concrete block walls prior to install-

ing the liner paper because the adhesive will bond to the spackling which may cause it (the spackling) to shrink. Otherwise, it would probably bridge over the grooves. It is not unusual for the liner to be pressed into some of the grooves during the installation, therefore, spackling over the liner in these places may become necessary.

Step 8: Clean all excess adhesive off the entire surrounding decorative trim or walls to prevent damage to them. Proceed to install the liner and always use a butt-seam technique for all of the seams.

Do not overlap them because the lap will show through the decorative surface.

Step 9: When an inside corner is installed, the liner paper should be cut directly into the corner, instead of rounding it in one piece.

Step 10: After the liner has dried, use a light bulb with an extension cord to inspect for any imperfections that may still be obvious. Re-spackle these and sand smooth after the spackling has dried.

Step 11: Apply the finished decorative wallpaper over the liner in the natural vertical manner. This will provide a cross seaming effect which will result in both layers supporting each other. **(Fig.92)**

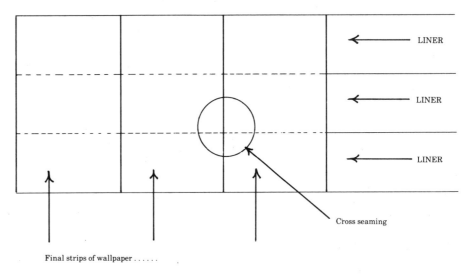

LINER

LINER

LINER

Cross seaming

Final strips of wallpaper . . . . . .

Fig. 92

Pre-Pasted Wallpapers

Place a small drop of iodine on the substrate (backing) of the wallpaper. If it turns brown, it means the company used a starch base. If it turns purple, it means they used a cellulose base. A purplish brown means that a mixture of starch and cellulose was used.

This refers to any type of wallpaper in which the substrate has been coated or sprayed with a water re-moistenable adhesive. There are several types of adhesives that may be applied by the manufacturer:

(a) a starch base of potato, rice, wheat,corn, tapioca, etc.,
(b) a cellulose base of wood pulp, wood fibers, cotton, plants, etc.,or
(c) a combination of the two (starch and cellulose).

Manufacturers suggest that all pre-pasted wallpapers be activated by submersing them into a water tray. Most all professional installers will prefer to reactivate the pre-pasted adhesive by repasting the dry adhesive with a diluted adhesive, however, certain procedures must be followed in order to prevent using the wrong adhesive or create an over abundance of adhesive according to the wall surface conditions that prevail. A simple test (suggested by various suppliers) can be made to determine which type of adhesive was applied at the factory:

If additional adhesive is being applied, it is imperative that the extra adhesive is diluted with at least 50% more water then is normally recommended for non-pasted wallpapers. If a starch and cellulose are mixed, it will generally not affect them chemically. The water-soluble adhesive must be fully activated to insure a uniform adhesion. If the added adhesive is too thick, it could cause a few problems:

■ It would require longer drying time which may cause the wallpaper to slightly shrink apart at the seam because of the time lapse.

■ Air pockets could be easily mistaken for adhesives, therefore if the air were not smoothed from under the surface, it could cause the adhesive to crystallize or become a hardened form.

■ It may not contain enough moisture to fully activate the water re-moistenable adhesive.

Most professional installers prefer to activate the water re-moistenable adhesive by applying the diluted adhesive; however, do-it-yourself paperhangers may still prefer, and have better success using the water tray process.

When the water tray is used to activate the pre-pasted adhesive; there are a few important steps and factors to consider:

■ Most all pre-pasted wallpapers will expand when wet and must be allowed proper time to relax before installing it on the wall. If it does not properly expand, it will continue to do so on the wall after it has been installed. This will result in the formation of vertical expansion blisters. The normal relaxing time for pre-pasted wallpapers is 5 to 10 minutes after the adhesive has been activated.

■ If the paper is submersed too long, the adhesive may wash off, and adhesion will be lost.

■ If the paper is not totally wet, the adhesive will not activate properly. This will cause an unsatisfactory bond to the wall surface. There will be dry spots which would cause a hollow blister to form or the wallpaper will not expand evenly in width. This would cause the wallpaper to be wider in some places than in others.

Since any or all of these problems are likely to occur, one may ask, "What can I do?" The following procedures are highly recommended when the water tray method of dipping the wallpaper is used:

Step 1: Pre-cut each strip and loosely roll the strip from the bottom to the top. **(Fig.93)**

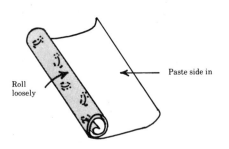

Fig. 93

Step 2: Fill the water tray about ⅔ full of lukewarm water and place it at the end of a work table on a large bath towel. Completely submerge the entire pre-cut strip (from Step 1) into the water for approximately 10 -15 seconds. **NO MORE!** Immediately start pulling the strip out of the water tray very slowly, about one foot per second. Be sure to allow excess water to drain into the water tray. Lay the wet strip, pattern side down on the top of the work table.**(Figs.94&95)**

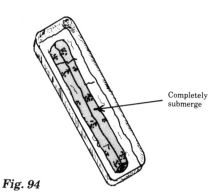

Completely submerge

Fig. 94

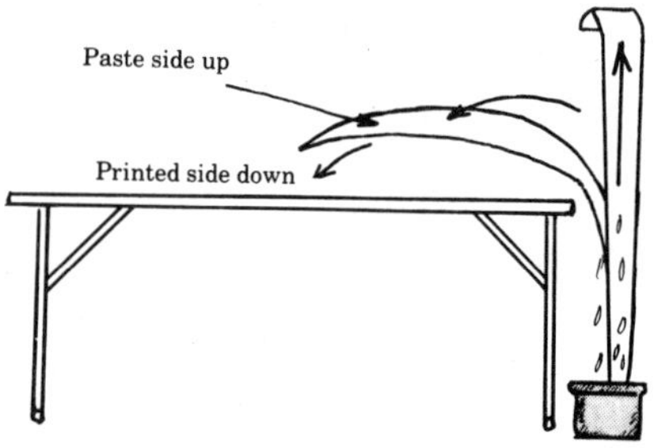

Paste side up

Printed side down

Fig. 95

Step 3: Book or fold the top half of the strip about middle way, being sure to fold paste side to paste side and perfectly align the edges of the wallpaper strip. **(Fig.96)**

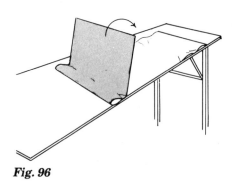

Fig. 96

Step 4: Immediately roll the booked end up, starting from the end that is folded, just like a loose newspaper roll. **Do Not crease the fold! (Fig.97)**

Fig. 97

Step 5: Fold the bottom half of the strip, paste side to paste side until it overlaps the end of the first fold approximately ½″. Continue to roll the strip from the top until it is completely rolled up. Again: Be careful not to crease either of the folds. **(Fig.98)**

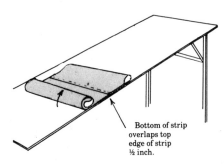

Bottom of strip overlaps top edge of strip ½ inch.

Fig. 98

Step 6: IMPORTANT!! Do not apply the wallpaper to the wall immediately after it has been submerged into the water tray. It must be allowed to relax and expand for a minimum of 5 to 10 minutes. It is completely normal for the wallpaper to expand between one and two percent during the relaxing period. This will commonly represent between a quarter and a half inch increase in width of the wallpaper.

Step 7: Once the paper has fully relaxed (expanded), proceed to install it on the wall. Unroll the relaxed strip and unfold the top fold only. **(Figs.99,100,&101)**

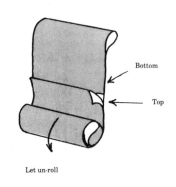

Bottom

Top

Let un-roll

Fig. 99

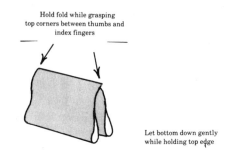

Hold fold while grasping top corners between thumbs and index fingers

Let bottom down gently while holding top edge

Fig. 100

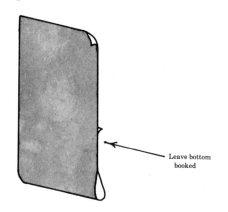

Leave bottom booked

Fig. 101

After the top section of the strip is positioned on the wall, unfold the bottom section and finish installing the strip.

If the pre-pasted wallpaper's adhesive does not perform or reactivate properly, it is advisable to apply a thin layer of diluted wallpaper adhesive onto the wall after the wallpaper has been submersed into the water tray and prior to installing it on the wall.

Important: NEVER attempt to apply a dry strip of pre-pasted wallpaper on a wet adhesive on the wall surface. This will force the wallpaper to fully expand on the wall which would result in a total disaster of expansion wrinkles!

See section on Pre-pasted Adhesives in the **Problem Solving and Trouble Shooting** chapter if further problems arise.

Dry Hanging

The dry hanging technique can only be used to install types of wallpapers that do not expand or shrink during the installation or drying-out period, such as foils and certain woven or non-woven materials. In these cases the adhesive may be applied directly to the wall surface rather than the wallpaper backing. There are several basic techniques that should be followed to prevent damage to the wallpaper during the dry hanging procedure.

■ Each wall should be carefully engineered to predetermine the seam placement of each strip.

■ The adhesive (usually a pre-mixed type) should be applied to the wall surface with an adhesive roller cover. The nap on an adhesive roller cover will resemble a commercial short-napped carpet.

■ The adhesive should be applied evenly and smoothly, being careful not to cause adhesive roller marks or ridges.

■ The adhesive should not extend past the predetermined width of the wallpaper more than 2-3″. Sometimes, it will start drying out and will not dissipate once it is

installed over. This is especially true with the clay-based pre-mixed adhesives because they dry much faster than the starch-based. If the adhesive dries prematurely, it could result in the textured effect of the adhesive roller showing through the newly installed wallpaper.

■ It is better to pre-cut all inside corner strips vertically before installing these types of wallpaper to prevent creasing it. (Do not pre-cut outside corner strips unless absolutely necessary!)

■ Use a tapered seam roller to secure the edges of the paper around door and window frames, moldings, etc. Be extra careful not to cut or rip the wallpaper while using the tapered seam roller.

■ Use a vinyl-to-vinyl adhesive to secure all overlaps.

■ When the double-cutting technique is being used during the installation to remove the selvage of untrimmed wallpapers, leave the exposed edge of the wallpaper lifted away from the wall until the next strip is ready to be joined. If the edge is left down it could dry prematurely and may cause damage to the wallpaper itself or the wall surface. If these lifted edges dry out before the next strip is ready to install, simply re-wet them using a small brush and fresh adhesive or use a household spray bottle with warm water to reactivate the dried adhesive.

When dry hanging a foil or Mylar wallpaper, it is advisable to use a very soft bristle smoothing brush or a soft rubber squeegee to remove the air pockets. Be extremely careful not to scratch or mar the finish with dirty tools because it would cause permanent damage!

Hint: If the squeegee tool is being used, apply some warm water (using a household spray bottle) to the decorative surface of the wallpaper to make the smoothing process easier and help prevent marring (scratching) the surface.

Caution: The dry hanging technique requires quality craftsmanship and speed; therefore, an installer with less than 5,000 rolls of installation experience should use extreme caution or preferably seek a highly skilled professional wallpaper installer for these applications!

Untrimmed Wallpapers

Today many types of wallpapers may come from the factory untrimmed; that is the selvage has not been removed by the manufacturer. The selvage is left on the wallpaper to protect it during shipping and handling. These types of wallpapers are commonly screen printed by hand, by hand and machine, or entirely by machine. Foils, burlaps, silks, suedes, textiles, etc., may also require manual trimming. The three methods to accomplish this are dry trimming, wet trimming, and double cutting.

■ **Dry Trimming:** This method requires very sharp razor blades along with a perfect straight edge as a trim guide. A good stable work table will also be required preferably with a zinc strip to be used as the cutting surface. The zinc strip will allow the razor blades to be more efficient and last longer and is recommended to protect the table top. The straight edge should be aligned perfectly along the trim marks on the selvage and within 1⁄64″ to the inside of the marks. The straight edge is held securely with one hand while the other is trimming the selvage away. A razor holder is highly recommended for this technique as opposed to holding the blade free-hand. The razor blade and knife should always be positioned at a 90° angle to the work table. **(Fig.102)**

Fig. 102

Caution: Any slight tilt of the razor blade may result in a bevel at the seam which may cause a white edge to show from the substrate.

■ **Wet Trimming:** Since most wallpapers either expand or contract after pasting, it may be advisable to pre-cut the strip, paste it, and fold it prior to trimming. Once the wallpaper has expanded after it has been booked, align the edges as perfectly as possible. **(Fig.103)**

Fig.103

Align the straight edge with the trim mark(s). If only one trim mark is visible, use a rule to measure the exact distance from the edge in at least three places to insure a true parallel cut with the edge. **(Figs.104&105)**

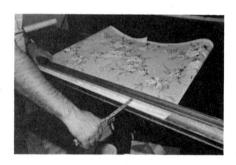

Fig.104

Fig.105

Cut through the booked strip of wallpaper and remove the selvage. Reverse the strip on the table and repeat the procedure for the other edge of the strip. After the selvage has been removed, the strip is ready to be installed.

■ **Double Cutting:** This method will eliminate the need for pre-trimming the wallpaper at the work table, either dry or pasted. This is the only method that will insure a perfectly fitted (butted) seam, therefore, it is preferred over the other two. This is the overlap and double-cut method which is accomplished by using the following steps:

Step 1: Use a pair of scissors to remove most of the selvage within ¼" to ½" outside the trim marks on all rolls to be used. (Be sure to leave the trim marks on the wallpaper selvage exposed.) **(Fig.106)**

Fig.106

Step 2: Establish a vertical guideline according to the pre-engineering requirements and paste the first strip. Remember a portion of the selvage is still remaining at this point. Book it and roll it up loosely like a newspaper, without creasing the folds. Allow the paper to relax the correct amount of time so that it will be able to expand and/or contract before installation.

Step 3: Carry the strip to the wall and align the trim guide marks on either side of the strip with the guideline. Trim the allowance cuts from both the top and bottom and immediately lift the edges approximately 3" away from the wall. This will prevent them from drying out until the next strip is ready to be installed.

Step 4: Cut the next strip, paste it, roll it up, and allow it to relax. While this is relaxing, re-paste the edge of the first strip that the second strip will be joining. This will provide a freshly pasted edge for double-cutting purposes once the second strip is over-lapped. It may only be necessary to spray some warm water from a household sprayer to the edges to reactivate any dried adhesive. It is generally not advisable to create an overabundance of adhesive along the edges of the wallpaper.

Step 5: Carry the second strip to the wall and align or match the designs perfectly by overlapping the second strip slightly over the first. An exact match should be possible. However, on hand-screen prints, the match may be off a little. Unless the misalignment is severe, it should be acceptable. **(Fig.107)**

Fig.107

Step 6: Once the second strip is in position and the allowance cuts have been trimmed, immediately lift the exposed edge 3" away on STRIP 2 as in Step 3. Use a straight edge such as a steel yardstick, a broadknife, etc., and a new sharp razor blade to double-cut the overlapped edges of STRIPS 1 and 2. **(Fig.108)**

Fig.108

Caution: Be careful when double-cutting on sheetrock (drywall). Applying too much pressure would cause the seams to separate when the adhesive begins to dry out. The torque that is associated with the drying of all wallpaper adhesives is strong enough to cause the wallpaper to pull apart if the sheetrock has been cut.

Remove the excess ends and lightly roll the seam with an oval seam roller. Be careful not to burnish or flatten the seam while performing the seam rolling technique. **(Fig.109)**

Fig.109

Several Cautions:

■ Be sure to allow enough overlap to remove the trim marks during the double-cutting process.

■ Do not cut through the wall surface, especially when installing over sheetrock (drywall).

■ Always use a perfectly new and sharp razor blade before double-cutting. This insures a good cut with minimal pressure.

Most all wallpapers that require trimming are generally expensive. It is not usually advisable for the novice do-it-yourselfer to start with these types of papers. Even professional installers require several thousand rolls of experience before they are comfortable installing these types of wallcoverings.

When a wallcovering such as suede or silk has to be trimmed, the front surface must be kept perfectly clean of adhesives. These types may require the slipsheeting technique. This is done by inserting a strip of wax paper, or the like, on the pasted and adjoining edge of the second strip, or applying a strip of masking tape to the adjoining seam of the last strip that was installed. The slipsheet will prevent the adhesive from damaging a previously installed strip. See section on Hanging Commercial Wallpapers.

Caution: Do not wash or scrub (even with clean water) any type of suede, grasscloth, silk, stringcloth, or any other type of wallcovering that stains very easily. These types of wallpapers will require extra care during the installation to protect the decorative surface from any residue of adhesive.

Commercial Wallpapers

Commercial wallpapers are very heavy in weight and usually require a heavy-duty adhesive. The adhesive is applied directly on the substrate (generally with an adhesive nap roller or a pasting machine) or directly on the wall. Whichever method is used, extreme care should be taken to keep the decorative surface clean.

The seaming process usually requires a lap and double-cut method. If the front vinyl surface is relatively smooth, any extra adhesive that gets on the front of the paper during the double-cutting technique can usually be washed off with a natural sea sponge and clean water. If the wall-covering has a deep textured effect, then the slipsheeting technique will be necessary. Slipsheeting can be accomplished by two methods:

Slip Sheeting
Wax Paper Method

Step 1: Cut 4"-wide segments of wax paper the length of the strips to be installed. This will serve as the slipsheeting tool. Some installers prefer to use scraps of leftover wallpaper or liner paper instead of wax paper. In either case, they should be pre-cut to the proper width and length.

Step 2: Paste and install the first strip of the commercial wallcovering and trim the allowance cuts. During the final cleansing process avoid smearing adhesive from the allowance trimmings into the texture of the wallcovering.

Step 3: Apply about 4-6" of additional adhesive beside the strip where the second strip will be joined. **(Fig.110)**

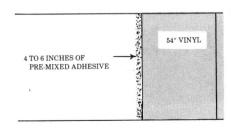
4 TO 6 INCHES OF PRE-MIXED ADHESIVE

54" VINYL

Fig. 110

Note: If the adhesive is applied directly to the wall for the first strip, be sure it extends past the seaming area at least a couple of inches. This will save having to apply the adhesive directly beside the edge of the strip previously installed. The couple of inches of adhesive is required to secure the slipsheet until the second strip is installed! **(Fig.111)**

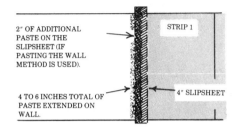
2" OF ADDITIONAL PASTE ON THE SLIPSHEET (IF PASTING THE WALL METHOD IS USED).

4 TO 6 INCHES TOTAL OF PASTE EXTENDED ON WALL.

STRIP 1

4" SLIPSHEET

Fig. 111

Step 4: Apply a strip of the 4" wide pre-cut slipsheet so it overlaps the first strip about 2" while the remaining 2" area sticks into the adhesive past the edge of the wall-paper.

Step 5: If the paste the wall method is being used to apply the adhesive, for the second strip apply additional paste on the front of the slipsheet approximately 2". This will secure the edge of the second strip to the slipsheet until it can be double-cut. **(Fig.112)**

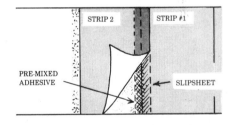
STRIP 2

STRIP #1

PRE-MIXED ADHESIVE

SLIPSHEET

Fig. 112

If the wallpaper substrate is being pasted, then paste the second trip and proceed to hang it by allowing the adjoining edge to overlap the slipsheet and STRIP 1 approximately 1". **Do not** overlap STRIP 2 past the slipsheet too far, because the adhesive on STRIP 2 will get on the front of STRIP 1. The whole idea of the slipsheeting technique is to protect the preceding strip from the adhesive, during the overlap and double-cutting process. If a 1" overlap is not wide enough to double cut for you as an individual installer, then a larger slipsheet may be used.

Step 6: Use a straight edge and **new** sharp razor to double-cut through all layers, which includes (a) the top edge of the second strip, (b) the slipsheet (middle protective layer), and (c) the edge of the first strip. **(Fig.113)**

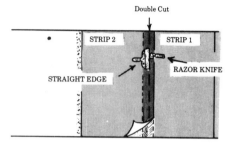

Fig. 113

Caution: If the wall surface being covered is sheetrock (drywall), do not cut through it when double-cutting. It will cause the seam and sheetrock's surface to separate once the adhesive begins to dry and dissipate.

Step 7: Remove all excess ends from the double-cutting step including the entire slipsheet. Lightly secure the seam together using a soft dry cloth or slightly damp sponge. **Warning:** Do not wet or roll suedes and linen seams because it could stain or burnish them. **(Fig.114)**

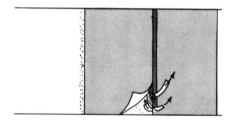

Fig. 114

Masking Tape Method

Everything is the same, except that 2″ or 3″ masking tape is used as the slipsheet to protect the top edge of each previously installed strip, as shown.

Fig.115

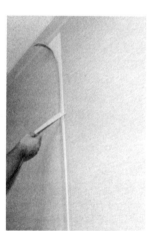

Fig.116

Fig.117

Stairways

Stairway installations cover a wide spectrum of special situation areas or types. These may include spiral (helix), multi-level, or single flight stairways.

■ **Helix or spiral stairways:** These will have a convex and/or concave circular wall structure.

■ **Multi-level stairways:** These will contain flights of steps that may either change directions at a platform landing, or continue up the same incline after a platform landing.

■ **Single flight stairway:** This type of stairway will have only one set of steps ascending or descending from only two levels. This is a standard type of stairway and is found in most residential homes.

Whichever type of stairway is involved, there are special techniques and safety requirements to be considered before attempting to install the wallpaper. Safety, above all, is very, very important. If the proper equipment (ladders, scaffolding, walk planks, etc.) is not available, the job should be nullified or passed on to someone else who has the necessary tools, equipment, and experience to handle these jobs and/or situations.

During the engineering process, it is important to understand and decide where the most difficult area or situation will be encountered during the installation. The engineering should begin from that point and proceed toward the easier areas. Normally, the most difficult place should be the starting point. Careful consideration should also be given to the direction of the installation and to where the scaffolding equipment for succeeding strips may need to be placed on the wall. Do not apply freshly installed wallpaper on an area where a ladder will have to rest for support during the installation of any consecutive strips.

Fig. 118 depicts a typical set up for a standard stairway.

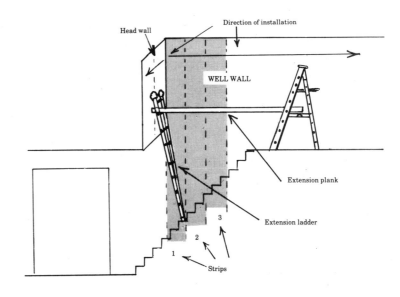

Fig. 118

Start the installation with the longest well strip; then move toward the top of the stairs using the walk plank. Next, paste and install the two head wall strips from the plank. Be sure to leave the bottom of the head wall strips booked until the walk plank can be rearranged. It is strongly recommended to paste and install only a couple of strips at a time because of the difficulty and safety required. If too many strips are pasted and booked ahead, the installer may feel forced to rush--creating a safety hazard!

After the top of the head wall strips are completely installed, arrange a support for the walk plank on the lower level with a step ladder. The other end can rest or be supported by the stair steps. Notice in **Fig. 119** that the two head wall strips are completed at the top section and the lower parts of the strips are still in the booked position.

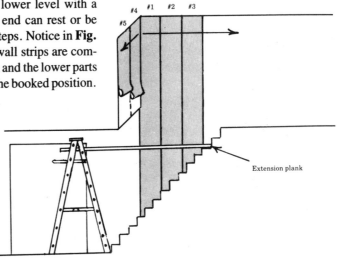

Fig. 119

This will require very careful seam placement engineering which must be employed so the head wall can be filled in later without causing a major mismatch to occur. This can be accomplished by using expanded spacers, which should be at least one full vertical repeat in length. Place spacers in the exact position where they will match the first well wall strip. **(Fig.120)**

Caution: If the stairway has two well walls (one on each side) and the ladder and walk plank method are being used as a scaffolding, then the head wall must not be installed until both well walls have been installed.

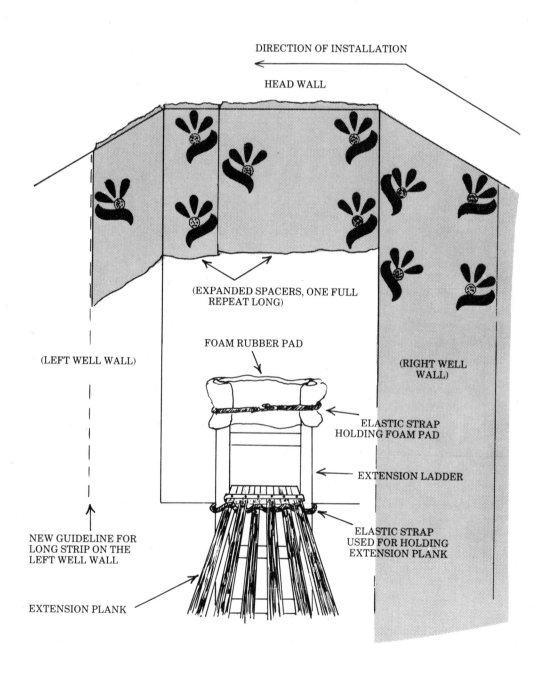

DIRECTION OF INSTALLATION

HEAD WALL

(EXPANDED SPACERS, ONE FULL REPEAT LONG)

(LEFT WELL WALL)

(RIGHT WELL WALL)

FOAM RUBBER PAD

ELASTIC STRAP HOLDING FOAM PAD

EXTENSION LADDER

ELASTIC STRAP USED FOR HOLDING EXTENSION PLANK

NEW GUIDELINE FOR LONG STRIP ON THE LEFT WELL WALL

EXTENSION PLANK

Fig. 120

Once the spacers are placed in position, you will be able to establish the exact position of the guideline for the first long strip of the opposite well wall, as well as predetermine the exact pattern placement and match to be used. After the guideline has been established, the expanded spacers

can be removed. Proceed to install the left well wall strips. Skip the head wall until the ladder and plank are not needed for the higher section of the stairway.

When the first strip of the left well wall is installed, it should overlap the head wall only ¼″ at the corner where they intersect

one another. Discard the remainder of the head wall section. **(Fig.121)**

After the well walls are completed, proceed to hang the head wall as described earlier. Remember to paste and install the top of both the head wall strips before moving the ladder and walk plank to the lower level.

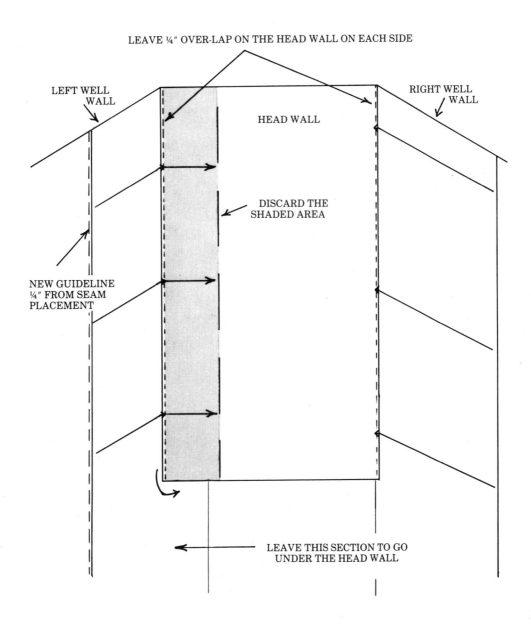

Fig. 121

Electrical Plates

Sometimes an extra touch of class can be added to a room by covering the electrical plates with the matching wallpaper. If careful steps are employed, the designs on the electrical plate should match very closely with the designs on the wall. Follow the step-by-step procedure outlined below.

Step 1: Cut a scrap piece of wallpaper to match the existing wallpaper area around the electrical plate. This should be cut approximately 1 or 2″ larger than the electrical plate and align or match the prescribed area as close as possible. **(Fig.122)**

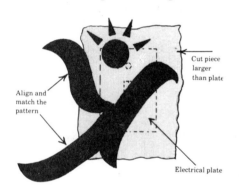

Cut piece larger than plate

Align and match the pattern

Electrical plate

Fig. 122

Step 2: Apply an adhesive to the back side of the wallpaper scrap. Fold and book it and allow it to set a few minutes. This will relax the paper. **Note:** A vinyl-to-vinyl adhesive or contact spray adhesive may be used to secure the wallpaper to the electrical plate, even if it is pre-pasted.

Step 3: Remove the screws from the electrical plate, but leave the plate in position. Make sure the screw holes of the plate and switch align together to be certain.

Step 4: Place your left hand at the lower part of the plate to hold it in place while applying the wallpaper over the top section of the plate with the right hand--making sure the pattern is aligned as closely as possible both horizontally and vertically. While the left hand remains in position, use your right index fingernail to make a sharp crease on the wallpaper across the

top edge of the plate. Press the paper down onto the face of the plate as far as possible, making sure the pattern matches. **(Fig.123)**

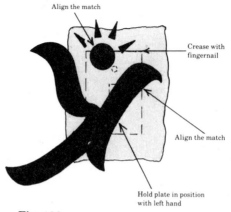

Align the match

Crease with fingernail

Align the match

Hold plate in position with left hand

Fig. 123

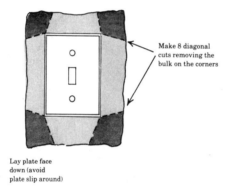

Make 8 diagonal cuts removing the bulk on the corners

Lay plate face down (avoid plate slip around)

Fig. 124

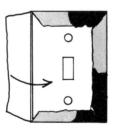

Fig. 125

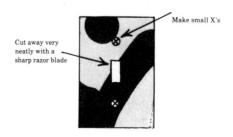

Make small X's

Cut away very neatly with a sharp razor blade

Fig. 126

Step 5: Hold this position firmly with the right hand, and using the left hand, lift the plate away from the wall so the bottom of the plate is removed first. This technique resembles a hinged effect, taking place at the top edge.

Step 6: Lay the plate face down onto a work surface with the underside of the plate facing upward. **(Fig.124)**

Step 7: Make 8 diagonal cuts (two at each corner) as illustrated.

Step 8: Fold the exposed edges around the plate and secure it to the back side. Start with the sides and do the top and bottom last. Allow to dry in this position. **(Fig.125)**

Step 9: Hold the covered plate up toward a bright light so the outline of the hole where the receptacle or switch is located, can be seen easily. Use a sharp razor blade to cut these areas out very neatly. Make a small "x" cut where the screw holes are to be inserted. **(Fig.126)**

Step 10: Apply the covered plate to the proper outlet or switch and secure it with the screws. **Do not** tighten the screws all the way until the paper is completely dry. This could cause it to twist and/or tear. **(Fig.127)**

Fig. 127

Repairing Wallpaper

There are times when it is much more practical to repair existing wallpaper than to replace it, especially when only a minor place is involved. The following steps will show techniques to camouflage a repaired place.

Step 1: Remove as much of the ripped paper from the damaged area as possible, simply by cutting around it with a razor blade. **(Fig.128)**

Note: If the wallpaper involved is a paper product, it may need to be sanded within the cut circle with a small piece of coarse sandpaper and wet with warm soapy water to soften the old adhesive.

Step 2: Remove the damaged area within the circle by either pulling it away or using a scraper to scrape it out. **(Fig.129)**

Step 3: Cut another scrap piece of wallpaper slightly larger than the remaining circle and make it match the remaining section on the wall. Paste it and allow it to relax in a booked position for about 5 minutes to allow for proper expansion. **(Figs.130,131,&132)**

Step 4: Place the repair piece over the damaged area until it matches the existing pattern. **(Fig.133)**

Step 5: Use a new sharp razor blade to double-cut through the overlapped area of the repair. Note: If there is a pattern outline to follow, double-cutting through this area would be less noticeable. **(Fig.134)**

Step 6: Remove the excess ends from the wall section as well as the outside part of the repair piece. **(Fig.135)**

The repair piece will be an exact fit for the area to be repaired on the wall.

Step 7: Insert the repair piece into the patch area and realign all patterns with their matching segments. Use an oval seam roller to secure the edge where the splice was made. **(Fig.136)**

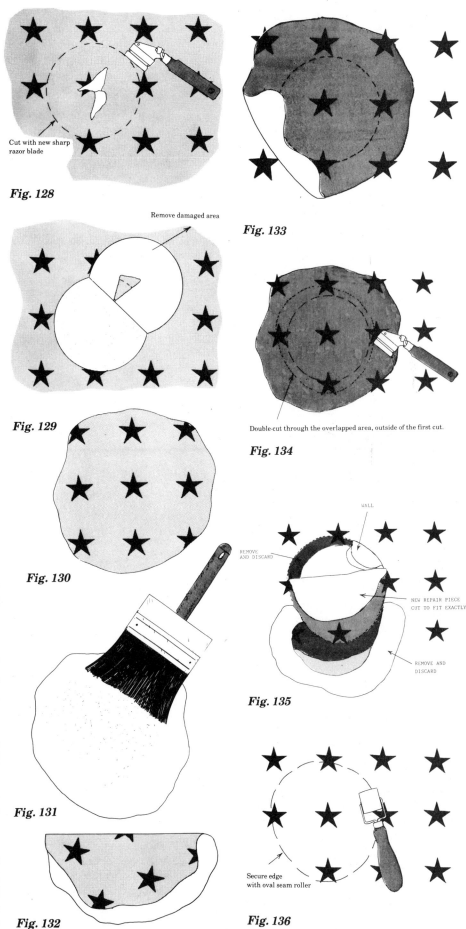

Cut with new sharp razor blade

Fig. 128

Remove damaged area

Fig. 129

Fig. 130

Fig. 131

Fig. 132

Fig. 133

Double-cut through the overlapped area, outside of the first cut.

Fig. 134

WALL

REMOVE AND DISCARD

NEW REPAIR PIECE CUT TO FIT EXACTLY

REMOVE AND DISCARD

Fig. 135

Secure edge with oval seam roller

Fig. 136

Cathedral Walls

A cathedral ceiling wall is one that follows the pitch of the roof or a sloped direction. **(Figs.137,138,&139)**

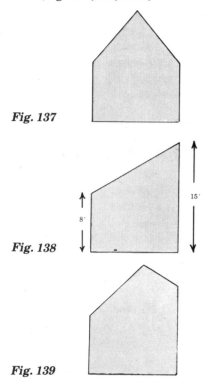

Fig. 137

Fig. 138

Fig. 139

Anytime a cathedral wall is being installed, the aesthetical pattern placement that will appear at a lower level should be considered before the engineering process can be determined. For example, in **Fig.138** the lower ceiling line of the wall is standard 8′ high and represents the back side of the house. If this were the case, the aesthetical pattern placement would be very important to follow the lower wall (8′) at the ceiling line. Once this height has been established, a horizontal guideline should be snapped across the cathedral wall at the 8′ height. **(Fig.140)**

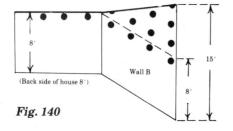

Fig. 140

The installation on a cathedral wall should always begin with the highest strip if at all possible. It is easier to align and install next to a strip that is higher than to join a strip next to one that is lower. (This is also true with stairways.)

Since the aesthetical pattern placement has been predetermined using a horizontal guideline, the highest strip can be installed first by adjusting the pattern to the proper height at the horizontal guideline. Once the corner strip has rounded where the lower 8′ high wall and cathedral wall intersect, the pattern placement will automatically fall into place.

To pre-cut the strips on a cathedral wall, measure the height over the horizontal guideline on each separate strip. The length below the horizontal guideline will always be 8′ high in this case. In every case, the higher measurement will be from the horizontal guideline to the highest point of the surface to be covered for each individual strip.

This method will eliminate the need to measure from the floor to the highest point for each individual strip. During the installation, it is easier to cut away the slant or pitch of the ceiling line rather than trying to install a pasted strip of wallpaper to the cathedral wall. This may be done by the following steps:

Step 1: Measure the expanded width of the wallpaper by pasting a small piece and allowing it to relax 5 to 10 minutes. (27″ is used for the example.)

Step 2: Establish a true vertical line with a spirit level or chalk line at any random place along the cathedral sloped ceiling line. **(Fig.141)**

Step 3: Establish another vertical line the exact width of the wallpaper strip away from the first line. **(Fig.141)**

Step 4: Use a spirit level to draw a horizontal line from the point where the second vertical line or lower vertical line meets the ceiling straight across until it intersects vertical LINE 1. **(Fig.141)**

Step 5: Measure the distance from where LINE 1 and LINE 3 intersect, to the top of the vertical LINE 1, where it touches the ceiling line. For illustration purposes, the distance is 15″. **(Fig.141)**

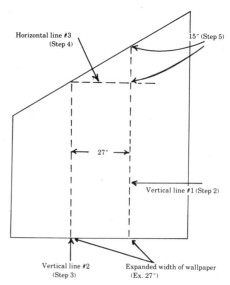

Fig. 141

Step 6: This calculation will tell you that the ceiling rises exactly 15″ vertically for every 27″ horizontally. When a wallpaper strip is cut, a simple measurement 15″ down from the allowance cut on the left-hand edge of the strip would be the amount you could remove before carrying the strip to the wall. **(Fig.142)**

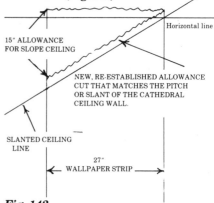

Fig. 142

Remember to cut the excess off the correct edge! It is important to remove the excess allowance from slanted cathedral ceiling strips during the table technique because it will create an unnecessary safety hazard during the installation. The hazardous situation will usually occur in a high area, and this will take longer during the installation. Also extra clean-up time will be required to remove excessive wallpaper adhesive from the ceiling.

Important: When working on high ladders and/or scaffolding, the less moving around and/or less work that is required during the actual installation, the safer the installation will be. **Safety should always take top priority even though the job may take longer!**

Borders

Basic Preliminary Information

Before the actual installation techniques of borders can be discussed; there are several factors that should be considered about the border itself, and its location on the wall.

Using borders can be a very effective way to accent a wall at the ceiling line, chair-rail, baseboard, doors, and window frames. It is important, however, to keep in mind that a border will attract dominant attention as the focal point of a wall and/or room. Therefore, it should be determined whether the focal point is level or plumb. In some situations, a border will possibly cause a room to look less attractive rather than enhance it.

Example: Suppose a border were planned to be installed at the ceiling line around a bedroom. If the ceiling line is visibly unlevel, the border would draw attention to this problem. **(Fig.1)**

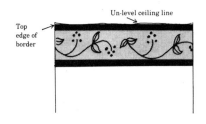

Fig. 1

If this were the case; it would be better to place the border at a lower level, such as at chair-rail height. By using the border at chair-rail height, the focal attention is drawn away from the unlevel ceiling line, and focused at a lower level. **(Fig.2)**

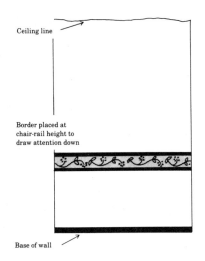

Fig. 2

Another Example: Suppose the border were planned to be installed over a kitchen cabinet soffit. If the bottom of the soffit is not parallel with the ceiling line; the border would emphasize the problem. **(Fig.3)**

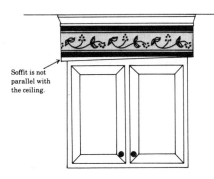

Fig. 3

Also, care should be taken so that a border will not overpower the soffit area when there is a companion wallpaper being installed directly on the soffit. **(Fig.4)**

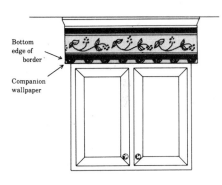

Notice in the illustration that not only did the border "over-power" the companion print, it overlapped the pattern as well.

Fig. 4

Another thing to consider about borders is the directional print. Make sure the correct type of print is installed around door and window frames so the pattern will not be upside down or sideways along these openings. **(Figs. 5,6, & 7) See page 96.**

Estimating Borders

When estimating for borders, use a yardstick to measure (in linear yards) the area where the border will be applied.

Borders are frequently packaged in 5-yard spools, 7-yard spools, or in continuous rolls. If the border is packaged in

Non-directional printed border

Directional printed border

Directional printed border

A non-directional print of this type would be fine around window and door frames. The pattern will appear upside down.

Fig. 5

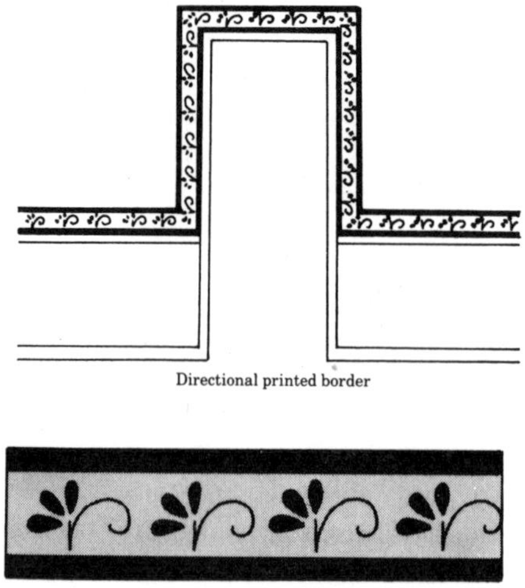

Fig. 6

A directional print of this type would not be aesthetically pleasing. The pattern will run upside down on one side of the door or window.

Fig. 7

spools; ½ yard should be added for each 5 yards that is measured. This will allow each individual spool to be rematched to the adjoining spool on the wall. If the border is packaged in a continuous roll, order at least 2 yards extra for correcting crooked corners and for any damage that may have occurred to the ends of the roll.

When installing borders around doors and windows, allow one foot extra for each mitered-double-cut that will be made. **(Fig. 8)**

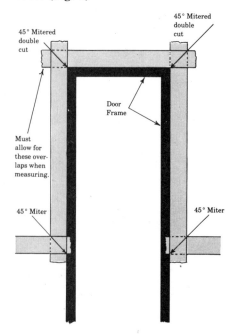

45° Mitered double cut

45° Mitered double cut

Door Frame

Must allow for these overlaps when measuring.

45° Miter

45° Miter

Fig. 8

Special Considerations Before Installing Borders

After deciding which border to use and where to place it on the wall, there are several factors to take into consideration before the actual installation begins:

■ Is the border being applied to a painted surface only?

■ Is the border being applied with a companion wallpaper?

■ Is the border being used as a chair-rail with two companion wallpapers?

■ Use the following steps and techniques for the proper situation.

Installing Borders
On Painted Walls

In every situation the wall surface must be properly prepared in order for the border to bond properly. If the border is being applied to a painted wall (without companion wallpaper), the **correct primer/ sealer** must be applied first. Use the following steps to insure a good installation:

Step 1: Reverse-Roll

Reverse-roll the border for inspection and to minimize curling. If there is a flaw present; now is the time to find it! **(Fig.9)**

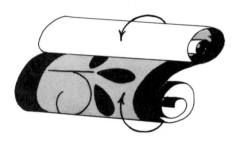

Fig. 9

Step 2: Measure the Expanded Width

Cut and paste (or wet, if it is pre-pasted) a 3″ length of the border. Allow it to relax in a booked position for approximately five minutes and then re-measure it. This measurement represents the actual width that the border will be after it has dried on the wall. **(Fig.10)**

Expanded border

Fig. 10

Step 3: Establish a Primer/Sealer Area

Make small pencil marks at 2 to 3-foot intervals at a distance below the ceiling line (or above the chair-rail or baseboard) of ½″ less than the expanded border's width. For example, if the expanded border's width is 6″, the pencil marks should be placed at 5½″ below the ceiling line. **(Fig.11)**

Fig. 11

Use a pencil and yardstick (or other straight-edge) to connect these marks to form a guideline for the primer/sealer. The reason for connecting these marks at 2 to 3-foot intervals is to establish a guideline as near parallel to the ceiling line as possible. **This will prevent the primer/ sealer from being applied below the border in the event the ceiling line is unlevel. (Fig.12)**

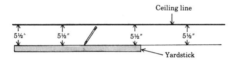

Fig. 12

Step 4: Apply Primer/Sealer

Prime the wall with an acrylic wallpaper primer/sealer within the guideline **only**. This ½″ allowance insures that the primer/ sealer does not extend past the border after it is installed. The ½″ un-primed wall will not cause the border to come loose. **(Fig.13)** Allow the proper drying time for the primer/sealer, and then proceed.

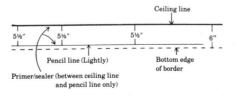

Fig. 13

Step 5: Paste and Book

Paste the border or submerge into water for only 10 seconds if it is pre-pasted. Fold the border in 2 - 3 foot intervals that resemble an accordion. This prevents the adhesive from getting on the front of the border and allows the strip to relax. **(Fig.14)**

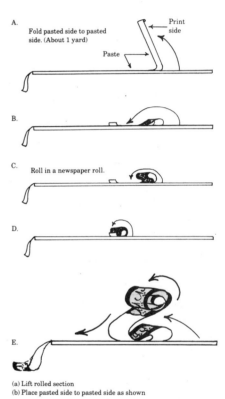

(a) Lift rolled section
(b) Place pasted side to pasted side as shown

After pasting the remaining end of the border, follow Steps A and B, only in the opposite direction. The border (if 5 or 7 yards long) should have at least 3 accordion type folds, each rolled separately, as shown:

Fig. 14

Step 6: Installing the First Piece

After about five minutes, the border will be ready to install. Begin in an inconspicuous place (the kill point). This is because the last border segment will most likely meet the first piece and result in a mismatch. **(Fig.15)**

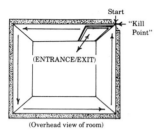

The border was started in the short corner over the door and ended in the same corner. In this case this corner was the most inconspicuous place. (NOTE: If you are a left handed person, work in the other direction.)
Fig. 15

When installing borders between doors or windows, be sure to balance the designs between these areas whenever possible, so the pattern designs will appear aesthetically pleasing. **(Fig. 16)**

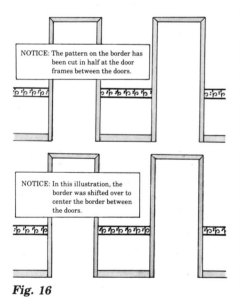

Fig. 16

When joining two border spools on the wall, the design on the ends of each spool must overlap until they match perfectly. **(Fig.17)**

Patterns must match exactly

Fig.17

Padded Double-Cut Technique

The ideal way to form a perfect seam when two layers of border have been overlapped is to use the padded double-cut technique **(Fig.18)**. This technique requires a small, thin scrap piece of wallpaper (or wax paper) to be applied on the wall surface underneath the overlap. The "pad" protects the wall while cutting through the overlapped layers of border. This will prevent cutting through the primer/sealer and the wall, which in turn will prevent a seam separation problem.

Double-cut through both layers, but do not cut through the pad. **(Fig.19)**

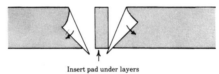

Insert pad under layers

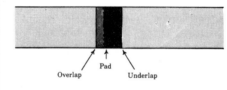

Overlap   Pad   Underlap

Fig. 18

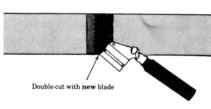

Double-cut with **new** blade

Fig. 19

Remove the excess ends and the pad. **(Fig.20)** Rejoin the remaining ends to form a perfect match, and use an oval seam roller to secure the seam. **(Fig.21,22)** Wipe off the excess paste with a clean sponge.

A.
Lift off   Lift away for removing excess

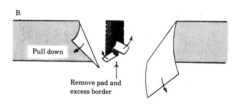

B.
Pull down   Remove pad and excess border

Fig. 20

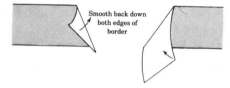

Smooth back down both edges of border

Fig. 21

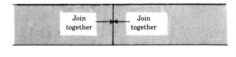

Join together   Join together

Roll seam down with oval seam roller

Fig. 22

With Companion Wallpaper

Before installing a border with a companion wallpaper, the aesthetical pattern placement should always be determined. This is very important in order to prevent the bottom edge of the border from overlapping into a dominant row of designs. (Figs.23,24)

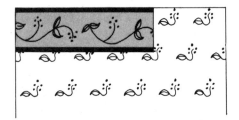

In this illustration, the companion wallpaper was installed first, placing the pattern at the ceiling line. The border was then hung directly over the wallpaper. No consideration was given to the aesthetical pattern placement. This is incorrectly installed, and the design on the wallpaper has been obstructed.

Fig. 23

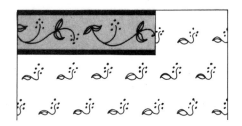

Before the companion wallpaper was hung, the wallpaper and the border were examined for aesthetical pattern placement. The end product was one that left the design of the wallpaper unobstructed and very pleasing. This is the correct method.

Fig. 24

The aesthetical pattern placement of the companion paper should start approximately 1 to 2 inches below the border. For example, when using a 6-inch border, snap a chalk line approximately 7 inches from the ceiling. This will serve as a guideline for the pattern placement. Important: Be certain that the chalk line is a very pale yellow to prevent show-through. (Fig.25)

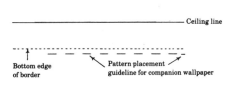

Fig. 25

As Chair-rail

The height of the border should be considered when it is to be used as a chair-rail accent. Commonly, the wall will be divided into exact thirds, therefore, the center of the border should be placed one-third (⅓) up from the floor on the wall surface. For example; a border should be centered 32″ up from the floor on a standard 8′ (96″) wall; on a 9′ wall, the border would be centered 3′ from the floor. (Figs.26,27)

The companion wallpaper should always be installed first. Use a vinyl-to-vinyl adhesive to install the border on top of the companion paper.

Caution: Before applying the border over the companion, check for transparency. If the companion is visible through the border, a white pigmented wallpaper primer/sealer must be used. (Follow Steps 1 through 5 from the previous section.)

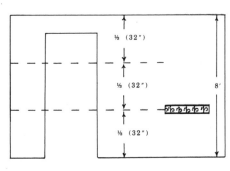

Chair-rail border is centered at 32″ from the BASE of the floor.

Fig. 26

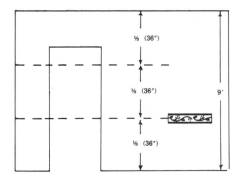

Chair-rail border is centered at 36″ from the BASE of the floor.

Fig. 27

Be sure to check the aesthetical pattern placement (if any) that will be used over and under the chair-rail border. (Fig.28)

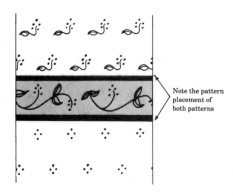

Fig.28

There are basically two methods to install borders as a chair-rail.

Method 1:
Snap a horizontal chalk line at the predetermined height (top of the border from the floor), to indicate the pattern placement of the wallpaper to be used over the chair-rail. (Fig.29)

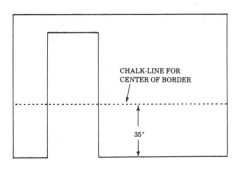

Fig. 29

BORDERS

Snap another horizontal chalk line to indicate the center of the border. **(Fig.30)**

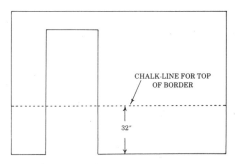

Fig. 30

Snap another horizontal chalk line to indicate the bottom of the border and placement for the dado (section under the chair-rail). **(Fig.31)**

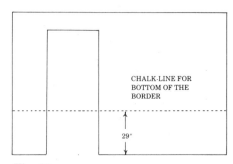

Fig. 31

First, install about three strips over the chair-rail border. **(Fig.32)**

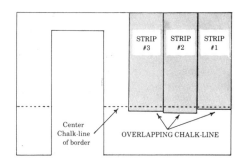

Notice: The upper strips overlap the center chalk-line.

Fig. 32

Then, install three dado strips, allowing them to overlap the upper strips at the center of the border's chalk line. **(Fig.33)**

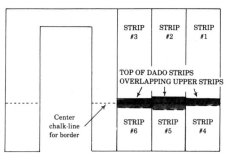

Fig. 33

Double-cut through the top strips and the dado strips where the center of the border will be located. **(Fig.34)**

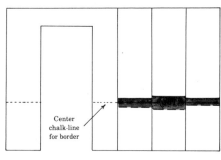

DOUBLE-CUT through both layers being careful not to cut the existing wall. Use new sharp razor blades and change as often as needed. Cut as close to the chalk-line as possible. If unsteady cutting freehand, use a broad knife or your 3″ putty knife as a guide. A straight edge may be used also, but may be a little bulky without help.

Fig. 34

Remove the excess ends. **(Fig.35)**

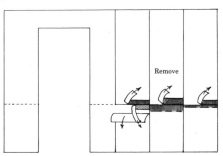

Remove the excess from the upper strips by lowering the tops of the dado strips just enough to free the excess. Rejoin the dado strips with the upper strips after this process is completed.

Fig. 35

Secure the seam with an oval seam roller. This provides a smooth surface to which the border may be applied. **(Fig.36)**

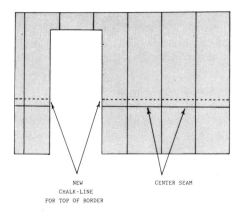

Roll the center seam with an oval seam roller to eliminate any overlaps.

Fig. 36

Proceed around the room until finished, then snap a new chalk line at the top of the chair-rail border to indicate border placement. **(Fig.37)**

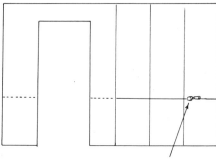

Fig. 37

The chalk line should be overlapped by the top edge of the border in order to hide it. **(Fig.38)** The chalk line is a guide only.

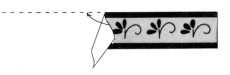

Cover the chalk-line with the border then wipe well with a sponge or damp cloth.

Fig. 38

Note: Remember to check for transparency before applying the border and apply the necessary primer/sealer to prevent show-through from the companion wallpapers. Use a vinyl-to-vinyl adhesive when applying borders directly over the existing wallpaper.

Method 2:

In this method, use the same steps explained in Method 1. The only exception is, hang the entire top portion of the room first, cutting the bottom of the upper strips approximately ¼″ short of the center border chalk line. Then install the dado strips. **(Refer to Figs.34, 35)**

Cut the tops of the dado strips ¼″ below the border's center chalk line. This will leave ½″ space between the top and bottom strips at the center of the border **(Fig.39)**

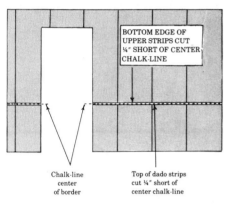

Fig. 39

Spackle in this ½″ space and allow to dry, then lightly sand. **(Fig.40)**

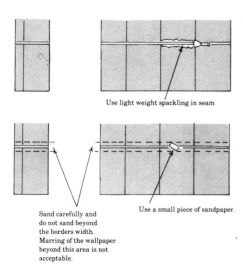

Fig. 40

Apply the border using the same techniques as in Method 1. Remember to consider the aesthetical placement for the top strips and the dado strips with relationship to the border. **(Refer to Fig.28)**

The following illustration is compiled to indicate proper chalk line placement. It assumes a 96″ wall height with a 6″ border being centered 32″ from the floor surface. The chalk line at the top of the border is placed 35″ above the floor while the chalk line at the bottom of the border is placed 29″ from the floor. This centers the border at 32″ from the floor. **NOTICE: Be sure to check the aesthetical pattern placement over and under the border.** Sometimes a border will need to be raised or lowered to develop a good aesthetical pattern placement at the ceiling line as well as at the top of a chair-rail border.

Using 32″ as the center is only a rule of thumb. **THE FINAL APPEARANCE IS ALWAYS THE MOST IMPORTANT! (Fig.41)**

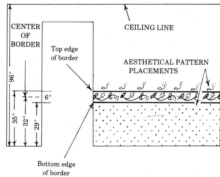

Fig. 41

Around Door and Window Frames

When installing borders around door and window frames, the border should extend past the end of the frame about 1″ farther than the width of the border. This allows the next strip around the frame to be overlapped. **(Fig.42)**

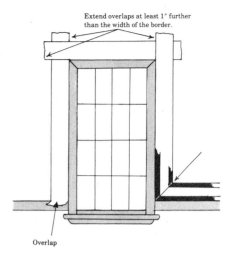

Fig. 42

After the border strips have been overlapped; double-cut at a 45 degree angle, through the two layers. Use the padded double-cut technique if necessary. **(Fig.43)**

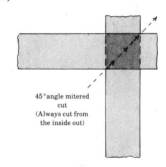

When double-cutting mitered cuts or splices, always use a new sharp razor blade for every cut. Be sure to match the designs on the miters.

Fig. 43

Remove the excess (and the pad if used), to rejoin the strips back together to form the 45 degree mitered corner, and roll the seam with an oval seam roller. **(Figs.44,45)** Wipe with a sponge or clean cloth.

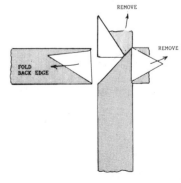

Fig. 44

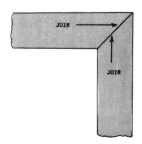

Fig. 45

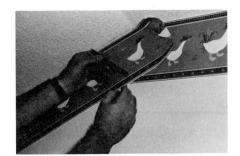

Fig. 49

Along Sloped Ceilings

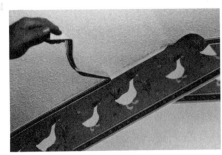

Fig. 46

Fig. 50

When borders are installed along the ceiling lines of attic rooms or sloped ceilings, they are especially attractive when special double-cutting techniques are used at the mitered seams. The following photographs are of an actual installation in which the border had to be mitered with special double-cutting techniques to prevent the cutting and distorting of a pattern. Other techniques have also been used to produce a pleasing effect.

In this case, the border is being applied on a painted surface. The walls within the border area were prepared with a primer/sealer and allowed to dry to insure a proper bond.

In **Fig.46** the border is being installed along a sloped ceiling that has an arch in it. In order to prevent the border from wrinkling at the bottom edge, the upper edge would have to overlap the ceiling at the arched area. The top accent edge of the border has been cut and separated from the border. This will permit the border to be installed straight without cutting the accent edge off at the ceiling line.

In **Figs.47 and 48,** the top accent edge of the border that was removed is now placed along the curved ceiling line and is overlapped onto the remaining border. This edge has been secured with a vinyl-to-vinyl adhesive. By using this technique, the arch of the ceiling line was absorbed within the border's background; otherwise, the accent edge (which is a focal point) would have to be trimmed off!

Fig. 47

Fig. 51

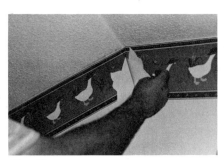

Fig. 52

In **Fig.49,** the actual place where the mitered double-cut angle should be made is shown. This is exactly where the top and bottom of the accent edge intersects.

Fig. 50 shows the actual mitered double-cuts for both the top and bottom accent edges ONLY. Notice that the entire border was NOT double-cut at this point. If it had been, the duck would have been cut in half. This would look very unattractive.

In **Fig. 51,** the exact outline of the duck is double-cut.

Fig. 52 shows the outline of the double-cut design after the excess has been removed. The outline forms the mitered angle. Notice the top and bottom accent edges are perfectly mitered even though the duck has been cut around.

Fig. 53 shows placing the two borders together at the double-cut. The finished product has eliminated cutting a major design in half, in this case the duck. The border takes the effect of a continuous strip without any dominant mismatch.

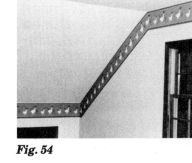

Fig. 54 shows the over-all effect of several mitered corners on sloped ceiling lines. This type of special mitering will take a little longer; however, the final results are well worth the trouble.

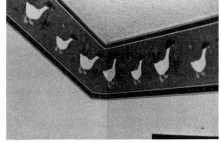

Fig. 53

Fig. 54

Figs. 55 and 56 show the special mitered effects of the lower section of a sloped wall.

Note: Try not to cut dominant patterns in half at the mitered cuts. This is unavoidable at times, but can be prevented by carefully planning ahead.

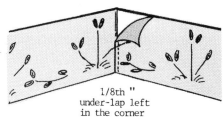

Fig. 55

Fig. 56

Around Corners

The technique of rounding (turning) an inside corner will need to be employed on almost every border installation. There are specific methods that should be used to prevent the border from pulling away from the corner once the adhesive has dried.

If the border is installed around an inside corner in a continuous strip, it will more than likely pull away from the inside corner leaving a void (hollow space).

The border installation should always begin in the corner where the kill point (final ending up place) will occur, however, allow ⅛ inch overlap on the wall where the final border strip will meet. This ⅛ inch overlap will hide the corner once

the final border strip has been installed and meets flush into the corner.

Once the first wall has been installed-- the border should be pressed (tucked) firmly into the following corner. Next, cut the border directly in the corner using a razor blade. Continue to install the remaining balance of the border exactly as stated in the preceding paragraph.

The remaining section of the border should be backed up just enough to hide the cut in the corner (approximately ⅛ inch). Lift the end of the border from the first wall and tuck the ⅛ inch overlap from the remaining segment of the border underneath the first wall border.

The end of border on the first wall should meet perfectly into the corner while the beginning of the remaining segment of the border on the second wall is placed underneath the first strip in the corner.

This technique should not distract from the appearance of the match in the corner since only ⅛ inch of the border has been backed up and covered. The cut in the corner will provide an expansion joint where the divided border intersects and will prevent the border from buckling during the movement of the structure which is referred to as thermo-expansion and contraction.

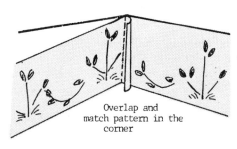

Overlap and match pattern in the corner

1/8th " under-lap left in the corner

WIR

Problem Solving and Trouble Shooting

Introduction

All too often, individuals have gone through a lot of work and effort installing wallpaper, only to end up with a failure. They must swallow their pride and be truthful in order to find out what went wrong, to prevent making the same mistakes twice. Many times, it will mean redoing the job, and since nobody likes to do a job twice, people sometime will not admit their mistakes.

An individual must be completely honest about a problem with wallpapering. In most cases a problem can be resolved if all the appropriate information is available to analyze the situation.

The most common problem that exists often deals with the wallpaper not adhering to the wall surface. In almost every case the final analysis will boil down to the lack of, or improper wall preparation procedures or the wrong adhesive and/or viscosity (referring to how thick the adhesive is mixed and applied) was used during the application of the wallpaper.

It is not uncommon for individuals to complain about these problems, simply because they probably were not educated or given the proper instructions to prevent such a dilemma. It is practically impossible for the manufacturers of wallpaper to cover every situation when they print the wall preparation instructions for wallpaper.

If the wallpaper has been on the wall surface long enough to dry, it is generally impossible to do anything to salvage the job except using a seam adhesive to resecure any loose edges, or maybe using artist water coloring in seams that may have gapped.

There are many times that wallpaper is printed incorrectly or it was not manufactured suitably; however, most every manufacturer of wallpaper will guarantee their products. It has been proven time and time again that if an installer will assume the responsibility of making the final inspection of the wallpaper prior to the installation, perform all aspects of necessary wall preparation, and use the appropriate adhesive (at the proper viscosity), almost every problem within the field of wallpapering would be eliminated.

Questions and Comments

Listed below are some of the major questions that must be answered in order to attempt to find a solution to a problem. The comments which follow the questions will describe why the question was asked and offer a solution to help work around the problem and/or salvage the job.

1. How long has the wallpaper been on the wall?

If the wallpaper has been installed for at least 24 hours, there is probably nothing that can be done to correct a problem, but there are a few ways to repair problems. For example, if it is simply coming loose, it may be possible to use a seam adhesive to secure loose places. Or, if seams are gapped open, you may choose to camouflage the gaps with seam colorants. See chapter on Wall Preparation.

2. What type of wallpaper is it?

The wallpaper must be identified in order to determine whether the proper adhesive was applied, or if the paper relaxed (set after the adhesive was applied) and if the proper amount of time. Check the manufacturer's instructions for the proper adhesive and the correct relaxing time. There are many times that professional installers must modify adhesive requirements based on the porosity of the wall surface and the wallpaper substrate. When this becomes necessary, the modification (adjustment) should be based on previous experiences or the results of using a test board. See chapter on Adhesives.

3. Was a primer/sealer or sizing used during the preparation?

This question will establish whether a primer/sealer was used. If so, exactly what kind was used and what was the approximate drying time? Primer/sealers will commonly dry within 2 to 4 hours; however, if the relative humidity was high on the day of the application, it should have been allowed to dry for 6 to 10 hours. Two of the main causes of wallpaper falling off is the lack of or use of the wrong wallpaper primer/sealer. See chapter on Wall Preparation.

4. How was the primer/sealer mixed?

Sometimes the primer/sealer is not mixed (stirred) properly. If this happens, the ingredients will not perform properly, therefore the application will be in vain. See chapter on Wall Preparation.

5. What type of wall surface is being covered? Examples: new drywall; poor latex paint; glossy enamel paint; existing wallpaper; paneling; cement block......

In order to determine the correct wall preparation procedures, the wall surface must be identified. See chapter on Wall Preparation.

6. What was the approximate temperature during the preparation procedures?

Here again, the primer/sealer application must have the proper drying time in order correctly dry. If the primer/sealer was applied below 40 degrees Fahrenheit, it may not have cured out properly, therefore the application was in vain.

7. What was the approximate temperature during the application of the wallpaper?

Wallpaper should never be installed below 55 degrees Fahrenheit. The adhesive may freeze or crystallize, which then becomes a hardened form and will not adhere properly to the wall surface. If the temperature was over 90 degrees Fahrenheit, the adhesive volatile factor was high; meaning it would evaporate very fast. This would cause the wallpaper to dry out too fast during the installation, therefore, an extra adhesive (or re-pasting) may have been required.

8. What was the condition of the wall surface?

The condition of the wall surface must be known in order to properly prepare it for the wall surface. Are they smooth, rough, sandy, porous, or non-breathable? See chapter on Wall Preparation to determine the proper preparation procedures.

9. If the paper is falling off, is there a mildew problem associated with the problem?

Mildew is an enemy to wallpaper adhesive. Mildew will destroy the bonding agent that holds the wallpaper to the wall surface. If mildew does exist, it must be properly cleaned and treated prior to the application of new wallpaper. See chapter on Wall Preparation.

10. How old was the primer/sealer and/ or adhesive?

If the primer/sealer was spoiled prior to its application it would not be as effective as it should. If the adhesive was spoiled it could cause a mildew problem to arise as well as forfeit its adhesion qualities, there-

fore any spoiled product should be discarded! See chapter on Adhesives.

11. How long has the sizing or adhesive been mixed?

If an individual is using a sizing (especially the starch type) or an adhesive that was powdered and mixed with water, it will spoil after a few days--especially if it has not been protected from excessive heat such as in a storage room or work vehicle. If the product has spoiled, it will prevent a secure bond of the wallpaper to the wall surface. See chapter on Adhesives.

12. Is the problem area exposed to high humidity, such as in a shower stall or basement?

Excessive moisture has always been an enemy to the adhesion of wallpaper to the wall surface. Anytime an area is exposed to an abnormal amount of moisture, such as in a shower stall or basement, the areas should have good ventilation such as air vents or exhaust fans. This will help remove the excess amount of moisture, therefore help eliminate the problem. Note: Anytime the wallpaper comes into direct contact with moisture areas such as around bathroom vanities, tub enclosures, or over kitchen counter tops around the sink, it should be protected by using a silicone-based caulking around the affected areas. See chapter on Wall Preparation.

13. The seams in my wallpaper separated a hairline amount within 24 hours after it was installed! What caused the problem?

The reason for the seam separation is often stated as the shrinking of the substrate (backing of the wallpaper) during the drying-out period. There is really no complete cure to eliminate this problem in every situation. The only way to help salvage the job, is to color in the seams with a special mixture of artist water colors and a pigmented primer/sealer.

14. We are installing now, and the seams are gapping open! What do we do?

If the installation is in progress, the viscosity (thickness) of the adhesive

should be spread as thin as possible in order to yield a faster tack time and still provide good adhesion. If the adhesive is too thick, it will retard the drying process, therefore the wallpaper may try to return to its original dry width.

The wallpaper that most often causes a shrinking problem is the pre-pasted type. The reason for the shrinkage has been stated as being the following: Once an adhesive has been applied at the factory, it is immediately dried in a heat chamber. During this drying-out process, the wallpaper is contracted and then re-rolled for packaging. The final process involves the shrink-wrapping process which holds the wallpaper in the contracted state until it is installed.

Once the wallpaper is re-wetted, it will expand between one and two percent in width. It is not exceptional for the wallpaper to recuperate its memory of contraction a fraction of an inch. This problem is especially dominant when installing dark-colored wallpapers, since even a hairline crack would be evident.

Manufacturers from all over the world have a battle with this problem, however they do perform certain tests for shrinkage. The substrates must meet decided standards in order to be used. Occasionally they barely match these standards, but are still used. Sometimes the wall preparation is the main culprit of the separating seams. A high quality acrylic or oil-based wallpaper primer/sealer should be applied to all wall conditions. See chapter on Seams and Seaming Techniques.

There are many problems that can arise during the process of wallpapering; however, most of the time every problem can be eliminated by committing to these four goals:

1. Insist that every necessary step of correct wall preparation is done properly! Don't ever compromise, whether you are the customer or the installer!

Home owners and general contractors should use extra caution when preparing their own wall surfaces for professional installers. If something goes wrong with the installation, it will probably result from poor or incorrect wall preparation procedures. If you are hiring a professional, make them responsible by allowing them to perform all aspects of the installation including the wall preparation. Then if something goes wrong, it will become the responsibility of the installer.

2. Re-check the quality of the manufacturing process!

No individual likes to re-check someone else's work; however, since the wallpaper installer is the final person to examine the wallpaper before it's installed, there is no choice but to assume the responsibility. This one special effort would eliminate almost every problem that results due to installing flawed materials.

3. Make sure the correct adhesive has been selected for the wallpaper being installed and that the viscosity (thickness of the adhesive) is proper for that particular application.

Many times the appropriate adhesive was used, but it was applied too heavy or too thin, and therefore caused an adverse reaction to occur with the wallpaper, such as shrinking or drying out at the seams. There are times when the adhesive may even penetrate through the substrate (backing) and stain the decorative surface if it is not mixed and applied correctly.

4. Perform every technique possible to make the wallpaper look appealing and attractive with the structure that surrounds it.

This may include tilting the wallpaper very slightly in order to make it appear level with an unlevel structure. Avoid installing dominant vertical patterns whenever the structure is noticeably off plumb. Avoid installing dominant horizontal pattern motifs, if the structure is obviously unlevel.

There are at least five major reasons why the professional installer must take responsibility for the final quality control inspection:

1. To protect personal liability
2. To deliver a professional job
3. To build customer's confidence
4. To eliminate wasted time (money) and energy during an installation
5. To establish professional status

If a problem with the manufacturing process is detected either before the installation or during the first double roll of the installation, the job should not be continued if it cannot be worked around satisfactorily. It should be returned to the supplier for credit.

Note: Any defective wallpaper that is returned to the supplier (retailer, distributor, manufacturer) should have the correct pattern numbers, dye-lot numbers, and an explanation of the problem. This will enable the manufacturer to analyze the problem and hopefully correct it and issue a credit where due.

Since most problems arise from poor wall preparation or the lack of wall preparation, it is advisable to review the chapter on Wall Preparation to solve many problems relating to poor adhesion of the wallpaper.

Problem Identification

Every individual that either sells or installs wallpaper should become very familiar with the following terms and understand the basic symptoms or problems associated with each of them.

This section is not intended to put the blame on, or remove the criticism from where the problem occurred. It is simply a means for individuals to recognize problems ahead of time and possibly work around them whenever feasible, in order to salvage a day's work and finish a job. This section will also provide retailers and wallpaper representatives with the knowledge that can be used to identify and solve many of the wallpaper and installation problems that exist or confront them on a daily basis.

Abrasive Detergents

Any type of harsh or abrasive detergent could cause ink flaking or mar the decorative surface of the wallpaper. Avoid abrasive detergents.

Warning: Never clean existing wall with a detergent that contains phosphorous. This will prevent the primer/sealers as well as adhesives from bonding properly to the wall surface. The primer/sealer will dry to a spongy or rubbery feel.

Adhesive Application

This refers to the process of applying adhesives. Adhesives may be applied to the substrate (backing) of the wallpaper or in some cases it may be applied directly to the wall surface if the wallcovering does not expand or contract. It is very important that the correct adhesive is selected for each individual wallpaper and wall surface. The viscosity, referring to the thickness that the adhesive is mixed and applied, is just as important as the adhesive selection itself. The porosity of the wallpaper's substrate and the porosity of the wall surface will be the determining factors used when mixing and applying the adhesive.

Do not apply an over abundance of adhesive during the installation of wallpapers because it will usually retard the drying process. This can result in shrinkage of the wallpaper or may cause an unnecessary mildew problem to arise because of the time lapse required for the adhesive to dry.

Adhesives may be applied using a brush, pasting machine, or roller. If it becomes necessary for the adhesive to penetrate into the substrate of the wallcovering to provide additional tack (initial bonding strength) during the installation--it is advisable to apply the adhesive with a brush in order to work (manually spread) the adhesive onto the substrate as opposed to applying the adhesive using a roller application.

Pasting machines have become very popular with professional installers especially when installing commercial wallcoverings. Pasting machines can be very efficient if the application of the adhesive is adjusted properly. However, since the adhesive viscosity is very important for the application of most wallcoverings it is advisable to know the proper adjustments that are required for different wallcoverings. Problems will usually arise when the adhesive is applied too heavy, therefore a pasting machine may not work as efficient as applying the adhesive by hand especially when lightweight or residential wallcoverings are being installed.

Applying adhesives with a brush requires additional labor for the installer, however, this method (if performed correctly) will provide the most accurate application. This is because the installer has complete control over the adhesive viscosity meaning that it (the adhesive) can be spread heavier or thinner depending on the porosity of the wall surface and the wallcovering being installed.

A roller application (whether manually or by machine) can only apply adhesive to the wallcovering. It cannot spread the adhesive as evenly as a brush application.

Adhesive Beading

Adhesive beading resembles water beading on a waxed car and is an indication that the PVC (polyvinyl chloride) has penetrated from the decorative surface and is present on the substrate (backing). This is a manufacturing defect and cannot be installed because this condition will prevent the wallpaper from properly bonding to the wall surface. See Adhesive Penetration

Adhesive Penetration

Adhesive penetration refers to the amount of adhesive that soaks into and relaxes the wallpaper and its backing (substrate) after it has been pasted. This is very important because the penetration factor has an effect on the initial tack (bonding strength) and/or final bonding strength. There have been many cases documented when the proper adhesive was used for installing a specific wallpaper, but since it was applied with a roller or pasting machine, there was insufficient penetration. Rollers and pasting machines can only apply an adhesive, whereas, using a pasting brush with a figure 8 motion will work the adhesive into the substrate of the wallpaper to add greater initial tack as well as enhance the adhesion.

It important to prevent the penetration of an adhesive through the substrate of delicate wallcoverings such as stringcloths, grasscloths, or fabrics. If the adhesive penetrates the backing and the decorative surface of these types of wallpapers, it may cause serious staining. See Adhesive Application, Adhesive Beading, and Adhesive Viscosity for problems resulting from inadequate adhesive penetration.

Adhesive Staining

There are times when an adhesive will discolor both underneath the wallpaper and at the seaming areas. When the problem exists underneath the wallpaper the stains will appear as yellow or brown splotches (both large and small). This is frequently caused by using a clay-based (brownish colored) adhesive to install semi-transparent wallcoverings. If the adhesive is a light brown or tan color it may appear as shadows or stains behind the wallcovering.

When a pre-mixed adhesive (whether clear or clay-based) is being used to apply wallcoverings, it is very important that the seaming areas are secured to the wall surface. If the edges are not secure and air is allowed to get underneath them, the adhesive will sometimes turn a dark brown color which will cause an unsatisfactory seam appearance. This problem is especially apparent when pre-mixed adhesives are being used on lightweight wallpapers. See Adhesive Application; Adhesive Viscosity.

Adhesive Viscosity (Thickness)

Different wallpapers will require different adhesive viscosities (thicknesses) in order to perform satisfactorily. The actual viscosity of the adhesive will vary with different types of substrates. It is not advantageous to apply the adhesive too heavily. This will delay the setting up period, and could cause the seam to shrink. This also makes it difficult to distinguish between the adhesive and air pockets. If the adhesive is extra thick, it may call for extra needed pressure to be applied with a smoothing brush (sweep). If the adhesive is forced out from beneath the wallpaper, it can cause a severe problem with keeping the decorative surface of the wallpaper clean.

If the adhesive is too thin, especially when installing over porous walls, it may dry too fast, which would be insufficient to bond the edges. A very thin adhesive will generate a fast setting-up period, and will shorten the amount of available working time. Some wallpapers will require a thin mixture or low-moisture adhesive to prevent shrinkage and/or staining from the adhesive penetrating through the backing (substrate) and onto the decorative surface. This is especially true with stringcloths, grasscloths, linens, fabric, textiles, etc. These types of wallpapers will require speed as well as the experience of a paperhanger; therefore, a beginner should be very cautious whenever these types of wallpapers are installed.

Aeration of Adhesives

Aeration of adhesives is a condition that exists when the adhesive is filled with tiny air bubbles, generally caused by excessive or vigorous whipping during the mixing process. This must be avoided because it may cause tiny blisters to form beneath the wallpaper, especially when installing non-breathable types. All adhesives must be thoroughly mixed to a creamy smooth consistency to prohibit the formation of lumps or hard places under the wallpaper once the dissipation or drying-out period is complete. A large manual restaurant type whisk is best suited for mixing the adhesive. An electric mixer should never be used unless it is made specifically for mixing adhesives.

The same reasoning also applies when the adhesive is mixed by hand. A slow continuous mixing technique is preferred over a fast whipping method. Whenever dry adhesives particularly the starch-based type, are mixed with water, it is imperative that the continuous stirring is employed. Never pour a dry powdered adhesive into the water without simultaneously stirring it, or the result will be a lumpy mixture. It is sometimes necessary to mix several containers of adhesive to an equal viscosity in order to provide a uniform thickness on the wallpaper substrate. This is especially true when using a pasting machine, otherwise the machine's viscosity setting would have to be adjusted continuously. The boxing technique (pouring from one container to another, beginning with a half-full container) may be used to provide uniform viscosity within several containers.

Caution: Pour the adhesive very slowly when using this method, to avoid aeration of the adhesive (suds mixture).

Alligation

This is a condition that occurs when a primer/sealer or adhesive will not properly bond to a wall surface--usually due to grease, wax, dirt, etc. The area should be cleaned with a solution of equal parts of ammonia and water. Never use a cleansing agent that contains phosphorous because it may cause the primer/sealer or adhesive to alligate or crack apart. The area should be sanded after it is dry. Alligation may also occur because the fusing or curing process of the primer/sealer was either halted or interrupted because of cold temperature conditions (below 45 degrees Fahrenheit). Improperly mixing or stirring the primer/sealer will also cause alligation. This is a field term that came into use because the cracking or cured-out product resembles alligator skin.

Available Lighting Conditions

Available lighting conditions refer to the amount of light exposed to a wall surface once the curtains, doors, room dividers, light fixtures, etc. are in place. The quality of the installation will be especially noticeable when the wall has a direct light reflection from either artificial or solar means. Any direct light reflection will also emphasize every slight overlapped seam or blister. Therefore, it is important to place a temporary (clamp) light in a position to simulate the actual lighting that will be present once all lighting elements are in position including artificial and solar.

Black Edges

These are caused by dirty trimming devices which are used to remove the selvage from the edges of the wallpaper at the factory. Black edges can often be eliminated by using a wire (ridge) seam to lap a clean edge over the dirty edge. Sometimes a very slight lap and double-cut will correct the problem. When these techniques are not practical, then the wallpaper should not be installed and should be returned to the supplier for credit. **(Fig.1)**

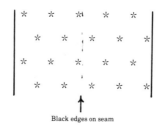

Black edges on seam

Fig.1

Blistering

This is a condition in which small air pockets or bubbles are formed during in-

stallation. They can be caused by several factors. See: Improper Relaxing Period; Crystallization; Porous Wall Surfaces; Soured Adhesives and Primer/Sealers; or Expansion Blisters

Contaminated Substances

Anytime the adhesive or primer/sealer contains hardened forms of foreign matter, it is usually because a dry powder product was not mixed properly or because the product dried in the container. Unless the product has soured, it can usually be salvaged simply by straining it.

Procedure: Cut an 8 to 10-inch section of nylon hose (stocking) that does not have a run or rip in it. Tie a knot in one end to form a funnel. Pour the contaminated product from one container into another. This technique will eliminate all the lumps or foreign matter so that the product may still be used.

Contaminated Decorative Surfaces

Sometimes the adhesive (especially a pre-mixed type) will contain certain solvents or chemicals that will cause wallpaper inks to flake off if it is not properly cleaned from the decorative surface, therefore, the surface is considered contaminated. This is especially true with dull or matt-finished wallpapers. Shiny or glossy vinyl surfaces will clean easier and therefore the problem is not as apparent.

All adhesives should be cleaned from the decorative surface of the wallpaper during the installation. A natural sea sponge works best because of its absorbency; however, it is very important to keep the rinse water as clean as possible. It is also advisable to immediately dry the wallpaper surface of some wallpapers to completely remove the adhesive residue from the decorative surface.

Crystallization

Crystallization takes place when the adhesive becomes a definite or concrete form, like salt or granular sugar. This is caused by hanging wallpaper in temperatures below 50 degrees Fahrenheit or installing wallpaper over an improperly sealed porous wall. The crystallized adhesive is shaped like a tiny snowflake and its hardened form will usually result in a small blister under the wallpaper.

Delamination

Delamination is the separation of a wallpaper substrate (backing) from the decorative surface or intermediate layer of vinyl. **(Fig.2)**

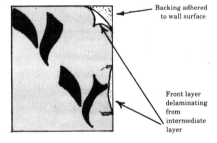

Backing adhered to wall surface

Front layer delaminating from intermediate layer

Fig.2

Delamination is caused by an excessive soaking (relaxing) period, after the adhesive has been applied. Some wallpapers like grasscloths, stringcloths, rushcloths, or jutes should only be allowed a relaxing period of 3 to 5 minutes to prevent delamination.

Dye Lot/ Run Number

This is a number, letter, or combination of each given to a particular batch of wallpaper rolls that are printed at the same time. This represents the inks, vinyl coat-

ing, embossments, etc. that were all created and applied at the same time. Each time a new batch is printed or the printing process is altered the dye-lot or run number will change to indicate it. This will alert the installer of a possible change in the printing process.

An additional number or letter may also be added to the dye-lot number to indicate the sequence in which individual rolls were printed and/or packaged, such as grasscloth or commercial wallcoverings. This will enable the installer to place each roll in its proper sequence on the wall, just as it was processed at the factory.

All wallpaper installers including the do-it-yourselfers should be sure all rolls have the same dye-lot number before starting, to insure uniformity during the installation. If odd runs are present, they may still be used. By knowing this information ahead of time, the installer will be prepared to stop and start in corners or inconspicuous places, therefore, minimizing the possibility of a dominant shading problem. It is very important to record all dye-lot and/or run numbers prior to the installation, in case additional wallpaper is needed to complete a job. Those numbers should be requested in the event a reorder is required.

Important: Do not ever stop installing wallpaper in the middle of a wall if it becomes apparent that there is not enough to complete the job. Stop the installation in a corner.

In the event the same batch of wallpaper is unavailable, it would be better the change dye-lots in a corner to minimize the possibility of shading, therefore, additional wallpaper may be required to complete an entire wall instead of ending up in the middle of it.

Edge Curling

Edge curling occurs when the laminating tensions are not properly adjusted at the factory, or when a paper substrate (backing) expands much faster than the decorative surface after the adhesive application. **(Fig.3.)** A couple of solutions to this problem are to place the wallpaper in a plastic bag for about 15 minutes after it has

been pasted, booked, and rolled up as a newspaper; or to apply a very thin layer of clay-based adhesive around all edges and seaming areas a couple of hours prior to the installation. This will help secure the edges by permitting the adhesive to set up much faster in the problem areas.

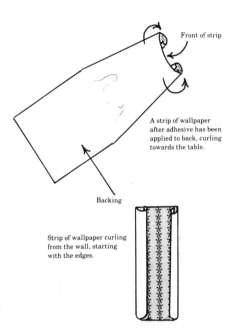

Front of strip

A strip of wallpaper after adhesive has been applied to back, curling towards the table.

Backing

Strip of wallpaper curling from the wall, starting with the edges.

Fig.3

Excessive Adhesive Moisture

Excessive adhesive moisture means the adhesive has been diluted too much with water or an excessive amount of adhesive was applied during the installation of wallpaper. In either case the excessive moisture will many times penetrate the substrate of the wallcovering and stain or ruin the decorative surface.

Whenever a polyester film is used, such as Mylars, too much moisture in the adhesive could cause the ink to deteriorate from the back side of the decorative surface. A liner paper may be required to absorb excess moisture, or a clay-based adhesive can be used because of its low water content. Excessive moisture may also cause the wallpaper to shrink because the drying process is delayed. See Adhesive Viscosity.

Expansion Blisters

Expansion blisters will form when an existing wallpaper is wetted. This may be caused when a wallpaper remover solution is being applied during the removing process, or when a primer/sealer is being applied in preparation for installing over the existing wallpaper. When a primer/sealer is being applied over an existing wallpaper--the moisture will cause every unsecured places to expand and swell. The expanded areas will appear as large and/or small blisters. Once the moisture from the primer/sealer has evaporated, the blisters will usually return flat to the wall surface without being noticeable. It is advisable, however, to cut and remove the blisters from the wall while they are still wet and visible. Once the primer/sealer has dried, the cut out areas can be spackled and repaired.

If the blisters are not removed they will swell and expand again as soon as the new wallpaper is installed. This is because there is moisture in the adhesive. These blisters or expanded areas will sometimes remain wet and swelled for a few days, however, they should dry out within a week. In the event a blister does not fully contract to the wall surface--it can be re-secured using a small hypodermic needle to insert adhesive underneath it. Once the needle is removed the fresh adhesive will bond the loose wallpaper to the wall while at the same time the hole where the needle was inserted will allow any trapped air to escape.

When removing old wallpaper, especially fabric-backed vinyl on drywall, it is important not to pull directly away from the wall surface because it will cause the facing paper of the drywall to come loose. Many times these loose places will not be visible until a primer/sealer (or moisture) is applied. Once the facing paper is wet it will swell and expand just as will unsecured wallpaper. It is important to cut all loose places from the drywall and repair it. The facing paper will not contract and tighten the same as wallpaper.

Vertical expansion blisters are created when a strip of wallpaper is installed too soon after it has been pasted. Most all wallcoverings will expand when wet (especially paper-backed materials), therefore they must be allowed sufficient time to relax after it has been wetted or pasted. The normal time required to relax is 5 to 10 minutes.

Extensibility Factors

This refers to the flexibility of a wallpaper, whether it has a woven, non-woven, or paper substrate. Extensibility is the amount that a wallpaper can be stretched or extended horizontally without distorting the pattern and/or causing shrinkage at the seams after drying out. Fill threads in woven substrates aid in extensibility and are useful on crooked or bowed walls. Stretching the wallpaper beyond its extensibility limit will result in a gapped seam after drying out.

Fabric Fraying

There are times when fabric (particularly the unbacked type) will fray during the installation process. One of the primary reasons for this problem is the lack of pressure from a trim guide along the edges while trimming away the excess allowance edges, or the adhesive is not the proper type and/or viscosity at the seaming areas.

It is advisable to use a small (three inch) slanted putty knife as a trim guide to help correct this problem. The trimming edge of the putty knife should be filed (sanded) to a fairly sharp edge in order to secure the fabric tightly against the decorative trim (woodwork) during the trimming process.

If the seams of the fabric are fraying, the seaming area (approximately 3 to 4 inches wide) should not be adhered to the wall surface until several strips have been installed. The seams should be secured by applying a clay-based adhesive very thinly (using a small brush) directly on the wall surface at the seaming area. Allow the adhesive to set-up for at least three to five minutes to establish tack, and allow most of the moisture to evaporate, which otherwise may penetrate the fabric and cause a permanent stain. Place the edges of the fabric together very gently and secure very carefully with a cloth seam roller or faint pressure with the palms of the hands.

Note: It is better to avoid the use of clay based adhesives unless it is needed to prevent fraying of the edges.

Also be sure to test the fabric for any shadow effect that may result while using the clay based adhesive, because of its light tan color. If this does show up as a contrast, the wall surface may need to be painted a light tan color to camouflage with adhesive.

Important: Whenever in doubt about the installation procedures to use, it is a good idea to establish a test board in order to determine the best method to use. If the fabric or wallcovering cannot be installed satisfactory, the job should be stopped until the manufacturer can be consulted for advice.

Feed Marks

Feed marks are caused from dirty or contaminated feed rollers on the printing presses. Feed marks generally cannot be eradicated so, if they are noticeable, the wallpaper should no be installed. **(Fig.4)**

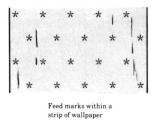

Feed marks within a strip of wallpaper

Fig.4

Flagged Roll

Flagging is a procedure used when an inspector finds a flaw during the printing process. As soon as a flaw is detected, the inspector will flag that roll, meaning rip out a section on the side of the roll, or apply a colored piece of tape to indicate a flaw, or draw a magic marker line across the damaged area. **(Figs.5,6,&7)**

Fig.5

Fig.6

Fig.7

The flagging process signals packaging personnel to eliminate the damaged area before shipping. However, if the manufacturing personnel do not catch the problem, then it must be detected by the installer. Important: It is very seldom that a flagged roll will exist without a flaw therefore, whenever an installer sees a flagged area, he or she should be alert to inspect it very carefully and closely.

Foil/Mylar Creasing

Foil and Mylar wallpapers will crease very easy. To prevent creasing is a real battle for most paperhangers, even professionals. Do-it-yourselfers should use extreme caution because of the nature of these types of wallpapers. Usually a low-moisture, high tack adhesive (such as clay-based) is used to install foils and Mylar wallpaper. The adhesive is frequently applied directly to the wall surface. Foil and Mylar products do not usually expand or contract after being wetted, therefore, they may be installed by using the dry hanging technique.

Gapped/Opened Seams

This refers to a seam that has slightly separated during the installation or after the wallpaper has dried. These are unsatisfactory, unsightly, and should be avoided. Sometimes a spring-loading technique or seam coloring technique can be used to correct or hide the problem. See chapter on Seams and Seaming Techniques. **(Fig.8)**

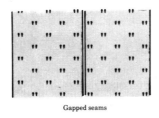

Gapped seams

Fig.8

Humidity

Humidity is the amount of moisture contained in the air, and has an effect on the drying process of both primer/sealers and adhesives. Anytime the relative humidity is high, extra time must be allowed for the primer/sealer to dry. High humidity

can also affect the wallpaper with its relationship to mildew problems. If the climate has a high humidity several months of a year, special precautions should be considered during the wallpaper selection, adhesive selection, and the wall preparation. Mildew (a result of high humidity) is an enemy to wallpaper as well as the adhesive bonding it to the wall.

Improper Relaxing Period

This is a term that describes an insufficient time lapse after a wallpaper strip has been pasted. If the paper has not fully expanded or relaxed, it will continue to expand after it is applied to the wall. This can cause blisters to appear in thin vertical shapes or force the entire strip to expand towards the seams. This will cause the edges to pucker away from the wall surface.

Ink Flaking

Ink flaking is a problem that occurs when the ink is not properly bonding to the decorative surface. There are several factors that can cause the ink to flake off the wallpaper surface. Caution: Creasing the wallpaper during the installation can break the ink away from the wallpaper surface. See Contaminated Decorative Surfaces; Abrasive Detergents; Excessive Adhesive Moisture; Over-Cured Wallpaper.

Ink Wash Off

There are rare cases when the ink on the decorative surface of the wallpaper will wash off during the installation. This condition usually means that the vinyl-coating was not applied properly during the manufacturing process, therefore, is a manufacturer defect. The wallpaper should be returned with an explanation along with the exact pattern number and dye-lot number for the manufacturer to inspect. Some wallpapers such as hand screen prints are very delicate to install and it is very important to prevent an adhesive from coming in contact with the decorative surface. In these cases the manufacturer will not be responsible if the decorative surface has been contaminated with a residue of adhesive. See Contaminated Decorative Surfaces; Ink Flaking; Abrasive Detergents

Liner Paper Problems

The major problem associated with liner papers is its application to the wall surface. Since liners are used to prepare wall surfaces such as paneling, concrete blocks, ceramic tile, or an uneven wall surface, it is important that the wall surface be properly prepared for each situation that prevails. The major problem is poor bonding to the wall surface. This is frequently caused by poor wall preparation or the failure to remove dirt, grease, wax, or other foreign substances from the wall surface. There are times when the decorative wallpaper will not properly bond to the liner paper. This is generally caused by using the wrong adhesive (or viscosity), or there is not an ample amount of adhesive on pre-pasted wallpapers. It is sometimes necessary to apply a wallpaper primer/sealer over the liner to prevent it from absorbing too much moisture from the adhesive of the decorative wallpaper. See Introduction (washing walls with phosphates); Alligation; also, see chapter on Wall Preparation.

Lumps Under Wallpaper

Lumps or hard places will appear under wallpaper when the wall surface is not prepared properly prior to the installation or the adhesive is not mixed or applied properly. Procedures such as sanding the walls to remove all uneven surfaces and scraping and repairing flaking paint are very necessary to insure a satisfactory job.

If the adhesive is not mixed properly, meaning lumps are present in the mixture, it (the adhesive) will dry into a hardened form. If the installation is done in low temperatures, the adhesive will crystallize,

meaning become a hardened form. See Crystallization; Flaking Paint

Marks On Paper

This is a manufacturer's defect caused during the printing process when small marks appear within a strip of wallpaper or on the edges. See Black Edges; Feed Marks; Screen Marks

Memory Factors

This refers to the original shape or position that a wallpaper may return to after it has been applied to the wall surface. Wallpapers with high memory factors may cause shrinkage to occur at the seams during the drying-out period. See Shrinking Seams.

Mildew

Mildew is a fungus that grows or flourishes in dark, moist environments such as bathrooms or closets. Existing mildew problems should be washed with a solution of bleach and water to remove the dirt associated with it. Then it should be sprayed with a germicidal spray.

Often mildew problems can form as a result of poor or non-existing vapor barriers in exterior walls, or by a leaking faucet or water line behind the wall. If a vapor barrier is not properly installed on the exterior walls of a structure, excessive moisture will be allowed to penetrate to the inside of the exterior walls. This could result in a mildew problem especially if a non-breathable wallpaper is installed on the inside walls. The non-breathable paper would stop the moisture where the adhesive's cohesion takes place, therefore, would create putrefaction or decay of the adhesive. This would result in mildew which will eventually penetrate the wallpaper and show up as dark discolored spots, usually in the colors of purple or violet. The mildew would also destroy the cohesion--consequently resulting in the wallpaper falling off the wall.

If an installer or wallpaper supplier is not advised of a poor or non-existing vapor-barrier prior to the installation, and a mildew problem occurs because of the fact, they (the installer and/or supplier) are not responsible for the problem, simply because it is a construction defect that can not be seen once the interior walls are in place!

If this type of problem does occur, the wallpaper must be removed and the mildew cleaned with bleach and water using a soft-scrub brush and sponge. Once the walls are dry, they should be sprayed with a germicidal spray. A breathable type of wallpaper should be recommended because it would allow air and/or existing moisture to pass through it, rather than be trapped. Care should be taken to prevent moisture from seeping under wallpaper edges around tubs, shower stalls, vanities, kitchen counter tops, etc., because mildew may form. A silicone-based caulking will generally prevent the problem. See chapter on Wall Preparation (section on Cleaning Mildew Problems) and chapter on Problem Solving (section on Humidity Problems).

Mismatched Seams or Patterns

This occurs when the print on the wallpaper will not match or line up with the print on the opposite side of the strip once they are adjoined. There are several factors that can cause this. See Undertrimmed Selvage; Overtrimmed Selvage; Pattern Repeat Inconsistency; Stretching; Overworked.

Missing Colors

Sometimes the ink of a pattern may be missing entirely, or it may be spotted on the decorative surface. This is referred to as mottling or blotches of ink. **(Fig.9)** If this condition exists and is very noticeable, the wallpaper should not be installed.

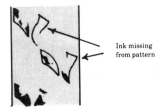

Ink missing
from pattern

Fig.9

Out of Register

This is a manufacturer's defect caused during the actual printing process when the pattern or design outlines and their colors are out of sequence. This will result in ghost-type or shadow-effect images to appear. When this happens a slight mismatch may occur at the seams. Wallpaper prints that are only slightly out of register may be considered to be within normal standards; however, the customer should give the final approval before the installation. If the problem is obvious, the wallpaper installation should not be done. **(Fig.10)**

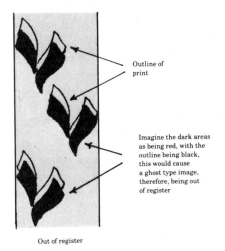

Outline of
print

Imagine the dark areas
as being red, with the
outline being black,
this would cause
a ghost type image,
therefore, being out
of register

Out of register

Fig.10

Over-Cured Wallpaper

If the wallpaper is over-cured during the printing process, or too much heat is used, the paper may become over dried. This will prevent the ink from bonding properly to the base, or ground coating, thereby, causing it to flake off. This is a manufacturing defect and the wallpaper should not be installed.

Over-Trimmed Selvage

This means that too much selvage has been removed at the factory. There is no cure for this problem on the job unless the pattern is duplicated many times across the sheet of wallpaper. If this is the case, one design may be overlapped by a duplicated design and then double-cut. This technique would obviously require more wallpaper. Generally, the wallpaper should not be installed if the problem is noticeable at a glance. Sometimes the over-trim may be so minimal, that it may never affect the overall design. **(Fig.11)**

Over-trimmed

Fig.11

Over-Worked Paper

This is a result of re-applying a strip of wallpaper several times in an attempt to successfully install it. The strip will be stretched beyond its natural extensibility limits, therefore, causing the wallpaper to mismatch as well as shrink. An individual should never force a strip of wallpaper to adjoin another pre-existing strip. The strip should be immediately and gently removed and realigned--beginning at the seaming edge.

Paint Deterioration

This refers to a major portion of problems associated with wallpapering on today's market. With fast construction time schedules, and low subcontract labor and material fees, it is practically impossible to get a high grade of paint and labor on a job--especially on new construction.

The painters get by simply because the wall looks good enough to the average customer. The fact of the matter is, the walls are usually painted with a very poor quality paint, and watered down at that. Consequently, the burden of providing a good foundation for wallpapering will fall directly on the installer. A wise professional or do-it-yourselfer will insist on taking care of all aspects of wall preparation before agreeing to install any wallpaper. Otherwise, any problem that results in paper falling off or coming loose at the seams will always come back to the installer. Paint deterioration commonly occurs when a poor grade of latex paint is applied to the wall surface. When the wallpaper adhesive soaks into the paint, the drying process soon begins. When the dissipation starts contracting the wallpaper tightly to the wall, the paint will not be strong enough to withstand the pressure, therefore, deterioration takes place.

This will always result in an unsatisfactory job. As soon as the seams begin separating and rolling up off the wall, the paint will be noticeable on the back surface of the substrate. To prevent the problem, a high quality acrylic pigmented wallpaper primer/sealer or an oil-based enamel undercoater (thinned with one quart of paint thinner per gallon) is recommended. The primer/sealer or the thinned down oil-based primer/sealer will soak into the bad paint and help re-bond it to the wall surface.

Wall sizing (the product) is used to provide uniform porosity on a porous wall surface; however, this product alone will not hold poor latex paint together. A great number of individuals still have the viewpoint that old methods never die. This is a false premise because paints, wall surfaces, adhesives, primer/sealers, etc., are constantly changing; therefore, the procedures and methods required to produce a satisfactory job must also change.

Paint Flaking

When paint is flaking from the wall surface, it must be scraped off and repaired prior to the installation of new wallpaper. This is done by using a broad knife, scraper, or putty knife, and spackling with a water-based spackling and sanded smooth. If the flaking paint is not repaired, it will produce a problem with the wallpaper's adhering properly to the wall surface. The problem will become visible as a hard, raised blister that feels like granular sand beneath the wallpaper. This is because the flaking paint has crumbled and cracked. Flaking paint will also create hardened ridges to form beneath the wallpaper because once the adhesive from the new wallpaper has contracted tight to the wall surface, it (the adhesive) will pull (force) the loose paint away from the wall surface.

Pattern Number

This is a number or combination of numbers and letters that are designated by the manufacturer or retailer to identify a particular pattern. These should always be consistent with each other to insure that two different patterns are not present. It is easy to get very close color ways (schemes) mixed up, especially when they are purchased from in-stock retail stores.

Pattern Repeat Inconsistency

This may result when the tension on the printing machine is not consistent, or when the wall surface is not perfectly even. This problem will cause the vertical pattern repeats to mismatch from the top to the bottom of the strip. A pattern may match at eye-level, for example, but will not match at a higher or lower level on the wall. Generally, the industry standard for this mismatch is ⅛ inch per eight feet. If the match is off more than ⅛ inch, the wallpaper should be returned to the supplier. **(Fig.12)**

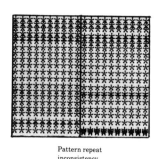

Pattern repeat inconsistency

Fig.12

Pieced/Spliced Rolls

At times a bolt or package of wallpaper will contain two separate sections or rolls, rather than one continuous piece. This is a result of a damaged area being removed before a complete bolt is filled during the packaging process. When this happens the company will include several extra yards of wallpaper to compensate for the splice. This should not affect the estimated amount of wallpaper required to complete the job.

Porous Wall Surfaces

Porous walls are very absorbent to moisture and should be sealed during the wall preparation procedure. If the wallpaper's adhesive does not have a uniform surface on which to bond, it will dry unevenly. This could result in crystallization or tiny hollow blisters forming under the wallpaper, because the moisture from the adhesive will be soaked up before it can properly dissipate. This problem is especially apparent on new drywall, poor latex paints, masonry block, and concrete slab walls.

Pre-Pasted Wallpapers

Manufacturers of pre-pasted wallpapers have applied a water re-moistenable adhesive to the substrate of the wallpaper. These types of papers are usually classified as pre-pasted, scrubbable, and strippable. The suggested procedures to install pre-pasted wallpapers are listed in the chapter on Hanging Techniques. However, there are cases when the water re-moistenable adhesive has too much or not enough insoluablizer to fully activate the adhesive. The following steps may be useful to solve these problems:

1. If the adhesive washes off too easily, add one teaspoon of vinegar to the water in the tray. This will help retard the insoluablizing process.

2. If the adhesive is difficult to activate, add one teaspoon of ammonia to the water in the tray. This will promote or speed up the insoluablizing process.

If the pre-pasted wallpaper does not have enough relaxing time, it will be forced to complete the process on the wall surface after the installation. This will result in long vertical expansion wrinkles and/or small vertical blisters or puckers to form. Important: These expansion wrinkles will not dry out or dissipate. Sometimes it may be necessary to apply an extra diluted adhesive to the back (substrate) of the pre-pasted wallpaper when the wall surface is extremely porous; or when the pre-paste was not evenly applied at the factory. This will enhance the adhesive as well as allow an extra amount of time to install it after the pasting process.

Note: When extra diluted adhesive is applied to pre-pasted wallpapers, it will destroy the dry-strippable feature that is classified with it! See chapter on Adhesives.

Most professional installers prefer to re-activate the water re-moistenable adhesive on pre-pasted wallpapers by applying a diluted adhesive. This is simply because they can control the viscosity (thickness) as needed for the wall conditions that are being covered. **One key factor** must be understood before re-pasting pre-pasted wallpapers.

Key Factor — when an additional adhesive is applied to a pre-pasted wallpaper the additional adhesive must be diluted with a minimum of 50% more water than the standard mixing instructions required for unpasted wallpapers.

The adhesive should resemble the viscosity of thick buttermilk or paint! Is is very important to apply enough water to re-activate the pre-pasted adhesive without clogging the pores in the substrate. If clogging occurs, unsatisfactory reactions will result such as improper relaxing/expansion or adhesive crystallization!

It is recommended to apply the diluted adhesive with a brush or a short nap roller to control the viscosity ratio. A long-nap roller will simply apply an additional amount of adhesive, therefore, causing an adverse reaction to occur such as wallpaper shrinking.

Note: The brush or short-nap roller will also make the adhesive penetrate the substrate of the wallpaper better than just submerging it into water; therefore, it will have better tack during the installation.

Warning: Unless you are a very experienced wallpaper installer, it is not **advisable to use a pre-mixed clay-based adhesive on pre-pasted wallpapers because of the solids in the clay.** Most manufacturers of pre-pasted wallpapers do not recommend re-pasting the water re-moistenable adhesive because of the adverse reaction that may occur from either using the wrong adhesive or improperly mixing the viscosity (thickness) of it.

Some pre-pasted wallpapers contain an ample amount of adhesive, therefore, re-activating it with lukewarm water is sufficient! Do not over soak the wallpaper in water, and be sure to allow the proper relaxing time. It is advisable to allow the wallpaper to remain in the water for only 5 to 10 seconds. It should be pulled out slowly and booked (folded pasted sides together) and allowed to relax for approximately 5 to 10 minutes. **Remember: Re-pasting a pre-pasted wallpaper will nullify the dry-strippability feature.**

Printing on the Bias (Out-of-Square)

One of the most important steps during wallpaper inspection and table techniques is checking the squareness of the wallpaper pattern with the edge of the wallpaper. Make sure the pattern design is printed square on the wallpaper, and not at an angle with the edge. If it is at an angle, then the pattern will run either uphill or downhill after the wallpaper is installed. This flaw is referred to as being printed on the bias or out-of-square.

Following are three methods for checking the bias of wallpaper:

Method 1: Measure the distance from a point of design on the wallpaper to the edge of the wallpaper. **(Fig.13)**

Then, using the same point of design, compare that distance with several identical vertical repeats, for a distance of 10 to 15 linear feet. The distance should be constant. If it is not, the print cannot be square with the edges of the wallpaper.

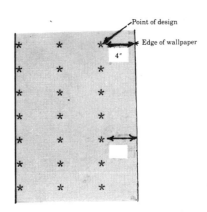

Fig.13

Method 2: This method will require a carpenter's framing square. Align one edge of the framing square with the edge of the wallpaper and compare either the horizontal pattern repeats, (motifs) or a divided pattern design on a straight across match, with the squareness of the edge. They should align perfectly. **(Fig.14)**

This pattern is printed square with the edge.

Fig.14

If they do not, the print is out of square, or on the bias with the edge. **(Fig.15)**

This pattern is printed on the bias, or out-of-square with the edge.

Fig.15

Method 3: Simply fold the wallpaper strip and align the edges perfectly together. While holding the wallpaper very securely in this position, flatten the paper to form a sharp crease at the fold. This crease will represent a perfect 90 degree angle with the edge of the wallpaper, therefore, any horizontal pattern repeats (motifs) should align perfectly with the crease, or the adjoining details of a straight across pattern will line up with the crease. If a one-half drop match is being checked, simply fold the wallpaper exactly from one vertical repeat to that identical vertical repeat. The crease will be exactly half the distance of the vertical repeats; therefore, you can examine the one-half drop pattern for squareness.

When a dominant vertical and horizontal pattern effect is on the bias, the wallpaper should not be installed. This refers to patterns such as plaids and checks. If the pattern design is a floral print, the wallpaper strips may be tilted slightly off plumb to compensate for the out of squareness. Using a framing square can tell you just how much to tilt the wallpaper.

Note: If a wallpaper pattern is only ⅛″ out-of-square across a single strip, the design will fall away ⅛″ from a level horizontal ceiling line or chair-rail which is equal to one full inch every eight strips.

The pattern squareness should always be checked before the installation begins. If you have already prepared the walls, removed the obstacles, unloaded your table and tools, etc., before checking the squareness, you may have wasted a lot of time and money. Important: Do not pre-

cut all the pieces for a room without checking the bias. Some manufacturers will not accept cut rolls for refunds, or anything over the first double roll. They emphasize: If there is a problem with their wallpaper, then it should be detected on the first double roll--especially if it has been installed on the wall. Do not proceed to install any wallpaper once you have determined there is something wrong with it and that it can not be installed satisfactorily.

Figs.16&17 illustrate an example of tilting a strip to make the design run horizontally level and parallel with the ceiling.

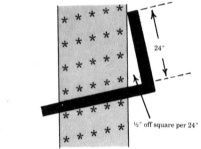

This is an exaggerated example of tilting a strip to make the design run parallel with the ceiling or horizontally level.

NOTICE that the framing square is lined up with the actual pattern designs, but is ½″ out of square with the edge of the wallpaper edge. This means the top of the wallpaper strips would have to be tilted ½″ to the right per 2 feet in order for the pattern to run level.

Fig.16

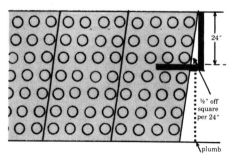

In this illustration, notice the aesthetical pattern design is level with the ceiling line, even though the strips are tilted ½″ off plumb every 24 inches.

Fig.17

Puckering

This problem usually occurs at the seams as a result of continued expansion of the wallpaper during the installation. The adhesive is still moist enough to force the expansion to the seam rather than in vertical blisters. These puckers can be eliminated by immediately removing the strip and re-applying extra adhesive (if needed) and allow extra relaxing time prior to hanging. Blisters and small bubbles from improper soaking or relaxing time are also referred to as puckers. When an outside corner strip is not installed properly, puckers may form on the outside corner's edge.

Sand-Painted Walls

These are walls that have been painted with a paint mixed with sand or a sand-type product. Sometimes a heavy textured paint is used such as ceiling textured paint. In either case, the finished product usually will not be suitable for the installation of wallpaper. The walls must be sanded or stripped smooth using a scraper and/or coarse sandpaper. The appropriate primer/sealer should be applied before installing wallpaper. If the wallpaper is installed over the sand painted walls, the paper will have a tendency to bond only to the outer tips of the sand, and a very poor bond (adhesion) will result.

Scalloped Edges

Scalloped edges result from the selvage being unevenly trimmed off at the factory, thus leaving a waving effect on the edges. This condition may be corrected by using a seam coloring technique or spring-loading technique. See chapter on Seams and Seaming Techniques. A slight overlapping wire seam is effective, but only about half the time. If standard butt seams are used with scalloped edges, then gaps will appear where the edges are not trimmed properly. If the seams cannot be joined satisfactorily, then the wallpaper should not be installed. **(Fig.18)**

Scalloped seams

Fig.18

Screen Marks

Screen marks are smears or smudges of ink on the decorative surface of the wallpaper which are caused when the screen printing device is either picked up or put down during the printing process. The marks may appear in either hand or machine screen printed materials. If these marks are very noticeable, the paper should not be installed. **(Fig.19)**

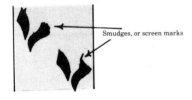

Smudges, or screen marks

Fig.19

Seam Curling

These are seams that have been joined but have pulled away for various reasons. They are caused by the same problems as those associated with seam shrinkage. Seam curling may be corrected by applying a thinned down clay-based adhesive to the seaming and trimming areas several hours prior to the installation. This technique is sometime referred to as the swatching technique or a velcro-technique. Once the clay-based adhesive has dried, it acts as a blotter or sponge within the seaming area. When the wallpaper is applied, the moisture within the wallpaper's adhesive will soak into the clay-based adhesive, therefore creating a high tack or bond to form. The clay-based adhesive will also force the seams or edges

to set up much faster than the other sections of the wallpaper strip which will also prevent wallpaper shrinkage and gapped seams.

The swatching technique is also used on very small corner returns such as soffits, recessed windows, or open doorways. If a heavyweight vinyl is being applied during cool temperatures, a heat gun (or hair dryer) may be required to soften the vinyl in order to relax it enough to adhere to the wall surface or corner. Seams may also curl because of paint deterioration which usually takes place within the first year of the installation. A seam adhesive may be used to secure curled seams; however, the wallpaper will eventually have to be replaced if this is the problem.

Shading

Wallpaper will shade if one side of the material is lighter or darker in color tonal value than the opposite side. This is a result of inconsistent color tones in the ground coating (background colors). Whenever inconsistent tonal values are joined, a shading result will appear. Sometimes inconsistent roller pressures during the printing or embossing process may also cause shading. Whenever shading problems are visible with a pattern or design other than a textured effect the wallpaper should not be installed. See chapter on Pattern Matches. **(Figs.20 & 21)**

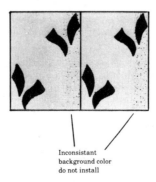

Inconsistant background color do not install

Fig.20

No shading of background OK to install

Fig.21

Whenever solid random textures are being used, every other strip should be turned upside down during the installation. This is referred to as the reversing technique. Reversing every other strip during the installation will join like tonal values. This will minimize any shading effects. **(Figs.22 & 23)**

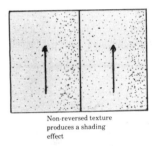

Non-reversed texture produces a shading effect

Fig.22

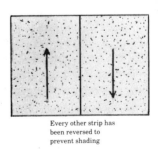

Every other strip has been reversed to prevent shading

Fig.23

On some types of wallpaper, such as real grasscloth, jute, rushcloth, or hemp, shading is considered natural because of the hand-made and/or natural materials being used. However, pre-sorting strips that are near the same shade can produce a more uniform job.

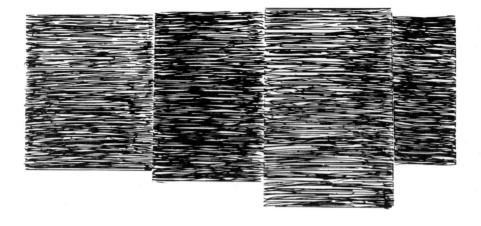

Fig.24

To sort individual rolls, lay the rolls on top of each other and shade (sort) them by putting the rolls together that are the closest in tonal values. Is is advisable to sort individual full length strips to obtain a more uniform effect on the wall. This is because the natural shading effect will sometimes vary within each roll. This technique is called shading. **(Fig.24)**

Shrinking Wallpaper

This is probably the major problem that installers have to deal with. The cause of wallpaper shrinkage is frequently unknown and cannot be explained. Listed below are some of the known reasons and helpful remedies:

1. Lack of Adhesive: When wallpaper is pasted (especially paper-backed) it has a tendency to expand approximately one to two percent of the width of the wallpaper. If insufficient adhesive has been applied, the wallpaper will probably shrink slightly to the original size. If the correct adhesive and viscosity are applied, the problem can usually be corrected.

2. Drying Out: The wallpaper was allowed to relax or sit too long after being pasted--allowing the edges to dry before it could be applied to the wall. Re-pasting may be necessary to correct the problem. See Memory Factors.

3. Excessive Moisture: This can cause certain types of wallpaper to contract, such as water does fabric. If this happens, an absorbent liner paper should be applied on the wall surface. This will absorb excess moisture from the adhesive. Sometimes a clay-based adhesive can be used due to its low moisture content.

4. Excessive Pressure: Too much pressure was applied at the seams during the installation. This should never be done. If an adjustment is necessary, the entire strip should be removed from the wall and re-aligned, beginning at the seaming area. A very slight tapping with the palm of the hand on the opposite side of the strip toward the seam will aid in small adjustments. This will move the entire strip rather than stretching it. **(Fig.25)**

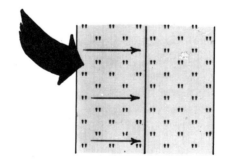

Fig.25

5. Adhesive Volatile Factor: This factor refers to how fast the adhesive's moisture will evaporate during the installation process. This may be a problem when work-ing on new construction during summer months. A high adhesive volatile factor means the adhesive's moisture is evaporating very fast, therefore, reducing the available working me.

Shiny Seams

Most shiny seams are created during the installation by applying excessive pressure with a seam roller at the seaming area. This pressure will cause friction to occur which will burnish the seam or cause a shiny streak.

Shiny seams are also visible when the decorative surface of the wallpaper is contaminated with a residue of adhesive following the installation of wallpaper. The shiny effect is a result of light reflection. The more available light that is present, the more visible the shiny seams will become.

There are other times when the seams will appear shiny (especially when the light reflection is at the right angle) because the vinyl coating was not consistently applied at the factory. Shiny seams will also occur when the embossment is not controlled properly during the manufacturing process especially when the hot-embossing process is being used. If the temperature is not set exactly consistent on both sides of the wallpaper during the embossing process, the wallpaper's decorative surface will appear shiny once the wallpaper is installed and the contrast of uneven embossment becomes visible.

When this is the problem, the wallpaper should not be installed if it is noticeable at a glance.

Soured Adhesive and Primer/Sealer

Often an adhesive will sour or spoil if it is left open or exposed in a warm climate for an extended period of time. This could occur in as few as a couple of days if the temperature is 70 degrees (F) or warmer. Any extra adhesive should be stored in a cool place when it is not in use. Starch adhesives tend to spoil much faster than cellulose.

It is possible for an adhesive to sour even after it was used to install wallpaper. This can happen when a non-breathable wallpaper is installed over a non-breathing wall surface such as high gloss enamel paint, existing vinyl wallpaper, or hard laminates such as Formica. The adhesive may remain wet for as long as a couple of months, which may result in putrefaction (mildew), and/or small blisters will form because of the soured (defective) adhesive. Steps for this problem will include:

(1) Removing the existing wallpaper.

(2) Washing the walls with a solution of equal parts of water and bleach. Allow to dry.

(3) Re-priming the walls with an acrylic wallpaper primer sealer. Allow to dry.

(4) Installing the new wallpaper (assuming a non-breathing type) using a low moisture adhesive, such as clay-based, or, installing an absorbent liner paper prior to the new wallpaper. This will help soak up the excess moisture from the adhesive.

Important: Do not ever use an adhesive or primer/sealer that you know or suspect has soured!

Stain Problems

Sometimes there are existing problems or wall conditions that a standard wallpaper primer/sealer will not correct. These may include smoke, grease, crayon marks, ink marks, water stains, food stains, graffiti, nicotine, markers, etc. In these cases a special stain primer/sealer should be used. This is a product designed specifically to secure or prevent these types of stains from bleeding through a wallpaper primer/sealer or an application of paint. However, it is not a wallpaper primer/sealer by itself, so a clear or white pigmented acrylic wallpaper primer/sealer should be applied over the stain-killer primer/sealer as well as the rest of the wall, in preparation to installing new wallpaper.

It is possible for stains to form beneath wallpaper after it is installed. This frequently results from a mildew problem. If this is the case, it will commonly show up as purple or violet circular or starburst colored-stains. The only cure for the problem is to remove the wallcovering and eliminate the mildew fungus. See section on Mildew Problems.

Stretching

Horizontal stretching refers to the excessive horizontal pressure that is applied at the seam of two adjoining strips. Vertical stretching is a result of allowing a long strip to suspend without being fully adhered to the wall surface, such as a stairway strip. Stretching is always caused during the installation and must always be avoided. An extra pair of hands will help relieve any excess weight or pressure on the wallpaper during the installation, or the installer should lightly press the wallpaper strip to the wall surface. The adhesive will help support the weight of the strip until the lower section can be properly aligned and applied to the wall. Never let the strip drop or unfold, bearing its own weight, while holding the corners of the strip. Allow the strip to lower slowly and gently, one fold at a time. Whenever stairway or extra long strips are being installed, it's important that the pattern matches at eye level, especially if the strip has been slightly stretched.

Structure Settling

This is a common problem that occurs when a structure gradually sinks down after construction. Settling frequently will appear as cracks in stress areas on walls, or when cabinet counter tops drop away a fraction of an inch from their normal position with relation to the wall surface.

Sometimes baseboards will even settle or sink away from the wall, especially on stairways. An installer cannot avoid this problem, therefore, must not be held liable for it, because these conditions are beyond his or her control. Settling that causes a wall to crack is referred to as a stress fracture.

Tensile Strength of Wallpaper

This refers to the amount of pressure or weight that can be applied to a wallpaper strip before it will rupture or tear. Some wallpapers have a weak tensile strength; therefore, extreme care should be taken to resist forcing or sliding the wallpaper horizontally during the installation. Also do not allow it unfold from a booked position without cushioning the unfolding process. If the weight of the strip (with the adhesive) is allowed to drop while holding it at the top of the strip, it could tear the paper while it is being held just prior to applying it to the wall.

Thermo-Expansion Contraction

This refers to the expansion and contraction that takes place within a structure during temperature changes. This may be caused by natural temperature fluctuations, or by artificial heating or cooling. An installer must be very careful about hanging wallpaper on individual plank boards, such as tongue-and-groove boards or knotty pine paneling, because they definitely have movement during thermo-expansion and contraction. If the wallpaper does not rip or tear during expansion, it will usually wrinkle or pucker during contraction. Even liner wallpaper will sometimes do this.

Transparency Problems

There is an enormous amount of wallpaper on today's market that has a semi-transparent quality. This means that any contrasting colors or tonal values of existing wall condition images may possibly show through the new wallpaper from the underlying wall surface. This is considered unacceptable; therefore, the walls should be treated or prepared to eliminate this problem. There are a couple of methods that can be employed:

1. Prime the wall surface with a pigmented wallpaper primer/sealer which generally contains titanium dioxide, the ingredient that produces opacity. The opacity of the primer/sealer will hide or at least camouflage the contrasting color under the wallpaper.

2. A liner paper may be used to prevent show-through on a semi-transparent wallpaper. The liner will also aid to prepare a smooth surface on which the wallpaper can bond. See chapter on Wall Preparation.

Undertrimmed Selvage

This is a problem that exists when a wallpaper's selvage has not been trimmed at the proper place on the edge. This will result in too much background showing at the edges. This causes a double image to appear at the joined seams. Sometimes a slight overlap and double-cutting technique can correct the problem. If this is not acceptable, the installation should be nullified. **(Fig.26)**

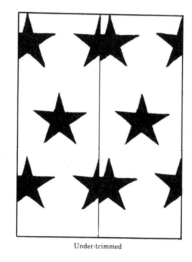

Under-trimmed

Fig.26

Uneven Embossment

This problem will cause shiny streaks to appear once two strips of wallpaper are joined at the seam. If the embossment is raised (or textured) more on one side of the paper than the other, it will create an uneven surface once the wallpaper is installed. If the wallpaper is embossed using heat (hot-embossed method) it will create a shiny (slick) appearance at the seams if the heat is uneven from one side of the paper to the other. Uneven embossment (whether hot or cold) is a manufacturer's defect and the wallpaper should not be installed if it is unacceptable after a double roll has been installed. See Shiny Seams

White Seams

These are seams that show up white when installing dark-colored wallpaper. The slightest little hairline crack or white edge is visible because of the contrast involved. It is important for the wallpaper installer to make sure that the wallpaper strips are not overworked during the installation. This will cause the seams to separate during the dissipation (drying out) process.

Sometimes the wallpaper will actually shrink because of the composition of the substrate. This is not an uncommon problem within the industry. Even though the seams are unsightly, it is not always the fault of the installer.

There are many cases when the seam may be butted perfectly; nevertheless, a white edge is still visible. This is due to the trimming process at the factory whereby the trimming device forms a V effect or the trimming blades are not adjusted at the proper angle. If the selvage is cut from the front (decorative surface), the V shape of the cutting device will usually expose a white edge of the substrate (backing of the wallpaper) a hairline amount.

Most all visible white seams can be camouflaged by applying into the seaming area artist watercolors or pastel chalks mixed with a water-based pigmented primer/sealer into the seaming area. A small brush or index finger is used to apply the paint into the seam and a slightly damp cloth or sponge is used to wipe away the excess paint. The cloth or sponge should always be wiped horizontally with the vertical seam, because a vertical stroke would wipe the coloring out of the seam. Some manufacturers trim the dark colored edges from the substrate side rather than from the decorative side. This eliminates the V shape of a cutting device on the front side.

Important: Do not use oil-based paints for this technique. This technique should never be used on absorbent decorative surfaces. It will stain or ruin the finish. Sometimes acrylic watercolors will cause a shine to appear where the colorant has been applied.

Therefore, a test area is recommended before applying any seam coloring on the decorative surface of a finished wall.

Wallpapering Tools

It is very important that the proper tools are acquired to do almost any job that can be conceived. The following tools will always be used at some time or the other to install wallpaper. The tools that will probably be used more often by professional installers is indicated with an asterisk (*).

* **Allen wrenches:** little hexagon shaped screwdrivers that are used to remove or replace certain types of towel brackets, handrails, bumper guards, etc. These are sometimes available as a set.

* **aluminum foil:** (a)used to store leftover seam colorants to prevent them from drying out; (b) used to check for mildew problems by taping to a wall surface for several days; (c) used to protect tv trays or other adhesive stands from the wet adhesive when using a pasting brush or roller.

* **appliance rollers:** used to move appliances that do not have existing rollers. Extreme caution should be used when moving any appliance over vinyl flooring--especially the floating type which is not secured by an adhesive.

bleach: used to clean and whiten mildew and mold; used to temporarily control mildew growth. Note: Once the bleach has dried, a germicidal spray should be applied to the wall surface to further control a mildew problem.

break-away knife and blades: used to trim hard-to-get-to areas such as around decorative moldings, window sills, spindles, chair-rail ends, etc. Some installers of wallpaper prefer to use the break-off tools all the time.

broad knife: used for spackling or repairing damaged areas or to aid in the removal of existing wallpaper; also may be used as a trim guide with a razor knife or as a tool to help smooth out excess adhesive wrinkles during the installation of wallpaper.

brushes: used for cutting in the edges around trim work when applying a primer/sealer or an adhesive. Generally a 3″ or 4″ brush is used for this purpose. A 6″ brush is commonly used to apply paste to the substrate of most wallpapers.

buckets: used to contain adhesives, clean rinse water, etc.

* **canvas tool bags:** used to store and carry the most frequently used tools and items. They make loading and unloading easier.

caulking: a material or substance that is used to seal around the edges of wallpaper--especially when there is a possiblity of contact with moisture.

caulking gun: a tool used to apply caulking.

* **chalk box and line:** used to establish a straight line (either horizontal or perpendicular) with the use of a chalk box. It is advisable to use a very light-colored chalk for this purpose in order to prevent showing through a semi-transparent wallcovering. Usually a white and yellow can be combined to obtain this color. Never apply a chalk line directly on a seam area. Always place the line at least ¼″ beside the seam in order to prevent the chalk from penetrating the seam once two strips of wallpaper are joined.

* **channel lock pliers:** used to remove light fixtures, nails, picture hooks, staples, etc., during the wall preparation. The large size may be used to remove wall-hung sinks.

clamp light: used to make light available wherever it is needed. It is important to position the clamp light so that it will simulate the lighting conditions that will be present once all structural elements are in place including wall light fixtures, table lamps, wall dividers, etc.

cleaning supplies: used to keep all scrap wallpaper off the floor, wash off all adhesives that may be on the decorative trim moldings, and any other necessary steps to insure that the job is left neat and clean. These tools may include a vacuum cleaner, broom and dustpan, trash can and replacement bags, paper towels, household cleaners, sponges, etc.

* **clipboard:** used to hold contract/estimate forms.

* **clothbacked vinyl:** used to protect tv trays or stands that are used for an adhesive bucket holder or may be used for providing a pad for the padded double cutting technique especially whenever hanging heavy commercial-type wallcoverings.

* **contract/estimate forms:** used to record all pertinent information that is available about every job, which should include room identification, pattern numbers, dye/lot numbers, type of primer/sealer, estimated preparation time, and the total price for each individual room that has been estimated. Any variables (different types of wallpapers, adhesive requirements, preparation time, etc.) that could affect the estimate should always be stated on the contract forms. Extra

copies should always be on hand in order to generate new business.

current tester: used to check the presence of electricity when removing or replacing electrical fixtures. This tool is inexpensive and is highly recommended for use by everyone.

dishwashing liquid: may be used with warm water as a wallpaper remover solution that will penetrate existing wallcoverings that have been scored with an abrasive sandpaper or other tool.

drop cloths: used to protect floors, furniture, appliances, etc., when preparing walls and installing wallpaper. It is highly recommended to use the rubber-backed type to prevent spills from soaking through and will also help prevent falling on slick floor surfaces.

* duckbill tin snips: used to cut plastic lids on pre-mixed adhesives and primer/sealer containers.

* elastic straps: used to secure belongings in the work vehicle and to strap protective foam padding to ladders to prevent marring the wall surface.

electrical tape: used to tape hot (live) electrical wires that are exposed during the wallpaper preparation or installation procedures. Electrical wire caps may also be used for this purpose.

extension cords: used to extend an electrical outlet. Used for clamp-lights and fans that may be needed when the current has been disconnected in the area where the wallpaper is being installed.

* extension walk planks: generally used in connection with scaffolding and/or ladders when installing wallpaper on staircases or higher elevations. Extra care should be taken to insure the stability of these and other climbing tools.

* fans: used to circulate air which will speed up the drying cycle of primer/sealers and spackling compound. They are also used to reduce humidity in rooms where existing wallpaper has been removed using hot water.

* fiberglass mesh tape: used to repair large holes or cracks in walls, especially when caused by the stress within the structure.

* file box: used to keep files neat and organized. Never throw away a work form; preserve it for future references. These are priceless records for installation dates and guarantees.

first aid kit: for use should an accident occur while installing wallpaper or preparing walls. An elementary kit including first aid cream, band aids, gauze, small scissors, waterproof tape, peroxide, and tweezers should be available at all times because of working with sharp tools such as razor blades and scissors. Important note: For deep cuts or wounds, always see a physician; and keep current on tetanus shots.

* foam rubber padding: used to pad ladders to prevent marring the wall surface; used to pad knees when working on hard floor surfaces.

* folding ruler: used to engineer the wallpaper seam placement as well as measure the length of the wallpaper strips that are to be cut. Hint: By cutting a folding ruler off at the 36″ mark, it will easily adapt to the installer's tool belt. A ruler with sixteenth inch increments is recommended.

* framing square: an L-shaped tool used to check patterns for squareness, both horizontally and vertically. Also used to form parallel guidelines.

germicidal spray or disinfectant: used after an area has been washed with water and bleach to help prevent a mildew problem from recurring.

* hacksaw: a small saw with very fine teeth that will cut metal and is used to shorten shower rods which otherwise may rip the new wallcovering. A hack saw blade with 32 teeth per inch is recommended to keep on hand.

hammer: used to re-secure popped nails, remove old picture hooks, etc..

* hawk bill utility knife: a curve-shaped razor knife that is used to cut old caulking from around counter tops or vanities.

* heatgun: used to soften heavy vinyls so that they will easily adhere to tight corners, especially on soffits, recessed windows, open doorways, etc. Heating vinyls will also give them flexibility when trying to secure a tight seam together. (A hair dryer could be used in a pinch)

* ink pens: used for recording information on estimate/ contract forms. They are not in any way to be used on a wall surface for the reason that the ink could penetrate the wallpaper's decorative surface.

* key tags: used to keep track of clients' keys. Never write a name or address on a tag. Use a code that only you can recognize.

ladders: used to reach areas beyond a normal reach. Do not ever try to over-extend when reaching from a ladder or walk plank. Having the proper ladder is critical in the safety of a job.

* levels: used to establish a plumb or perpendicular line when installing wallpaper. Several different sizes are recommended to keep on hand for the various circumstances that may evolve. A do-it-yourselfer may use a level, however it is important that the vial is read properly. Frequently it is easier to use a weighted plumb chalk-line.

light bulbs: used to highlight any defects on the wall surface during the preparation procedure and also gives better lighting during the installation. A 150-watt bulb is recommended.

* map book: used for directions. City map books are especially useful. Update these as often as possible. If a map book is not available, use county and city maps. These are generally available at the local Chamber of Commerce.

* molly bolts and expansion shields: used to secure towel racks and light fix-

tures to the walls. Keeping several different sizes on hand can eliminate a return trip to a job.

* **mouthwash:** used to freshen breath before talking with clients. Nobody wants to be offended by bad breath. It is good to have mints available at all times.

* **nail punch:** used to re-set protruding nails in paneling before installing wallpaper or liner paper.

* **offset screwdrivers:** an "s" shaped screwdriver used to remove and replace fixtures during the wall preparation of objects in hard to reach places.

open end wrenches: used during wall preparation to remove fixtures such as light fixtures, bi-fold doors, wall-hung sinks with pedestals, etc.

* **oval seam roller:** an oval-shaped roller used to secure the seams of wallpaper and make them lay down. Nearly all seams should be secured to insure a good bond. Heavily embossed wallpapers such as grasscloths, stringcloths, or flocks should never be rolled with a seam roller because it could burnish or flatten the seam.

* **palette knife:** used to mix watercolors with a pigmented primer/sealer base when coloring seams that have pulled apart during the drying out process.

* **paneling nails:** used to secure loose seams or bows in the paneling. **plumb bob:** used as the weight of a chalk line when establishing a plumb line or vertical guideline. The chalk line should always be covered with light-colored chalk to prevent its showing through a semi-transparent wallpaper.

putty knife / scraper: used in conjunction with a razor knife when removing the allowance edges from the wallpaper during installation. A three-inch tapered (slanted) putty knife is recommended.

razor blades: used for trimming allowance cuts during the installation of wallpaper. Single edge blades are generally suitable for wallpapering. They can be purchased in small packs or in boxes of 100. A dull blade will tear and/or pull the paper.

razor knife holder: used to hold a razor blade while it is used for trimming excess allowances from the wallpaper. It is recommended to use the holder instead of just holding the blade free-handed. Note: Never hold a razor blade in your mouth. It is dangerous as well as contaminated with adhesives from the wallpaper.

roller cover: used in conjunction with a roller frame when applying primer/sealers and adhesives. The disposable double packs are economical because they can be used and eliminated to reduce clean-up time.

roller extension handle: used to make the application of primer/sealers and adhesives easier in high or hard-to-reach places.

roller frame: used to hold the roller cover during the application of primer/sealers or adhesives.

roller tray: a tray used to hold primer/sealers or adhesives. The tray should be cleaned after each use. A one-gallon tray is recommended.

sandpaper: used to sand the wall surface or spackling during the wall preparation. The different types and their applications are listed below:

    a. 50-grit is used to rough up enamel wall surfaces or hard laminates to provide tooth (tack) to it.

    b. 80 or 100 grit is used for all latex-painted surfaces, new drywall, and spackling.

    c. 4-grit (floor sandpaper) is used to score vinyl-coated wallpaper prior to applying a wallpaper remover solution. This process allows the moisture to penetrate the vinyl coating.

sandpaper holder: used to give more power and protection to the hands during sanding a wall surface. This tool is especially recommended when using a coarse sandpaper.

* **schedule book:** used to keep track of names, addresses, client phone numbers, and dates of the installations.

scissors: used to cut wallpaper. Six-inch stainless steel blades with plastic handles are recommended. Keep clean at all times. Dirty scissors will not provide a sharp cut and will tear the paper. Stainless steel is rust proof and easy to clean.

* **scrapers:** used to remove excessive caulking from around counter tops and excessively rough paint from around architectural trims; also used to remove wallpaper from hard finished surfaces.

screwdrivers: used to install or remove screws. Small flat, medium flat, medium Phillips, etc. may be required to remove different types of fixtures. Professional installers need to have all sizes available on each job.

* **"S" hook:** used to lift and secure low-hanging light fixtures up and out of the way.

* **sheetrock screws:** used to secure sheetrock to a wood or metal stud. These are good to have on hand in case special repairs are needed on a job site.

smoothing brush (sweep): used to smooth out wrinkles or air from behind wallpaper during the installation. A 12-inch long bristle brush is recommended for most wallpapers. This type does not deface most wallcoverings and will last a long time. A short-bristle brush would work better for heavyweight vinyls. Sometimes it is advisable to use a plastic wallpaper smoother to remove the trapped air when installing certain types of wallpapers. It is always important to keep all smoothing tools clean to prevent marring the surface of the wallpaper.

sponges: used for cleaning adhesives from the surface of the wallpaper and from the decorative trim molding during wallpaper installation. A natural sponge will work much better than the man-made types.

spray bottle: used to test the strippability reactions before any major preparation steps are taken. Highly recommended to mix bleach and water to spray-mist mildewed walls.

* **staple gun:** used to re-staple telephone wires or special types of curtains after installation of wallpaper.

step stool: used to stand on when installing wallpaper on standard 8-foot walls. They should be built high and wide enough to use over toilets.

* **straight edge:** used as a guide when manually trimming untrimmed wallpaper or borders. A 6 or 7-foot length is recommended.

strainer: used to remove foreign matter from primer/sealers or adhesives. It may be made from wire or a nylon stocking.

tape measure: used for measuring. A 30-foot retractable steel tape with $\frac{1}{16}$ inch increments is recommended. It is used to measure long strips of wallpaper or borders; or for engineering.

* **temporary lights:** used to replace light fixtures overnight for the convenience of a client. A 60-watt bulb is recommended for this purpose.

* **three-way plugs:** used to connect two or three extension cords to a single electrical outlet; especially useful when working on new construction.

* **toggle bolts (wing nut bolts):** used to secure towel bars, pictures, mirrors, etc. to walls. These are good to keep on hand in case one falls behind the wall after removing bathroom or other fixtures from the wall. The 1/8 inch size is the most common.

trim guide: any tool used to guide the razor knife when trimming the allowance edges around obstacles during the wallpaper installation.

* **tv trays:** stands that provide a place for the paste brush and for placing wallpaper strips in a systematic order after they have been pasted. This makes carrying the strips from the pasting area to the installation area much easier. Using two tv trays on each job is recommended.

* **water colors:** used for mixing seam coloring to fill in seams that slightly separated after the wallpaper has completely dried. This has been a major problem with many professional paperhangers because some wallpaper substrates shrink; however, the installation is usually satisfactory after the seams are colored. Caution: Do not ever use a seam colorant until it has been tested on a scrap piece for an undesireable reaction. (such as staining the wallpaper or leaving a smear)

* **wax paper:** used when double-cutting delicate or easily stained types of wallcoverings (suedes, stringcloth, textiles, etc.) and heavily textured vinyls to prevent the adhesive from getting on the front of the material during the double-cutting process. Also used as the pad for the padded double-cutting process.

* **window crank:** a device used to open and close roll-out windows. These cranks have often been removed or lost and are not available, particularly on new construction.

* **wire caps:** plastic caps used to secure electrical wires when installing light fixtures, doorbells, etc. Keep large and small sizes on hand in case they are needed when replacing electrical fixtures.

wire whisk: used to mix pastes (adhesives). The standard household type will work fine for do-it-yourselfers; however, a professional may prefer to use a commercial restaurant type.

yardsticks: used to measure strips on the wallpaper table; used to smooth wallpaper behind toilets; used to engineer the seam placement of the wallpaper prior to the installation. Always have a spare.

* **zinc strip:** used underneath the wallpaper and on top of the work table to protect the working surface while cutting with a razor knife (blade). Some factory-made tables have a zinc strip built in the top.

Wallpapering Terminology

The following terms and definitions should be reviewed carefully to help build a knowledgeable foundation for wallpapering. These will help you to better understand the terminology used by the industry and throughout this book.

abstract design: a pattern or arrangement that does not resemble or correspond to natural forms. These designs have characteristics that are unique within themselves and are unlike any other object or specific design.

accent wall: the wall in a room on which special or extra emphasis has been given to attract attention from the adjacent walls.

accordion folding: the technique of booking a strip of wallpaper or border several times, resembling an accordion. This keeps pasted sides together and allows relaxing or soaking time. This technique also makes long strips easier to manage during the installation.

adhesive penetration: the process whereas the adhesive is soaking into the wallpaper substrate (backing). This happens during the relaxing or soaking period.

adhesive viscosity: the property of the adhesive that resists the force tending to cause the adhesive to flow or spread. This is generally referred to as the amount an adhesive can be spread at a given thickness. The adhesive viscosity can increase or delay the amount of drying time that the wallpaper will require.

adhesive wrinkles: the wrinkles or ridges that are apparent and visible immediately following the installation of wallpaper. These wrinkles become visible because the adhesive is still damp and has not had time to dissipate and disappear. All adhesive wrinkles will normally dry out within 24 to 48 hours. Some environments may cause the drying to take longer, such as: high humidity, a non-porous wall surface, viscosity of the adhesive, and/or use of a non-breathable wallpaper. **Note: Whenever a clay-based adhesive is used, it should be continuously smoothed throughout the application of wallpaper because of the solids within the adhesive. This type of adhesive does not dissipate as evenly as other types.**

aeration of adhesives: a condition that exists when the adhesive is filled with miniature air bubbles, frequently caused by extreme or vigorous whipping during the mixing procedure. This must be avoided for the reason that it may cause small blisters to form underneath the wallpaper, especially when installing a non-breathable type.

aesthetical pattern placement: the location of a distinct pattern or design at the ceiling line, chair-rail, baseboard, etc., to look appealing and attractive at initial glance. This ought to be considered in advance of hanging all patterned wallpapers and when a border is used in association with them.

alligation: a condition that occurs when a primer/sealer or an adhesive will not suitably bond to a wall surface because of grease, dirt, wax build-up, etc. Alligation likewise can occur when the fusing process of a paint or primer/sealer is not complete due to low temperatures during the application or inappropriate mixing of the product. As the product dries, it cracks and resembles alligator skin.

allowance: the extra amount of wallpaper that is allowed at the top, bottom, and/or sides of a strip, that is trimmed off after the strip is placed on the wall. This allowance should be approximately 2 to 3 inches long or wide.

alternating rolls: the technique of working with two separate rolls of wallpaper to prevent excess waste while installing a drop-match patterned design. This technique should be used only if a significant amount of wallpaper is wasted while matching consecutive strips.

American single roll: a quantity of wallpaper containing between 34 and 36 square feet. These rolls vary from 20.5 to 36 inches in width, and from 4 to 7 yards in length.

archway: an open doorway which has a dome or oval shape at the top of the opening.

artificial break and/or ending point: an area where a decorative wood strip, a spindle, or other object has been placed to create a break or termination place. Such a point is oftentimes essential so that the wallpaper or border ends attractively and appears to be there by design.

available lighting conditions: the amount of light that is existing when the doors are opened, the drapes are open, and room dividers, shutters, etc., are in place. All of these elements can bring about the glare of light reflection on a wall surface. The more light that is available, the more the imperfections will be emphasized. An installer must take available lighting conditions into consideration throughout the wallpaper installation for the reason that a direct light reflection will display overlapping seams and poorly prepared wall conditions.

back-splash: the extended, perpendicular section of a counter top that is positioned on the wall, generally used in kitchens and bathrooms.

back-splash wall: the perpendicular wall surface that is directly behind the counter top in a kitchen or bathroom.

baseboard: the molding or trim attached to the wall that follows the base of the wall next to the floor.

basket weave design: a pattern or arrangement that simulates the over- and-under weaving effect of basket weaving. This can be achieved on wallpaper by using hot or cold embossing during the manufacturing process.

bay window: a window arrangement with three or more separate windows normally fixed in a circular or oval fashion, and projecting from an exterior wall.

blister: a small bubble (air pocket) which forms under the wallpaper during the installation. Blisters are usually caused by: (a) inadequate soaking or relaxing time after the adhesive has been applied to the backing; (b) installation temperatures below 50 degrees Fahrenheit; (c) air trapped between the wall and the paper; (d) wallpaper installed on an extremely porous wall that was not properly sealed; or (e) aeration of the adhesive.

bold pattern: any pattern or arrangement that is conspicuous, flashy, or showy to the eye; strong and vivid; non-conservative.

bolt: a continuous roll of wallpaper that is equivalent to two or more single rolls, and packaged as one unit. 48 and 54-inch commercial wallpapers are normally packaged in 30-yard bolts. Bolts are packaged this way to increase the usable yield.

booking: the technique of folding (not creasing) a recently pasted strip of wallpaper with the pasted sides together, the edges of the strip in perfect alignment, and the ends overlapping about ½ inch at approximately mid way of the strip. This process allows the adhesive to penetrate (soak in) the wallpaper. Booking also relaxes the strip and keeps it from drying out until ready to hang. The relaxing period varies with different types of wallpaper.

borders: a strip of wallpaper usually less than 15 inches wide, which is used to accent around doors, windows, and/or along ceiling lines. Borders are also used as chair-rails or in combination with a wood chair-railing.

breathable wallpaper: any wallpaper that has a porous surface through which air can pass.

builder's flat: a mixture that is used as paint (usually on new construction), that is nothing more than sheetrock compound (mud) that has been diluted with water and applied to the wall surface as paint. This provides a decorative surface, however it is one of the worst enemies of a good wallpapering job. This type of surface must be thoroughly washed with a mixture of ammonia and water and then a good grade of acrylic primer/sealer or an oil-based primer/sealer thinned down should be applied to help protect the wall surface and insure the wallpaper will properly bond to the wall. Note: A poor quality Latex paint is sometimes referred to as builder's flat.

burnished seam: a seam that has a slick or glossy look that was caused by excessive pressure from a seam roller. This must always be avoided particularly when installing embossed or raised wallpaper patterns.

busy patterns: patterns that are cluttered with small or inharmonious detailed arrangements. Occasionally, even small-scaled patterns or mini-prints will emerge as busy patterns in large rooms.

butted seam: the most popular type of seam in wallpapering in which two strips are merged without any overlap. Once the paper is butted together, the seam should be very lightly secured with an oval or flat seam roller. (After approximately ten minutes of setting-up time, check the seam and roll again if necessary.) See: burnished seam

casing: any molding or decorative trim that is used around door frames, window frames, etc.

cathedral walls/ceiling lines: walls which are created when the ceiling line follows the pitch of the roof or is at an angle.

cellulose paste: a paste that is derived from wood pulp, cotton, plants, etc. These are non-staining and ordorless adhesives that are frequently used in hanging natural materials such as grasscloths, linens, silks, stringcloths, etc.

center point: the center in between two given points on a wall. Example: the center point of an eight foot wall would be four feet from each end. The center point must be established throughout the engineering process when hanging murals or positioning a given pattern or seam on a wall.

chalk line: a tool used to establish a plumb line on high walls such as where the 4′ level is not long enough. Chalk lines are also used to establish both horizontal and vertical guidelines. HINT: Replace the line in a chalk box with a cloth fishing line for a more refined line and a minimum of chalk on the wall. Be sure to use a light-colored chalk when a semi-transparent wallpaper or border is being installed.

clay-based adhesive: an adhesive that is usually of a starch origin and has heavy solids that enhance its tack (holding power). This type of adhesive will stain and/or cause the ink to flake off of many types of wallpapers. Most clay-based adhesives will not dissipate (dry out) as evenly as other types of adhesives; therefore, they ought to be completely smoothed out during the installation.

coat: an individual application of either the primer/sealer or an adhesive. Two coats of an adhesive means that two separate applications were made.

coating: the protective layer of plastic or vinyl applied to the decorative surface of a wallpaper to make it more durable.

coherence: the degree of stick that is present when wallpaper is installed and has dried onto the surface.

cohesion: the act or state acquired when a wallpaper is bonded or joined with the wall surface or primer/sealer, as a result of the adhesive.

color way: a group of colors (tonal values) that are used during the printing process.

When different color schemes of the same pattern are printed, they are referred to as a color ways. Most wallpaper patterns are printed in two or more different color ways.

concave walls: walls that curve like the inner circumference of a circle. This could be the internal stairway wall of a circular staircase.

convex walls: walls that curve like the outer circumference of a circle. This could be the wall on the external side of a spiral staircase.

coordinating wallpaper: a wallpaper which blends with another wallpaper by color, design, or other factors. Coordinating wallpapers are often used to tie together two different rooms or walls. Sometimes they are used over and under chair-rails as companions.

cornice: the decorative wood box affixed over a window which may be painted, wallpapered, or covered with fabric. Cornices are sometimes used around the top of a wall for indirect lighting.

correlating: a term which refers to bringing together different items so they will have an orderly connection, such as correlating fabric with wallpaper.

coved ceiling: a ceiling that is formed in a coved or arched manner at its junction with the side walls. Example: a coved attic ceiling.

creasing technique: the act of making a crease into the wallpaper by using a trimming tool or putty knife. This should be avoided except when it is used as a technique to establish a trim mark in areas such as behind door frames or in tight places along ceiling lines lacking a crown molding.

cross seaming: the technique used when a wallpaper liner is installed horizontally and the decorative wallcovering is installed vertically, so that the seams do not fall in the same place. The resulting lattice-type arrangement provides a more secure bond.

crown molding: the molding or trim that follows the ceiling line around the top of a room.

curing-out period: the time it takes for a primer/sealer or wallpaper adhesive to completely dry out.

cutting in: the technique of using a brush to apply the primer/sealer or adhesive where a roller cannot reach.

crystallization: results when an adhesive becomes a definite or concrete form, such as that of salt or granular sugar. This is caused by installing wallpaper in temperatures below 50 degrees Fahrenheit or installing wallpaper over a very porous wall that lacks the proper primer/sealer. These crystals may be shaped like tiny snowflakes.

dado: the area of wall space between the chair-railing (or chair-rail border) and the baseboard.

decorative surface: the front (also thinnest) layer that the consumer sees on the wallpaper's surface. This surface is generally printed by a flexographic, rotographic, or rotary screen printing machine. Some are actually hand screen printed. Most printed surfaces are coated with a clear solution to add extra protection. A clear laminate is sometimes applied over the printed design to provide even more protection.

deep soffit: a soffit with an underside area that is deeper than the vertical area is high; for example, the soffit underside is 20″ and the perpendicular profile height is 12″.

delamination: a condition when a substrate (the backing) of wallpaper separates from either the front or the intermediate layer of vinyl. This is frequently caused by an excessive soaking period. Some wallpapers such as grasscloth, stringcloth, etc., should not be allowed to relax more that 3 to 5 minutes after the adhesive has been applied.

depth: an effect that wallpaper will create in a room regarding its size. If a room has light colors, it will become visibly larger. Darker or bolder colors will make the room appear smaller. Note: Dark colors will always confine space.

design: any sketch, outline, decorative composition, etc., that is formed by an artist, for printing patterns onto wallpapers. The recurring of the art is what determines the vertical and/or horizontal repeats within a wallpaper decoration.

designer: a person who constructs, invents, or plans a design to form a scheme or pattern for wallpaper.

diagonal pattern: a pattern that appears at a slant; an oblique pattern.

diagonal pattern effect: an effect that will become noticeable on a small-scaled pattern, as well as a large-scaled pattern, especially after it is installed on a large wall. A consumer should be made conscious of the possibility of this effect appearing on the wall, because it may not be evident in a small catalog sample or on a single strip of wallpaper.

diagonal pattern sequence: the diagonal recurring of a pattern or design across the wall surface that appears at an angle other than true horizontal or perpendicular. Example: The diagonal sequence of a half-drop match pattern will repeat itself at an angle exactly one-half the distance of the vertical repeat.

directional print: a pattern or design on either wallpaper or borders that must be installed in a particular direction to appear aesthetically pleasing.

disparate patterns: two or more patterns that are each distinct in nature, meaning they are each essentially different. Example: plaids and floral prints. Combining disparate patterns should be carefully coordinated when continuity is important. They could clash or distract from the overall appearance of the environment.

dissipation: the process that occurs as the adhesive is drying out. This is what eliminates the adhesive wrinkles.

door frame: the molding or trim that is placed around a door opening; the casing.

double-cutting: the technique used by many professionals to obtain perfectly fitted seams by simply overlapping one strip over the other until all patterns are perfectly matched, and a new sharp blade is used to cut through both layers. The excess edges are then removed for a perfectly fitted seam.

double roll: a bolt which contains the equivalent of two single rolls of wallpaper in a continuous piece. This bolt is priced as two single rolls and is packaged this way to minimize waste during the wallpaper installation, which allows more useable yield from the wallpaper itself.

drop-match: sometimes referred to as a half-drop match. A match in which every other strip will have the same pattern design at the ceiling line, assuming it is level. This forms a diagonal pattern sequence, rather than a horizontal sequence comparable to the straight- across match.

drying-out period: the time that it takes for a primer/sealer to completely dry and cure out. Also refers to the time that is allowed for wallpaper to completely dry out after the actual installation. Different types of wall conditions, adhesive viscosities (thicknesses), and/or humidity levels will affect the drying-out period.

drywall (sheetrock): a gypsum composition that is sandwiched between two layers of kraft paper. Drywall is used primarily as the wall surface on most new construction. This provides a smooth surface for the wallpaper to be installed on. A primer/sealer or strippable adhesive is recommended to protect it for later removal of the wallpaper.

dye-lot number: a number, letter, or combination of both, that is given to a particular batch of wallpaper rolls that are printed at the same time. This represents the inks, vinyl coating, embossments, etc. that were all created at the same time. Each time a new batch is printed, or the printing process is altered, the dye-lot or run number will change to indicate it. It is very important to record these numbers in case additional wallpaper is needed to complete a job. All wallpaper installers including the do-it-yourselfers should be sure all rolls have the same dye-lot number before starting, to insure uniformity during the installation.

edge curling: a condition when the edges

of the wallpaper curl away from the wall during the installation. This may be caused by improper laminating tensions during the manufacturing process. Sometimes a low- water-content adhesive (clay-based) or an extra relaxing period will help solve the problem. Edge curling can also result from the use of an improper primer/sealer and/or adhesive. If the adhesive has dried prematurely on the wallpaper backing before the installation, this may also cause the edges to curl. If the edges of the wallpaper continue to curl, the installation should be stopped.

embossed paper: wallpaper which has been run through a cold or hot embossing machine at the factory. This machine takes a smooth paper and creates a raised, textured effect. Sometimes embossing will create a pattern or design on the wallpaper itself. These particular types of wallpapers are especially useful when installing over imperfect wall conditions. Do not use a seam roller on embossed papers because it can flatten or burnish the raised effect which would cause a shiny streak to appear.

ending point: the point where the wallpaper stops at an obstacle. Examples: fireplaces, accent walls, kitchen cabinets. Unlike the kill- point, the ending point does not result in a mismatch, because it never meets itself.

etching technique: the technique used to scratch or roughen an existing wallpaper surface to prepare it for the wallpaper remover solution application. The etching of the vinyl-coated surface will allow the solution to penetrate through the wallpaper and dissolve the old adhesive, which in turn will aid in the removal of the existing paper.

expanded spacer: a small scrap piece of wallpaper, which is the full width of the wallpaper being installed and approximately 2 to 3 inches long, that has been pasted and allowed to relax and/or expand the same amount of time as the wallpaper being installed. Expanded spacers are used during the engineering of the installation of wallpaper to pre- determine a vertical guideline. Expanded spacers represent the actual width of an expanded strip. (Allowance trimmings may

be used for this purpose, provided they are fully pasted and have relaxed.)

extensibility factor: the amount that a wallpaper can stretch or extend horizontally, without distorting the pattern or causing shrinkage after the installation. The fill threads in woven substrates add extensibility and are an advantage when installing wallpaper on crooked or bowed walls.

flight: a series of steps (stairs) that are between one landing and another, or between one floor level and another.

floating flooring: a vinyl floor covering that is NOT secured with an adhesive. Extreme care should be used when moving heavy appliances across the vinyl, because it will easily tear or rip.

floral patterns: any pattern or arrangement of flowers printed as the decorative surface of wallpaper.

flowing: describes the uniformity or compatibility of wallpapers and colors as they appear from one room to another. This should be considered when choosing wallpapers for adjoining rooms, so that one room does not take away or distract from the appearance of another.

focal point: the first wall you see upon entering a room. If a room has multiple entries, the main focal wall is the one facing the room's dominate flow of traffic.

gapped seam: a small space (gap) between adjacent strips of wallpaper. This is usually caused by improperly prepared walls or excessive force being used during the installation. If the edges of the wallpaper have not been properly trimmed at the factory, the seam will meet in some places and be gapped in others. This is referred to as scalloped edges. If this condition is very noticeable, the wallpaper should not be installed.

geometric patterns: any pattern or design characterized by straight lines, triangles, circles, etc.

grit rating: refers to the coarseness or texture roughness of sandpaper. The higher the number, the finer (smoother) the grit. Example: 80-grit is much rougher (coarser) than a 220-grit rated sandpaper.

ground coating: the acrylic coating on the upper surface of the substrate. The ground coating is usually an off-white or a colored surface. The wallpaper pattern is printed and/or embossed on top of the ground coating.

headboard wall: the wall in a bedroom where the head of the bed is located.

headwall (face wall): the wall that faces you when walking down a stairway.

helix stairway: a stairway that has a spiraling curved effect; sometimes referred to as a spiraling staircase. These structures have convex and/or concave walls.

horizontal guidelining: the technique of using horizontal guidelines during the installation of wallpaper. These guidelines are usually made with a light-colored chalk to prevent its showing through a light background wallpaper.

horizontal pattern sequence: the horizontal recurring of a pattern or design across the wall surface. This sequence may be within one strip; however, it is usually defined as being across several strips. Example: a straight-across match will have the same pattern at the top of every single strip.

inconspicuous place: the place in a room that attracts little or no attention. This should be considered before engineering or installing wallpaper so the final ending mismatch or kill point will not be noticed.

ink flaking: a problem which may occur when the chemicals are not balanced in the ground coating of the substrate. This will prevent the ink from bonding to the substrate which, in turn, may cause the ink to flake off. Leaving adhesives on the decorative surface will also cause ink deterioration and flaking and this is usually the major cause of most ink flaking problems. Do not use abrasive detergents on wallpaper, as this may also cause ink flaking.

inside corners: a corner that is formed when two walls join, facing each other, usually at a 90 degree angle.

inside corner molding: a molding that usually has a concave or convex shape facing the center of a room and flat surfaces on the other sides that attach to the walls, usually at 90 degree angles. This type of molding is recommended for use on inside corners when there is a void space or when the corner is exceptionally out of square. The inside corner molding will also help hide a mismatch of wallpaper in a crooked corner.

intermediate colors: any color that is formed by mixing an adjacent primary and secondary color.

intermediate layer: the middle layer in some types of wallpapers that is between the decorative surface (front layer) and the substrate (back layer). This layer provides extra strength and is where the background shades are colored. The intermediate layer provides extra opacity, especially if it contains a color other than white or off-white.

kill point: the position where the final strips of wallpaper join together, usually resulting in a mismatch. For this reason, the kill point should fall in an inconspicuous place.

kneading the wallpaper roll/strip: the technique of lightly pressing a roll or strip of wallpaper to further minimize the curl factor which originates from the packaging process. This is done by placing a fully reverse-rolled strip or bolt on the work table surface and rolling it back and forth between the hands and the table top, while applying slight pressure at the same time. This simulates the technique and use of pressure that is applied to a rolling pin when rolling out dough.

knee space: the area that is located underneath a vanity counter top. This section will sometimes have a wall space that will be wallpapered with the other walls in the room, and should not be overlooked during the estimating and installation processes.

knee wall: the lower vertical wall usually below a sloped ceiling, such as in an attic room.

laminated wallpaper: wallpaper that has a decorative surface which is bonded to a backing usually made of paper or fabric.

Examples: grasscloth, cloth-backed vinyls, solid sheet vinyls, etc.

lamination: the process of adhering two thin layers together, such as a wallpaper intermediate layer and the substrate (backing).

landing: a platform between flights of stairs or steps.

large-scaled patterns: patterns that have large design repeats or motifs, and a background with an ample amount of open space. Generally these patterns are used in large rooms, stairways, etc.

lath: the wood strips that are nailed horizontally to the studs of a wall and is used to provide the foundation of plaster.

light sources: all the places from which light is provided. Different lighting variables should be considered before choosing colors, textures, shiny or dull finishes, etc. These variables may include: direct or reflected light, natural or incandescent, white or pink florescent. These different lights, or light colors, can actually change the way a wallpaper will look once it is away from the retail showroom.

lightweight spackling: a patching or spackling compound that is very light in weight, non-shrinking, and requires very little effort when sanding. When the spackling drys, the substances do not evaporate and, therefore, do not shrink.

linear feet: pertains to length. Could refer to the length of a wallpaper roll, strip, border, or the height of wall surfaces.

liner paper: a wallpaper which is blank stock and is recommended for smoothing out a rough surface or covering paneling or cinder block walls. Liners are available in a variety of weights for different surfaces. They are also used for preparation under expensive hand-printed murals and foils. Liners minimize the possibility of mildew as they absorb excess moisture between layers of non-breathing wallpapers and/or a non-breathing wall surface. They are generally installed horizontally to provide cross-seaming. When liner paper seams are installed horizontally and the final wallpaper seams are installed vertically, an increased bond is attained without the risk of having two seams overlap. Also, by hanging liners horizontally, seams will not fall on perpendicular grooves of paneling. Liners should not be used on individual plank or tongue-and-groove boards, because the wood will expand and contract with weather changes, which will stretch or rip the liner during expansion, and/or wrinkle during the contractions.

matching: the technique of joining two strips of wallpaper so that partial designs will line up suitably or a sequence of designs will line up properly. Coordinating different wallpapers and/or fabrics is also referred to as matching.

matte finish: a refinement or finish on the decorative wallpaper surface that has very little shine or light reflection; dull finish.

memory: the original shape or position that a wallpaper may return to, even after it has been installed on the wall. Wallpapers with high memory factors may cause shrinkage at the seams during the drying or curing out process.

metric roll (Euro roll): an amount of wallpaper containing 28 to 30 square feet per single roll. This is about 25% less than the standard American sized single roll. The metric single roll is usually 21 inches wide and 16½ feet long; however, some manufacturers are making metric size single rolls 27 inches wide by 13½ feet long. Metric double rolls contain 56 to 60 square feet. These are sometimes referred to as Euro-bolts.

mildew: a fungus growth which flourishes or grows in dark, moist environments such as bathrooms, shower stalls, basements, and closets. It appears in different colors such as black, grey, yellow, green, or purple. Mildew problems should be treated before installing new wallpaper by washing with a diluted household bleach and spraying with a germicidal spray.

mismatch: a situation when patterns on wallpaper do not line up evenly from one strip to another.

moiré: a watered silk wood grain finish effect printed or embossed on the decorative surface of wallpaper.

monochromatic: having only one color or the various tonal values of one color. A monochromatic wallpaper pattern contains all the same color blends.

motif: the duplicated designs of vertical and/or horizontal repeats in a wallpaper pattern. Motif refers to the recurring subject matter.

mottling: a condition when spots of ink are present on the surface of the wallpaper where they are not supposed to be. This is a manufacturer's defect.

multi-level stairway: stairways that have two or more separate levels or flights. The step intervals are usually divided by a small platform (landing), which changes the direction of the steps.

multiple-drop match: a drop-match pattern that is neither a half-drop match nor straight-across match. The multiple-drop match will repeat itself at the ceiling line every third, fourth, fifth, sixth, seventh, etc., strip, depending on the distance of the horizontal pattern match drop, compared to the vertical repeat. If the match is neither a straight-across nor a half-drop, then it is most likely a multiple- drop.

mural wallpaper: a picture or scene of the countryside, a historical event, modern art, etc., which usually comes packaged in paneled strips that join together to form the scene. Extreme care should be emphasized during the installation as there are only a few numbered panels, and no room for error.

netting: this refers to the warp and weft woven materials of grasscloth, rushcloth, jute weaves, etc.

non-breathing wallpaper: non-porous wallpaper which does not allow air to penetrate the decorative surface. This type of wallpaper usually requires longer drying time because the adhesive must dissipate into the wall surface. When both the wallpaper and wall surface are non- breathable, liner paper is sometimes used to absorb moisture to prevent a mildew problem.

oblique patterns: patterns that are neither perpendicular nor parallel to a given line or surface. This refers to patterns that follow a diagonal angle across the wall or may refer to patterns that are printed on the bias.

opacity: the state or quality of being opaque. In wallcoverings, opacity refers to how transparent or how translucent a wallpaper is, relative to the underneath wall conditions. If the opacity is poor, it usually means the wallpaper is a light color and/or does not have an intermediate layer between the decorative surface and the substrate. Primer/sealers that contain titanium dioxide will have an opaqueness to help prevent show-through from existing wall conditions such as new drywall, old wallpaper, etc.

open doorways: door openings that have no casing or decorative trim placed around them.

opened seams: seams that have separated between two strips of wallpaper. This is usually caused by poor adhesion, usually because of improper wall preparation or the wallpaper was overworked during the installation.

out of register: when two or more ink colors on a pattern of wallpaper are printed out of line with one another. This results in a ghost-type image or total misalignment. Out-of-register wallpapers are defective and should not be installed. If only a very slight misalignment is present, it may be still be installed satisfactorily.

outside corner: a corner that is formed when two walls join, not facing each other, usually at a 90 degree angle.

outside corner molding: a molding that has been pre-grooved to fit on an outside corner of two walls that meet at a 90 degree angle. These moldings are sometimes used to protect corners from abuse and/or to hide mismatched patterns that occur when correcting the corner.

overlapped seams: a seam where one edge of wallpaper laps over another. This is rarely used except when correcting outside corners, archways, and soffits. Overlapped seams should be secured by a vinyl-to-vinyl adhesive.

overpowering patterns: these are patterns that dominate a room or wall setting. One must be careful that large, bold patterns do not detract from every other decorative aspect of a room. Sometimes borders can be overpowering.

overtrimmed wallcoverings: a result when too much selvage has been removed either at the factory or by the installer. This results in a mismatch on the edges of the wallpaper because part of the print will be missing.

overworked: when a wallpaper strip has been stretched or pulled away from the wall an excessive amount of times. Also refers to washing or scrubbing a piece too much during the installation. Care should be taken not to overwork any wallpaper strips because it could damage it or cause the seam to gap apart after drying.

padding double-cuts: the technique of inserting a small thin, scrap piece of wallpaper or wax paper between the wall and the two layers of wallpaper before double-cutting. This pads the double-cut area and helps prevent cutting into the wall. This will also help prevent the double-cut seam from separating.

paint deterioration: a condition when a poor latex paint or builder's flat application breaks down underneath the wallpaper because of improper wall preparation. Anytime a poor grade of latex paint is on the wall surface, the paint will not be able to withstand the drying pressures that take place while the wallpaper is drying out. All wall surfaces should be primed with a high-quality wallpaper primer/sealer to insure a satisfactory job and a secure bond.

pastel colors: any light, delicate shade of color; pale and subdued; tone of a hue that has been reduced in intensity or strength.

pattern placement: a particular point or line at which a pattern will follow. Example: Pattern placement would be important when hanging a design that would present a dominant pattern at the ceiling line, border line, chair-rail, etc.

peelable wallpaper: a wallpaper from which the decorative surface (front) and

intermediate layer (middle) layer may be stripped away from the substrate, leaving a continuous solid layer of backing paper on the wall. Most peelable wallpapers are paper-backed vinyls and are sometimes referred to as solid-sheet vinyls. During removal, the paper backing (substrate) may serve as a liner paper; however, it usually can be easily removed by wetting with hot water mixed with a wallpaper remover or mild dishwashing detergent.

photo murals: wallpaper that simulates photography that is enlarged to be placed on a room-sized wall or door. Photo murals are usually divided into quarter panels for installation purposes, and portray nature scenes such as mountains, seashores, forests, or woodlands.

pieced roll: a roll containing more square footage than an average roll (bolt). During packaging, the roll ended before the proper square footage had been filled. The manufacturer has added several yards of wallpaper to compensate for the splice. This usually occurs when a damaged area has been removed during the production of the wallpaper.

pigmented primer/sealer: a type of primer/sealer that drys white instead of clear and therefore blocks out discolorations and spots on the wall. This is mainly used when installing new wallpaper over existing wallpaper or new drywall (sheetrock). It is usually necessary to use a pigmented primer/sealer before the installation of semi-transparent wallpapers.

plumb bob: a tool used as the weight of a chalk line when establishing a plumb line or vertical guideline.

point of design: a specific detail of a design within a strip of wallpaper. In a mural, the point of design refers to the highest or lowest point of the image portrayed. Point of designs must be established in order to center the image vertically.

popped nails: nails that have backed out of a wall because of vibration and/or structure settling. It is usually advisable for a structure to settle for at least six months before wallpaper is installed.

porosity factor: the state or quality of a product with relationship to being porous or permeable by water, air, etc. This factor should always be considered before the application of a primer/sealer to the wall surface. If it is very porous, it should be sealed with an oil-based sealer or a pigmented (universal) acrylic latex primer/sealer. The porosity factor should also be considered with different substrate backings of wallpaper. If it is very absorbent, a second application of adhesive may also be required.

pre-pasted wallpaper: wallpaper that has a water-soluble adhesive either sprayed or coated on the substrate. The wallpaper adhesive (which is usually a cellulose or starch base) is activated when the wallpaper is soaked in a water tray or bathtub. One must be careful not to oversoak the wallpaper, because it may dissolve too much of the adhesive from the backing. Pre-pasted wallpapers should always be allowed an ample amount of time to relax (between 5 and 10 minutes) prior to the installation to prevent vertical expansion wrinkles.

pre-trimmed wallpaper: wallpaper in which the selvage has been removed at the factory by machines. Most wallpaper comes this way to make the installation process easier.

primer/sealers: an alkyd or acrylic-based liquid used to prime and seal walls prior to the wallpaper installation. Most primer/sealers on the market are of acrylic (latex) form. These types of primer/sealers soak in a porous wall surface such as a sizing would; however, primer/sealers go an important step further. They soak into a poor latex paint or builder's flat application and re-bond the paint to the wall surface. Most wallpapers expand when they are wet with an adhesive; however, during the dissipation or drying-out process, the wallpaper dries tight to the wall and a poor latex paint will pull away, simply because it cannot withstand the drying pressures. Some oil-based primer/sealers are still used today and are referred to as alkyd.

putrefaction: the decomposition of organic matter by bacteria and fungi; rotting mildew that forms underneath wallpaper is a result of putrefaction.

quality control: the inspection of the manufacturing and installation process to make sure that every specified job is completed with the desired quality. Even though the inspection of the wallpaper may or may not be the installer's job, it is very important that the individualized inspection of the wallpaper be done. It is practically impossible for the manufacturers to produce this kind of inspection.

railroading: the technique of hanging random-textured wallpaper horizontally, rather than vertically, over window or door headers. This technique is also used for installing borders and liner paper.

reaction test: a test to pre-determine the effect that an adhesive, cleaning solution, or wallpaper removal solution may or may not have on a specific wallpaper or wall surface.

relief cut: a cutting technique used during wallpaper installation to relieve the pressure (the weight) from the strip when positioning it around an obstacle such as a door or window frame, vanity cabinet, soffit, etc. Relief cuts are usually a mirror angle of the mitered cut of the wood or obstacle.

reverse rolling: the table technique of reversing a bolt of wallpaper to uncurl or reverse the window shade effect. This helps the wallpaper lay flat while cutting and pasting the wallpaper. A visual inspection of the wallpaper should be made during this reversing technique.

reversing strips: the technique of installing every other strip of wallpaper upside down. This technique assures that the lighter (or darker) edges on textured wallpapers will come together and minimize shading.

roller marks: small ridges that are made from the excess pressure of a roller cover during the application of paints or adhesives. If these ridges are not smoothed out while they are wet, they will usually dry in a hardened form. These should be spackled and sanded smooth to prevent them from showing through the wallpaper. All adhesive wrinkles will dissipate and dry out with the exception of clay based types which should be smoothed out be-

fore the wallpaper has begun to dry.

room continuity: the continuous flowing of wallpaper patterns and/or colors from one room to another.

sand-painted walls: walls which have been painted with a rough-textured paint or a paint mixed with sand. This finish does not provide a satisfactory surface for the wallpaper to adhere to without a lot of sanding preparation.

scoring walls: a technique of sanding, scraping, or etching a wallpaper surface in preparation for wallpaper removal. This process allows the wallpaper remover solution to penetrate the vinyl-coated decorative surface and dissolve the old wallpaper adhesive.

scrim backing: a cotton or linen fabric of open weave used for the backing (substrate) of some wallcoverings.

scrubbable wallpaper: wallpaper that has either a sprayed vinyl or solid vinyl surface and is durable enough to be scrubbed with a mild soap or detergent and warm water. These are ideal for kitchens, baths, and high traffic areas. Even scrubbable wallpapers should never be cleaned with abrasive cleansers.

semi-transparent wallpaper: a wallpaper that is usually light in ground (background) color and permits darker colors to show through from the wall surface. A pigmented primer/sealer should be applied to the wall surface if there is any possibility of this condition.

sequence: a continuous or connected series of wallpaper strips, patterns, designs, techniques, etc.

setting-up time: the time it takes for the wallpaper and its adhesive to start drying out. Once the adhesive is set up, the wallpaper can not be adjusted on the wall surface without completely removing it. Occasionally, attempted removal of the wallpaper soon after it has set up will result in severe wall damage, especially if a re-wettable primer/sealer was used during the wall preparation.

settling: a condition when a structure

sinks or settles over a period of time. Example: a kitchen counter top or bathroom vanity top may drop as much as a half inch away from the wall surface during the first two years after the original construction.

shade: a slight graduation or variation of a color (hue); usually refers to a darker tonal value of the hue. Wallpaper is considered shaded whenever there is inconsistent tonal value from one strip to another.

shading: the technique of sorting rolls or strips of wallpaper so that they are uniform in color or tonal values. Wallpapers such as grasscloth, rushcloth, etc. will still contain various inconsistencies in tonal values because this is a natural effect associated with them.

shallow soffit: a soffit whose underside is more shallow than its profile is high. Example: The soffit underside is three inches deep and its profile height is twelve inches.

single roll: an amount or unit of wallpaper used for pricing. An American single roll contains between 34 and 36 square feet. The metric or European single roll contains between 28 and 30 square feet. Even though wallpaper is generally priced by the single roll, it is customarily packaged in double or triple roll bolts to minimize waste during the installation.

sizing: the technique of preparing a wall surface prior to the application of wallpaper. Sizing when used in the noun form, refers to the actual product which is a powder mixture of starch and cornflower, or cellulose and pine flower. These mixtures provide uniform porosity as well as increase the tack of the wallpaper during the installation. Sizing should NOT be mistaken for the liquid pre-mixed wallpaper acrylic primer/sealers or pigmented primer/sealers.

sloped walls: walls which follow either a roof line or staircase slope. These are usually found in attic rooms or underneath stairways.

small-scaled patterns: patterns that have small design repeats or motifs and are usually spaced very close together. They are generally used in small rooms or as a background to crafts, bookshelves, pictures, etc. One must avoid using patterns that will appear busy in large areas. Small-scaled patterns are sometimes referred to as mini- prints.

solar light exposure: the angle or direction of direct sunlight that a structure is exposed to. This will have an effect on colors that are chosen within the wallpaper. Examples: (a) East and West get full morning or late evening sunlight and could use cool, light colors such as blue or silver. (b) North may have no direct sunlight; therefore, warm colors should be used. (c) South normally has light available all during the day; therefore, natural or pastel colors should be used.

solid-sheet vinyls: wallpaper that has a paper substrate laminated to solid vinyl. These wallpapers are peelable and scrubbable. Solid sheet vinyls are appropriate in heavy wear or traffic areas such as children's rooms, bathrooms, halls, and stairways.

solid-vinyls: wallpapers that contain a woven or non-woven substrate (backing) and are laminated to a solid vinyl decorative surface.

spacing technique: the technique of using expanded spacers to determine the plumb line placement around inside and outside corners, or to establish a vertical guideline past wall obstacles such as windows or doors. Spacers are also used to measure the distance of several strips under a multiple window or to predetermine the pattern placement when hanging around bay windows, so they can be adjusted to look aesthetically pleasing.

spackling: the technique used in repairing popped nails or repairing seams or damaged areas in drywall or plaster. Spackling as a product can be made with a dry mixture and water, or it may be purchased pre-mixed.

straight-across match: a match in wallpaper where a pattern is matched from one strip to another by a direct straight-across sequence. Once a pattern sequence has been established, the pattern design at the top of the straight-across match strip will always be the same on every strip.

straining technique: the technique of pouring an adhesive or primer/sealer through a screen wire strainer, or nylon stocking funnel, from one container to another. This process eliminates any foreign matter in the product such as; dried adhesives, dried primer/sealers, sand, and grit.

stress fracture: a crack that forms in a wall because of the stress (weight) that occurs during the settling of a structure. These should be repaired using a mesh-type repair tape and spackling.

stretched wallpaper: a condition that occurs when a wallpaper strip (that has already begun to adhere to the wall surface) is forced horizontally to join an adjacent strip. Vertical stretching results from the weight of long strips hanging without being adhered to the wall. Stretching should always be avoided as much as possible in order to prevent gapped and/or mismatched seams.

strippable wallpaper: wallpaper that can be easily removed from the wall surface without damaging the wall.

thermo-expansion/contraction: the movement that takes place within a structure as it changes temperatures, either by natural or artificial means. It is not recommended to install wallpaper over tongue-and- groove boards because of the adverse reactions that may occur such as buckling or ripping the wallpaper during the movement of the boards during the expansion/ contraction process.

tint: a graduation or variety of a color (hue), which has been diluted from the maximum purity of the hue.

trimming: the technique of removing the selvage from untrimmed wallpaper or removing the excess wallpaper allowance from around door, windows, ceilings, and baseboards. This is generally achieved by the use of a straight edge (trim-guide) and a razor knife (blade).

unpasted wallpaper: wallpapers that have not been pre-pasted at the factory. All wallpapers require specific types of adhesives and should be installed according to the manufacturer's recommendations or according to recorded test procedures.

untrimmed wallpaper: wallpaper in which the selvage has not been trimmed at the factory and must be done by the installer. This can be done with a straight edge and razor knife (blade) or can be double-cut on the wall.

usable yield: the quantity of wallpaper that is actually installed on the wall. Waste factors such as allowances, matching patterns, etc., are important in pre-determining the useable yield for a room or wall.

vapor barrier: a plastic film, sheeting, or other product that is used on the exterior walls of structures to restrain or prevent vaporescence (production or formation of vapor) from forming behind the interior walls that adjoin the exterior walls of the structure. If a vapor barrier has not been properly installed, a mildew problem may arise within the interior of the structure, and may cause a mildew problem to form underneath the wallpaper.

variegated pattern: any pattern or design that contains different features in character, form and appearance. Examples: floral and stripes; wide stripes and narrow stripes.

vertical guideline: a perpendicular upright line that is commonly plumb. Sometimes it is not plumb, but is parallel to an obstacle such as a door frame or outside corner. The parallel vertical guideline should always be used with expanded spacers when installing wallpaper around obstacles such as windows. Guidelines should be made with a light-colored chalk line or pencil mark to prevent their showing through light-colored wallpapers.

vertical pattern repeat: the span or distance from one point on a pattern design of wallpaper to the identical point vertically. Every patterned wallpaper will have vertical repeats, with the exception of murals and random patterns.

volatile adhesive factor: the time element associated with the evaporation of water (moisture) from an adhesive once it has been applied to the wallpaper substrate (backing). A high volatile factor means that the adhesive's moisture will evaporate very quickly. This should be considered during hot summer months, especially when working on new construction with no air conditioning. The amount of working time is greatly reduced with each strip if it is drying out very fast because of heat and evaporation.

wainscotting: paneling or woodwork covering the dado of a wall. This area is customarily equal to one-third of the wall height.

wall preparation: various techniques used to prepare a wall surface for wallpapering which should include but not be limited to the following: wallpaper removal if necessary; sanding and washing walls; repairing places with spackling; removing fixtures from walls such as towel racks, mirrors, light fixtures, shower rods, etc.

wastage: the amount of wallpaper that is cut away (lost) from a roll (bolt) in order that one strip can be matched to another. The amount of wallpaper that is actually installed on the wall is considered the useable yield.

working time factor: the amount of time an installer has to work with a strip of wallpaper from the time it has been fully pasted until it must be in the final position on the wall surface. This time factor should be considered before pasting too many strips of wallpaper in advance of the actual installation, because delamination of the wallpaper itself and drying-out of the adhesive could occur.

Summary

I have been a consultant for many wallpaper retail stores, distributor representatives, professional installers, and do-it-yourselfers during the past 20 years. I have discovered that almost every individual is willing to perform all the right procedures that are necessary to obtain a successful wallpapering job. However, there has never been a source for them to turn to for information or advice.

Most every failure or problem with wallpapering results because an individual, whether consumer or installer, does not know the appropriate questions to ask in order to obtain the proper advice.

The Complete Guide to Wallpapering has set forth many standards for the industry. This includes everyone who buys, sells, or installs wallpaper. Each person involved with wallpapering and the products associated with it needs to understand the other's liability.

Consumers and installers must realize that manufacturer instruction sheets cannot possibly contain enough information to deal with every situation especially in the area of wall preparation. The information that is provided is very basic and many times very inadequate because of the many different field conditions that exist.

Installing wallpaper can be very fruitful and rewarding-- provided you know the right questions to ask and receive the correct information prior to the installation.

The Complete Guide to Wallpapering is written to provide the right questions and the right answers to insure a satisfactory job.

Effective communication and proper execution will always produce satisfied customers!

DMG

The Complete Guide to Wallpapering Answers The Most Commonly Asked Questions

The paper on my walls is falling off! What can I do?

Can I hang new wallpaper over old?

How do I set up my work area?

I cleaned my walls with a detergent! Why did the wallpaper fall off?

How do I determine where and how to hang a border?

Why did gaps appear after the wallpaper dried?

What causes bubbles or blisters to form during the installation?

What do I do if my adhesive has soured?

My adhesive has lumps in it! Can I still use it?

What makes my grasscloth look shaded?

What causes the ink to wash off the front of my wallpaper?

What are the pink spots showing through my wallpaper?

Why are the seams on my wallpaper shiny?

What caused the ink to flake off the front of my wallpaper?

What kind of tools do I need to install wallpaper?

The edges of the wallpaper won't stick! What's wrong?

What types of wallpaper must be reversed and why?

What caused the adhesive to stain my wallpaper?

How do I remove old wallpaper?

Can I paint over my old wallpaper and hang a border?

Can I hang wallpaper over paint?

Why did the crayon marks and ink show through my wallpaper?

How do I hang cathedral walls?

What are the special techniques required to install murals?

What should I expect from a professional installer?

What is the difference between American and metric rolls?

Why is wallpaper packaged in double and triple rolls?

How do I repair damaged sheetrock?

Why are the sheetrock seams showing through my wallpaper?

How do I repair the hole in my wall?

What is "builder's flat"?

Can I hang wallpaper on a metal surface?

Can I hang wallpaper over plywood?

How do I mix my adhesives?

What caused the suds in my adhesive?

What caused my wallpaper to pucker at the seams?

How can I avoid excessive waste when installing wallpaper?

Why wont my pre-pasted wallpaper stick?

Where do I hang the first strip in my room?

How do I get the wallpaper straight on the wall?

How do I hang wallpaper on a ceiling?

How can I install a border with my companion paper?

How do I hang a stairway?

How do I repair my wallpaper?

Does pre-pasted wallpaper ever need additional paste?

How do I hang around corners?

How do I install wallpaper around my recessed window?

How do I deal with manufacturer defects?

What caused my wallpaper to shrink?

Why do my seams look white on my dark wallpaper?